The Oboe

A Reed Blown in the Wind

MARION WHITTOW

With illustrations by the author

Published by Puffit Publications
47 South Hill Park, London NW3 2SS

© Copyright Marion Whittow 1991
Illustrations © Marion Whittow 1991

Reprinted 1992

Cover Design: Northlight Design

ISBN 0 9518072 0 X
A CIP catalogue record for this book
is available from the British Library

By the same author: *Great Fermentations*
From the same address: Puffit Greetings Cards

Manufacture coordinated in UK by Scriptmate Editions
20 Shepherds Hill London N6 5AH

Electronically typeset in Century 10/12pt

This book is dedicated to
ALL BROKEN REEDS

Foreword

This well-researched book is full of sound and detailed information on all aspects of oboe-playing. It is comprehensive, and full of hints and tips which should be invaluable to the student and amateur, and may even be new to many professional players and teachers. Written with a delightful sense of humour as well as with common sense, Marion Whittow has produced a worthy addition to the oboist's library.

EVELYN ROTHWELL (Lady Evelyn Barbirolli)

Acknowledgements

I would like to thank everyone who has assisted with the research and production of this book.

My special thanks to Evelyn Barbirolli, who so kindly spared me time from her busy schedule, for her patience and encouragement, and to Howarth's for their help and support.

Also to John Cowdy, David Fingerhut, Neville Gardner, Nora Knox, Francisco Médir and the L.S.O. library.

Anecdotes and stories contributed by:

Lady Evelyn Barbirolli, Ted Brake, Jack Brymer, Anthony Camden, John Cowdy, Peter Craen, Peter Davies, Andrew Denyer, Jim Hunt, Max Jaffa, Aubrey Johnson, Paul Lowdell, James MacGillivray, Sir Charles Mackerras, Peter Mentzell, Malcolm Messiter, Charles Morley, Paul Mosby, Celia Nicklin, Barbara Rhodes, Sidney Sutcliffe, Richard Taylor, Roy Thackray, Steven Trier, Penny Veryard, Tony Walker and Geoffrey Wareham.

Instrument-making photographs kindly supplied by David Fingerhut. Photograph of *Dalbergia melanoxylon* reproduced by kind permission of Photography Department, Royal Botanic Gardens, Kew.

Other photographs, Peter Watson.

Extracts from Bleuzet's *La Technique du Hautbois* and from Gillet's *Studies for the Advanced Teaching of the Oboe* reproduced by permission of Editions A. Leduc, Paris/United Music Publishers Ltd.

Extracts from Hinke's *Elementarschule* reproduced by permission of the original publishers, Peters Edition Ltd.

Extracts from Poulenc's oboe sonata and from Manuel da Falla's 'Three Cornered Hat' reproduced with the kind permission of the copyright owners, Chester Music Ltd.

Extracts from Stravinsky's 'Orpheus' and 'Rite of Spring' and from Rachmaninov's second piano concerto reproduced by permission of Boosey and Hawkes Music Publishers Ltd.

Extract from Lalliet's 'Prelude and Variations on Carnival of Venice' reproduced by permission of Nova Music Ltd.

Extract from Ronald Binge's 'The Watermill', copyright 1959 Josef Weinberger Ltd., reproduced by permission of the copyright owners.

Preface

To most people the phrase 'a good read' refers to a good book; to oboe-players it means something completely different.

Reeds—good *and* bad—is just one of the subjects included in this book, in which I've tried to consider every angle of oboe-playing—in particular, aspects not covered before.

Playing any instrument should be *fun*—the more so the better you play. Whatever your standard there will always be others to enjoy making music with. It's a wonderfully absorbing and fulfilling occupation, whether hobby or profession.

If you choose the oboe you will not only share the joy of being able to play one of the most beautiful and expressive of all instruments, but have the satisfaction of finding yourself—hopefully!—more in demand than performers on more usual instruments—whether you prefer playing orchestral or chamber music, or with piano accompaniment.

Today the oboe is taught in most schools and there are thousands of amateur players, yet there are few books about the instrument, and these are mainly in technical language for serious students or professional players. *A Reed Blown in the Wind* is aimed at this gap in the market—easily understood by amateurs, or even those with merely a love of or passing interest in the oboe, as well as being of interest to advanced and experienced players. I have enjoyed lightening the text, not only with cartoons, but amusing tales of disaster and embarrassment, collected from many players, and all, to my knowledge, absolutely true.

Opinions and methods will always differ. Everything in this book is simply what has worked for me as student, teacher, and during years of professional playing. I hope it will not only give food for thought, but be enjoyed, by novices and experts alike, whether you're looking for a good reed, or just a good read...

M.W. London 1991

Contents

Oboe   Oboe d'amore   Cor anglais

Overture

What is an oboe? A few facts

One player's answer to this question is 'A column of air with wood round it', and if you think about it, the wood merely serves as a reminder of where the column of air is as it is the air, not the wood, that vibrates. As a small child I misused the word 'oboe' for a joint in my arm. But here are a few facts:

The oboe is a woodwind instrument approximately two foot long, with a conical bore. It uses a 'double' reed, with two blades of cane, unlike the 'single' one-bladed clarinet reed. Its sound is activated by these blades vibrating together. There are three 'joints'—or sections—and the reed fits into the top one.

The name derives from 'haut bois' ('high wood'), the term used for a group of higher pitched instruments in the seventeenth century. It has a comparatively small range of two and a half octaves, from Bb below 'middle' C up to F or G an octave above the treble clef—even higher in some contemporary pieces:

The oboe has an attractive, reedy quality, hopefully *not* sounding like its ancestors, which were raucous out-of-doors type instruments.

Early oboes were often made of—softer—boxwood or rosewood, but today the very hard African blackwood (or grenadilla) is generally used. The mechanism consists of an intricate system of rods and springs, with sometimes as many as over three hundred components. The keys are cast, usually from nickel-silver, then silver- or even gold-plated.

There are normally two oboes in a chamber or Mozart-sized orchestra, and three, or even more, in a full symphony orchestra, when one player may be required to play cor anglais as well.

In the absence of a piano, organ or harpsichord the principal oboist gives the 'A' for the orchestra to tune to—an unwelcome task.

The oboes are usually positioned centrally in the orchestra, opposite the conductor, between the flutes and clarinets, with strings in front and—less popular—brass and percussion immediately behind.

The *cor anglais* and *oboe d'amore* are close relatives of the oboe, with similar fingerings, but their larger sizes give them different tone qualities and lower pitches. They are 'transposing instruments', i.e. notes when played sound lower than written (see 'The Oboe's Relatives', Chapter 17). Their bells are pear-shaped, whereas the oboe's is trumpet-shaped or flared, and each uses a crook—a small curved metal tube—inserted into the top joint, onto which the reed fits.

The oboe is the highest pitched of the three instruments, or 'soprano' voice, the oboe d'amore the middle, or 'mezzo-soprano', and the cor anglais, the 'alto' oboe.

All three use different reeds.

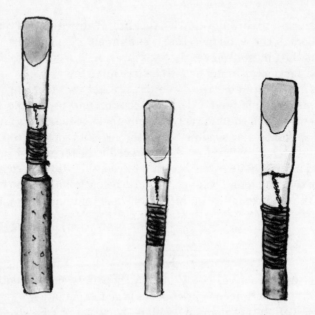

Oboe reed   Oboe d'amore reed   Cor anglais reed

The oboe is a key member of the symphony orchestra, besides having important roles in smaller ensembles and chamber music and a varied solo repertoire.

The cor anglais is used almost exclusively within the orchestra, and the oboe d'amore, with few exceptions, for the music of Bach.

Bass oboe, heckelphone and *Eb oboe* are among other, less commonly played, members of the oboe family.

Chapter 1

The Basics

How to start; Breathing; Posture; Embouchure

How to start

Things you need: An oboe. A reed. A teacher. Plus reasonable health and a good pair of lungs.

Start with the reed on its own. Moisten its tip thoroughly in your mouth, or by immersing it in a little water. Roll your lower lip over your bottom teeth to form a cushion for the reed. Rest about one third of the cane part on this 'lip-cushion' and close your mouth. Say 'tee' firmly, letting your tongue touch the reed's tip to start the sound (called 'attack'). This should produce a sustained 'squeak'. Later you will learn to avoid squeaks but at this stage a squeak is the object of the exercise. Repeat this until you can produce a confident sound each time.

Next, assemble the instrument. There are three joints or sections of an oboe besides the reed, which must be put together with care. NEVER use force or grip the instrument tightly, but use gentle turning motions until each joint is eased into place with the keywork aligned. Care of and respect for your oboe is as important as learning to play it. Unfortunately this is all too often neglected with disastrous results (see 'Nursing Care', Chapter 15). Lastly, insert the reed into the top joint as far as it will go, its flat sides parallel with the finger-holes of the oboe, thus completing the instrument. Now you are ready to play your first note.

And there I'll stop!

I stress the need for a teacher! Fingerings on the oboe are less complicated than on many other instruments, for instance clarinet or bassoon—certainly stringed instruments. They can be picked up from a chart, or even by experimentation. But don't be complacent. The hardest things to master on an oboe are correct blowing and breathing, making a good sound and playing in tune. These must all be studied properly, with practical help from an expert. So I don't advise trying to teach yourself the oboe without proper guidance from an *oboist*.

I believe it is important for teachers of beginners in particular to be oboe-players themselves. Basic breathing and blowing are very different on a flute or clarinet, or brass instruments. I have had to 'unteach' problems with talented pupils who have studied with teachers whose instrument was *not* the oboe. It is the very first lessons which are the most important—so is your first teacher. Specialist tuition is particularly important for mastering such things as embouchure control, and, most important of all

Breathing

Proper breathing technique is of *utmost importance* for oboe-playing and it's essential to understand it fully from the start. It is amazing and frightening how many players breathe incorrectly. It seems to be a rudiment often badly taught, which can be a great hindrance to playing progress and quality—even health. Good breathing is the basis of good playing. (We professional players literally 'breathe for a living'!)

In day to day life we don't give breathing a thought 90 per cent of the time—we even do it in our sleep. When the body needs oxygen we inhale a breath automatically, probably unaware that we are exhaling used-up air (or CO_2) when we breathe out. We only become conscious of the need for oxygen after vigorous exercise or when 'out of breath'.

When speaking, singing, even playing a wind instrument—other than the oboe —the only problem is to take IN enough breath for comfort, stale air being EXhaled naturally. But with the oboe it's different.

1) Look at the tiny aperture of the reed; you can imagine how very little air will pass through it during playing. Meanwhile your body is using up oxygen as usual—quite quickly if you're playing energetically, or you're nervous. So, what happens? Your lungs will still be three-quarters full of 'used-up' air by the time you need to inhale a fresh breath (to stay alive). So before you are physically able to inhale more air you must make room for it by first *exhaling* all the CO_2.

The first vital lesson is, therefore, *always breathe out before you breath in*—NEVER INhale before EXhaling. If you don't follow this rule a) you will lose control of your playing through lack of breath support, and eventually *have* to stop and gasp, and b) you will start to feel dizzy as your body is, literally, starved of the oxygen it needs, and eventually you may even pass out.

2) Although such a minute amount of air is used in playing, a high *pressure* is required—almost similar to that needed for playing a trumpet, if you compare the air being forced through the small aperture. To produce and control this pressure and airflow, we use our diaphragm and stomach muscles—as in a cough or sneeze. Try coughing (or sneezing) with your hand on your stomach and feel the muscles jerk. You didn't realise you had such strength did you? Even when 'squeaking' the reed (described above) you should have been aware of a tightening of these muscles. One word of warning though: Beware tight clothing or weak waistbands which might let you—or themselves—down while you are putting this muscular control into practice in public (see 'Concert Dress', Chapter 19)...

3) It is important to breathe fully and make use of your entire lungs. Avoid 'shallow breathing'. This, too, can lead to dizziness and lack of control in your playing. Our lungs are pear-shaped, so it's vital to use the lower—larger—part.

The stomach is pushed out by the automatic movement of the diaphragm when we breathe in; it contracts when we breathe out.

Here is a good exercise for testing breath control. Stand straight with the backs of your hands on the sides of your ribs. Inhale a deep breath and feel the sideways expansion of your chest (or observe it in a mirror). There should be NO upwards movement of your shoulders. Now exhale slowly whilst counting eight slow beats in your head, saying 'sssssssss' (later count twelve, sixteen beats etc.). Listen to the evenness of this 'sssssssss' sound. Is it free from any wobbles—even after ten counts?

You are now learning breathing or 'diaphragm' control, which ultimately leads to playing control—though in fact we cannot actually govern the diaphragm itself.

Using the muscles in this way controls the flow of air by preventing it bursting out too fast at first, and gradually pushing air out as the lungs empty. Proper widthways chest expansion needs room. It is impossible if you are slouched and your lungs restricted—therefore good posture is essential (more later).

4) Allow *time* to breathe fully. Don't leave it till the last second. In the orchestra breathe on or *before* the *upbeat* depending on the speed of the music—(several bars before in fast pieces). For example:

Breathe through your mouth, not your nose, which takes too long.

If you breathe too late, i.e. almost *on* the downbeat a) there won't be time for a really good breath and b) certainly not time for a cough, or other adequate preparation for your first note. To make a late entry because of taking too late a breath is as bad as a singer or newsreader missing out the beginning of a word.

We have to breathe, but breathing can and should *add* to the music, not interrupt it (see 'You the Musician', Chapter 7).

5) *Never* break a phrase or slur in order to breathe. This can be equated with a newsreader breathing in mid-word.

Staggered breathing, i.e. breathing out—(usually marked 'O')—continuing to play, and breathing in—(marked '√' or '𝕵') —a few bars or notes later (depending on the tempo of the music). This is a useful practice when, as is so often the case, there is not time to breathe out and in at the same place without interrupting the flow of the music or missing a note or notes. It's especially useful in fast and busy or continuous pieces such as much of Bach's music e.g. 'Jesu, Joy of Man's Desiring':

Practise staggered breathing at first in simple tunes, e.g. Hinke No 1:

(see 'Recommended Publications')

or in slow scales:

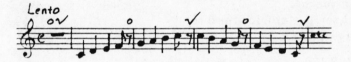

Circular breathing. This is a technique whereby air is breathed in through the nose while the player continues to play using air puffed out with the cheeks, giving the impression of going on for ever without taking a breath. This should not really be necessary if you have learned good breath control, as described. Breathing should divide music into natural phrases as it does speech. Music, like speech, can be dull if it just goes on and on. (In recordings it's possible to cheat—by splicing tapes and cutting out breaths taken—'no breaths'.)

In extreme instances of *very* long notes, however, this perhaps might be useful, and I recently heard of a well-known player having to be carried from a rehearsal on a stretcher, after passing out during such a passage.

Some recommend circular breathing as being 'good for you', saving you from 'bursting' by keeping natural breathing rhythm.

One reason why you might feel it worth learning the technique, I'm told, is that it has the dubious asset of enabling you to pass the breathaliser test, however much alcohol you've consumed! This was recently proved by a woodwind member of one of our orchestras who passed the test after drinking fourteen pints of beer! (*not* that I am recommending drinking and driving).

Posture

Good posture is vital for oboe-playing. Bad posture hinders good breathing which is the key to good playing.

For correct breath control to be possible your back must be straight during playing (whether you are sitting or standing), your head held up, and arms held away from your sides to allow for sideways chest expansion. It is best to practise standing up—some of the time at least—but when you play sitting down use a hard chair, keep both your feet on the floor and your oboe held up. The angle of the oboe in relation to your body should be 40°-45°. Don't let it—and you—sag, not only impeding breathing but projection of your playing—don't play to the floor.

'Sagging' posture will also affect your tone, tuning and general technique.

Remember, good posture makes breathing easier. Good breathing makes playing easier. Don't make things harder for yourself.

Heighten the music stand to encourage you not to slouch...

Embouchure

This term refers to the muscles around your mouth. Beginners, at-first you will find that your embouchure tires quickly when you play and that you cannot control the sound (or 'noise') you make. Don't worry, this is natural. These muscles are not normally used, so will not be developed. Never try to go on playing once you start to get tired and lose control. If you stick to the 'little and often' rule of practice (ten to twenty minutes at a time until you're able to play for longer) your embouchure muscles will soon develop. It may only be a few weeks, if you persevere, before you'll be able to control sound and intonation for reasonably long periods.

Avoid pressure on the reed. It is important not to 'grip' or 'pinch'. Not only will a 'tight' embouchure produce a hard 'tinny' sound, as the vibrations of the reed will be impeded, but it will also make high notes sharp and bottom notes squawk. A 'loose' relaxed—*but controlled*—embouchure will help you to produce a good 'round' tone as well as aiding general intonation. It can be likened to a mother dog carrying her puppies; she holds them tightly enough to know she won't drop them, but not so tightly that her teeth cut into their flesh.

The secret of a relaxed embouchure is to think of an 'OOOO' mouth shape and not an 'EEEE' or tightened shape when you play (except on the very high register). This is especially important for low notes, when almost an 'OW' shape is needed, or a more 'dropped' jaw. Pout—don't smile. This *should* be easy—one doesn't usually feel like smiling when trying to play low notes, especially quiet ones, on the oboe!

Think of your teeth as a frame and your lips merely as a cushion for the reed —or as a draught excluder preventing air leaking from your mouth. A teacher of mine would demonstrate this 'slackness' of embouchure by purposely letting air escape from the sides of his mouth while playing. Try it. It's *not* easy and is a good exercise. For very low notes *even less* lip pressure is needed, but more 'diaphragm' support. If the music is marked pp, or you are worried about notes splitting try to get 'below' them—i.e. relax even more—you need nerves of steel, but lips of velvet.

A—*slightly*—tighter embouchure is required for very high notes (top E''''* upwards) when your lips must be more stretched over your teeth, i.e. the reed vibrates against a harder surface—it will be vibrating faster for high notes. However, since avoiding pressure is harder, especially for those who find it difficult to relax, I feel it best not to think of this tightening of the lips as 'pressure', which might encourage you to 'pinch'. You will be more aware of it on high notes when ascending while diminuendoing. For this, 'diaphragm' (or stomach muscle) control is needed rather than lip pressure, to prevent the top notes petering out. To develop good embouchure control practise accented long notes with crescendos and diminuendos, for example:

Or play slow legato intervals from high to low notes:

Think consciously about the change from 'EEEE' on the very top notes to 'OOOO' or 'OORR' on the lower notes (or 'dropping' your jaw) while listening critically to your tuning. (Surely you've heard donkeys doing this exercise?)

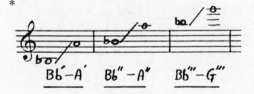

25

Chapter 2

Technique

Tonguing / Staccato; Legato; Vibrato

Tonguing/Staccato

Before attempting staccato playing, it's important to have mastered tonguing. Don't try to run before you can walk.

To tongue a note for the first time blow a long note firmly, then divide it into four by saying 'ter' four times, letting your tongue touch the reed. Keep the tone smooth with no sudden little puffs of air. (N.B. The note actually starts as your tongue *leaves* the reed.)

When you come to staccato, practise t u t at first, slowly but crisply, stopping as well as starting each note with your tongue, and making each as short at possible. Don't try fast staccato yet! 'Staccato' means daylight between each note, however quick; a positive silence, however short, and always crisp; 'ter' not 'ther'. Feel your stomach muscles jerk as described in chapter 1.

In busy music aim for each beat rather than thinking of every note. Otherwise it can easily run away or become unrhythmic (more so than in slurred passages, which are easier to play).

It's better that the first note of each bar or beat is in the right place, on time, than that all the notes are played, but in the wrong place, out of time (or rushed and unrhythmic). Students often place too much emphasis on playing *every note* (showing off fast fingers or a quick tongue?) at the expense of the music.

Your tongue and fingers must be absolutely co-ordinated.

In long fast staccato or tongued passages this is particularly important. Examples are: Mozart's 'Marriage of Figaro' overture (not solo):

the last movement of Haydn's 'Clock' symphony, (tutti):

the last part of Strauss' 'Die Fledermaus' overture, (tutti):

and Rossini's 'Silken Ladder' overture, a notoriously tricky solo:

Don't 'let the side down' by uncontrolled tonguing in a fast 'tutti' passage.

Of course you can cheat (better than playing unrhythmically) by adding the occasional slur, though this *can* change and spoil the desired effect unless done unobtrusively and logically. E.g.:

Even just slurring the first two notes of a piece like 'The Silken Ladder' can help to get you off to a good start and save a fall, viz:

Double-tonguing. This means saying 'ter ker' (instead of 'ter') on every note, and is useful for rhythms such as:

An instance is Suppé's 'Light Cavalry' overture:

Though easier for brass players and flautists, some oboists prefer to double-tongue the whole of a long staccato passage:

But as the 'ker' is softer than the 'ter' less tongue must be used, for evenness.

Learn double-tonguing by playing simple 'appropriate' exercises, for example Hinke (see 'Recommended Publications') numbers 7 and 8:

Triple-tonguing ('ter ker ter') can help such rhythms as:

which occurs in the second movement of Debussy's 'La Mer':

Hinke's excercise 9 is a good 'practice' one for this:

I find that if I keep my single tonguing in practice it's unnecessary to bother much with these 'antics', except sometimes in the sorts of rhythms quoted. For even the fastest performance of 'The Silken Ladder' overture (once engagingly programmed 'The Silken *Larder*'), I feel single tonguing should be adequate, but tastes and abilities differ. In this piece it's usual for the conductor to ask the first oboist what speed he or she likes it, and they trust he'll abide by their wishes. For me it's easier very fast than at a medium tempo—others ask for it to be 'as slow as possible'. One should, I suppose, be prepared for *any* tempo just in case.

Flutter-tonguing (notated in various ways), easier for flautists and more common in flute writing, crops up in some twentieth-century oboe music. It is a sort of 'purring' effect and it's helpful if you can roll your RRs (which rules out many of us). Otherwise fake the effect with a gargle-like 'grrr' instead. I don't think your future as either an amateur or professional player will be jeopardised by an inability to flutter-tongue, though for much avant-garde music it may be useful and sometimes essential. Stravinsky asks for it in his 'Rite of Spring':

Legato

One should, ideally, be able to play any interval within the oboe's range absolutely smoothly, whatever the rhythm, tempo or dynamic—like intervals sung on 'aaah' without consonants. The voice is the 'king of instruments'—using a man-made substitute should not make the listener aware of mechanics (artificial aids). (A 'cellist asked to pay an extra air fare for his 'cello replied, "My instrument is my voice. Singers don't have to buy a ticket for theirs".)

To achieve overall fluency, intervals requiring simultaneous—therefore coordinated—movement of several fingers, or worse, a slide (usually for the little—weakest—finger on the furthest—heaviest—keys) needs *practice*. There is no substitute. Always listen for 100 per cent smoothness and be very particular. Don't tolerate the slightest sound or audible break between notes. Repeat an 'untidy' interval VERY SLOWLY until it's *absolutely* 'clean', in different rhythms, before increasing the tempo *gradually*. Don't leave any interval until it is perfect (see 'Practice', Chapter 4). How to practise this is set out brilliantly in Bleuzet's *La Technique du Hautbois* (see 'Recommended Publications'). For example:

Use full fingering not trill keys. Follow this method for *every* interval in every key and rhythm. For instance practise legato scales in thirds, repeating each interval slowly until clean, then in triplet and other rhythms. For example:

and:

And like this:

Later practise scales in fourths, fifths etc., the same way. For example:

and:

And don't forget arpeggios (Bleuzet volume 3) and chromatic scales, and scales in chromatic seconds, thirds etc. For example:

(seconds)

(minor thirds)

These are good examples of how to work at every interval within the oboe's compass, and not only make an excellent backbone for smooth legato playing, but marvellous groundwork for a sound overall finger technique.

Trills may be practised this way too, slowly and evenly in increasing tempi— not only tones and semitones, but larger intervals. Trill keys on some oboes and alternative fingerings facilitate fast trills, but for slow practice always use full fingering. Be governed by the hardest interval or key when choosing your tempo. Don't start too fast, then come unstuck.

B-B*b* (middle or top octave)—on thumbplate models—is one nasty interval which must be practised slowly until absolutely smooth. Only use trill keys (in this case the spatula key—see Chapter 18 page 188) for fast trill practice (32+ notes per bar), aiming for each beat. All trills and intervals should sound equal no matter what notes they are or whether full fingering or a trill key is used (for 'fake' and 'alternative' fingerings see chapter 18).

Persist, as with all practice, slowly and patiently, until 100 per cent sure, and you should develop a good legato and finger technique and be able to play smoothly and fluently in any key.

Legato playing will also be facilitated by good diaphragm and breath control and support (see 'Breathing', Chapter 1), and by blowing 'through' rather than 'into' the instrument (see 'Mixed Bag', Chapter 18)...

However hard, a legato passage should sound smooth and 'easy' to the listener, who should not be aware of fingering difficulties. The second movement of Brahms' first symphony has a typical example—a solo on awkward notes, which needs beautifully co-ordinated finger movement for it to sound 'singing' and 'effortless':

and:

Another example is the opening solo in the second movement of Tchaikowsky's fourth symphony:

This is also a good reed tester—if a reed sounds okay in this it is definitely okay. (More later, see chapter 12.)

The opening of Ravel's 'Tombeau de Couperin' is another awkward exposed passage which is impossible to play smoothly without thorough fingerwork practice:

These examples are all common audition pieces.

Vibrato

Though usually a natural thing, there are various ways of producing vibrato deliberately if necessary—with the throat or with the lips—(some people even appear to do it with their heads!)...

But the most usual and, I think, satisfactory method is from the diaphragm—'hoo-hoo-hoo' as in laughing, using the stomach muscles.

If it is not there naturally leave the positive production of vibrato until your general playing technique is well advanced. Treat it as the final polish, the gilt on the gingerbread. Don't worry about it or try to force it too soon. Vibrato too early can hinder playing progress by concealing a multitude of sins. (Conversely it can be used on purpose to this end—but I don't want to go putting ideas in your head.)

Even when you are a 'vibrato expert' it's always important to practise without it sometimes so that you can listen acutely to your 'unadulterated' sound.

It's essential to be able to control, and eliminate, it. Some contemporary composers specify 'no vibrato', and it should not always be used, for example in held woodwind chords. Use vibrato as a colouring, or to increase intensity, especially on long sustained notes (with crescendos), for example the start of the second movement of Mozart's oboe quartet:

or the long top C''' after the oboe enters in the first movement of his oboe concerto—uninteresting if played the same throughout:

or the Brahms I solo mentioned in 'Legato'. Start without vibrato and introduce it gradually for intensity, atmosphere and colour.

Don't let yourself get into the habit of always playing with the same vibrato (or tone colouring). This is boring and meaningless. Use different speeds (or intensities) to suit the music and give the effect you want. Apply it imaginatively to give your music interest, life and meaning. A fast deep vibrato can make a short phrase exciting, a slower 'shallower' one adds expression to a gentle, sustained melody. Experiment for yourself once you can produce and control it easily.

To practise vibrato play long notes (sixteen slow beats or more) pp with a crescendo (see 'Practice', Chapter 4) starting without vibrato, gradually introducing it as you crescendo, and reversing this exercise as you diminuendo through the note to end pp and vibrato-less. This is useful for tone, lip, breath, diaphragm and embouchure control, too.

At the beginning of Rossini's overture to 'The Barber of Seville' the oboe enters on a sustained G#", first with a long diminuendo (which can seem endless if taken slowly) with vibrato as well as volume dying away, then crescendoing and adding vibrato, increasing in intensity through to the end of this longish phrase. In some editions these dynamics are reversed. Either is good practice in use and control of vibrato. (This piece is known, for obvious reasons, as '7-8-pom pom'...):

Instances of vibrato (intensity) and volume decreasing to nothing often occur at the end of pieces or movements (for example the cor anglais solo in Mahler's fourth symphony—see page 83).

Finally, NEVER use vibrato when giving an 'A'. (Sir Thomas Beecham once told the orchestra, cheekily, following an oboe 'A' given with vibrato, "Take your pick, gentlemen".) 'A's are purely a clear pitch for the orchestra to tune to—*not,* as many oboists appear to believe, a chance to show off their very best sound, 'vib an' all'.

Chapter 3

Using Your Ears

Listening; Pitching; Tuning; Tone

Listening

Listening to yourself in minute detail is only really possible when playing alone. Solitary practice is, therefore, vital—there is NO substitute. Playing with others can hide faults, imperfections and bad habits, which are harder to eliminate the longer they're allowed to persist.

SLOW practice of EVERYTHING is also imperative, to enable you to listen critically to yourself (see 'Practice', Chapter 4). Small imperfections are easily missed when you're trying to play lots of notes and, perhaps, are too preoccupied with reading, fingerings, or tonguing to listen properly to detail.

Playing without music helps concentration too, even just scales. It's better to do this in the dark without distractions. (You'll know this if you've ever listened to music in the dark…Try it.)

Practise at home in different rooms, or parts of a room. For instance, play into a wall or mirror, then into a curtain or bed; hear the contrast. (More later, see 'Mixed Bag', Chapter 18.)

Do some of your practice without vibrato, to listen to your true sound (see 'Vibrato', Chapter 2).

When playing with others listen not only to yourself but to those around you. If playing second oboe listen to the first. If you are first oboe listen particularly to the first flute. These are the players you are most likely to be playing with. Always try to hear the bass line, too. This can be helpful for keeping the beat in your head, especially in fast music where there may be a tendency to rush, besides being a reliable 'anchor' pitch-wise, especially in chamber music. Blame the second bassoon!

Keep your ears open for whoever is playing 'the tune' (if you're playing the kind of music that has one). If somebody is, and you cannot hear them properly, you are probably playing too loudly.

Listen, then, to balance and blending, as well as tuning, pitch, articulation and phrasing, and, of course, your own vibrato and tone quality.

Pitching

Pitching each note is essential on woodwind as well as stringed instruments. It is a false belief that a woodwind player has only to put down the correct fingers and blow for exactly the right note to come out. How I wish it were that easy! The oboe is difficult to play in tune, and it is as crucial to 'hear' each note before you play it as it is for a singer.

This applies especially to high—more flexible—notes, and to solo entries at the start of a piece or movement. An example is the opening of Tchaikowsky's

36

ballet 'Swan Lake', when it's important to have the first note in your head before the performance starts (unless you have perfect pitch):

Another is the opening of Beethoven's seventh symphony where, after the first short loud chord from everyone, the oboe is left on a high A″, feeling very lonely indeed:

A similar nasty entry, again on high A″ (a note that could be all over the place if blown carelessly) is in the third movement of Tchaikowsky's fourth symphony:

The opening of Beethoven's violin concerto also needs careful pitching; just four drum beats to give you your note. There are many such instances. If you 'just blow' a note you will be lucky if it's anywhere near in tune, however good your instrument and reed, let alone 'spot on'.

The tricky opening and closing wind chords in Mendelssohn's 'A Midsummer Night's Dream' are a case in point, needing careful pitching and relating of every note. Aim for perfection. Being 'nearly in tune' is still being out of tune!

It's hard to sing out of tune *on purpose*. If you listen and 'pitch' in your head as you would to sing, every note should be in tune—always (assuming you're in control of your playing). It sounds easy doesn't it?

It's a matter of concentration too. If you use your ears efficiently you'll find you adjust your embouchure automatically, tuning each note, as you would to sing or whistle in tune. It's harder to 'hear' every note, however, in twelve-tone or 'serial' music—called 'snap, crackle and pop' music or 'knitting pattern' music as it's made up of a pattern of notes—but *perhaps* it's not *quite* so vital in this kind of music. Even if you can't actually hear yourself, once you are a reasonably accomplished player, you'll instinctively tune by 'feel'. Make sure, of course, that your instrument is properly warmed up, basically in tune, and assembled properly, that you are familiar with any notes needing 'lipping' up or down, and that you know your reed and have as reliable a one as possible.

Tuning

To learn to play in tune is crucial. Out of tune playing spoils any performance for the other musicians and is not something anybody will want to listen to.

Intonation is more important even than tone. It's better to have a 'poor' sound (a matter of taste after all) and be in tune, than to play 'beautifully' out of tune (though a good sound *and* perfect intonation are best). Funnily enough one will follow on from the other. Concentrate on tuning and you'll find this leads to tone improvement. (I speak from expert advice *and* experience.) Having understood the necessity to 'pitch' in your head it's then a case of controlling your embouchure, playing, and reed, and listening meticulously, in order to *play* the pitch you 'hear'.

Every instrument has notes which need minor 'lipping' adjustment to tune them. Don't *over*-compensate though. You may find that you actually play a 'flat' note sharp (or vice versa) as you're thinking too hard about it being a flat note.

As a first-year student I had oboe lessons at my teacher's home, where he kept a mynah bird. I was studying Malcolm Arnold's sonatina, I remember, and finding it hard to get all the top notes in tune. The bird would whistle them for me, perfectly (it obviously knew the piece) which did *not* help my confidence.

Once you can control and adjust tuning in detail there is little excuse for out of tune playing, despite influencing factors which must be overcome (see 'Physical Hazards', Chapter 6). There is certainly no need for the lame excuse made by some nineteenth-century players: "Sir, we played out of tune on purpose to make it in character, for whoever heard of music being in tune at the Lord Mayor's show?".

It's important always to play and practise at correct pitch, even on your own. Constant playing flat or sharp will accustom your ear to faulty pitch, which is no good when playing with others. So if you play regularly with a piano make sure it's tuned to standard British 'A=440' (440 vibrations per second). A tuning-fork (referred to by an ex-farm worker pupil of mine as a 'pitch fork') is useful to have, especially if you make (or alter) your reeds, or have to give 'A's. Don't rely on your piano.

When checking pitch with the tuning-fork—a good habit—don't just play 'A'—often an unreliable note. One's instinct is to tune or adapt the 'A' (with lips/embouchure) to the fork without even realising it. Rather, check intervals between more reliable notes on your instrument—say, D, E or F—and 'A'. Listen to the fork *after* playing the note rather than the other way round—a more reliable test.

You can flatten the overall pitch *slightly* by pulling your reed out of the oboe, but only a *fraction*—1-2mm—or general intonation will be affected. Notes nearest the reed (i.e. middle B″ and C″) will be affected first. You can, however, pull the crook out quite a way to flatten the pitch of a cor anglais before this occurs (see 'The Oboe's Relatives', Chapter 17).

If you make your own reeds (much more later) make them 'to the fork', i.e. to British standard concert pitch, or, if you buy them from a shop check their pitch if possible (take your tuning-fork with you)—*hopefully* unnecessary with 'professional' reeds.

And, of course, buy a standard pitched oboe (see 'Choosing an Instrument', Chapter 14).

(For more about reeds and tuning see chapters 9 and 12.)

Emergency alterations, such as pulling the reed out, should only be resorted to, for instance, in extreme temperatures (heat makes wind instruments sharper and cold, flatter), or, God forbid, to match a flat piano, or, more likely, organ. But find out about such things first if you can and be prepared. I was recently accompanied at a service on a church organ which was nearly half a tone flat (unfortunately not quite half a tone or transposition could have solved the problem). I had to use the longest ever reed with the longest ever scrape, to match it, but had been able to check its pitch in advance and prepare a special one.

On another occasion, performing Bach's 'Jesu, Joy of Man's Desiring' in a London church, the organ was, mercifully, exactly a semitone flat, so I played it in G, as written, and the organist transposed it into G#!

To adapt to sharp conditions is a worse problem unless there is time for reed alterations. It can 'ruin' your lip to play, for instance, with a *sharp* piano, when you will instinctively 'pinch' the reed to try to play sharper, soon making your mouth sore, as well as distorting the sound.

For minor tuning of individual notes it's simpler to adapt your playing, I think, than to 'tinker' with reeds or with the instrument's mechanism. See if you can imitate an ambulance on your oboe. Simply play C″ and A′ repeatedly, 'lipping' down further and further, i.e flattening the pitch drastically by 'dropping' your jaw (see 'Embouchure', Chapter 1). It's most effective:

This experiment should bring home to you the relatively huge amount it is possible to alter pitch, especially in the middle or upper—more flexible—registers, by simply tightening or slackening your embouchure. Use this method—in moderation—to tune notes as you play them—'EEE-OOO-ORR'—(see 'Embouchure,' Chapter 1). Try this using the reed only. You'll find you can alter the 'note' by several tones. In fact it's possible to play 'God Save the Queen', or similarly ranged tunes, on the reed in this way.

Giving 'A's. Although 'A' is an unreliable note on many oboes it's the oboist's job to give the 'A' for the orchestra to tune to if there is no piano, harpsichord or organ ('fixed pitch' instruments). The oboe has a penetrating sound, easy for all to hear, and a less flexible pitch than many instruments. 'A' is a convenient note for most to tune to (brass and clarinets would prefer B♭, but, except in wind bands, they are in the minority). If it falls to you to give the 'A' make sure your oboe is warmed up and use a tuning-fork to be sure the 'A' you give is correct.

String players, especially violinists, often tune sharp—and think they're right. (Oh dear! Now I'll be in trouble with my string-playing friends—in fact now I may not have any!) 'Stick to your guns'—and the fork—and ignore the inevitable moans. It's an unenviable job, and means arriving early (or at least on time). String players don't realise how fortunate they are.

One well-known oboist got so fed up when the conductor said, sarcastically, "Could we have an A=440 next time?" that next day he simply held up a sign reading 'A=440'. Another was told by a violinist, "That's sharp, I've got perfect pitch", to which he replied, "You don't need an 'A' from me then."

Tone

The oboe is described as having a 'wondrous sound that sings alone above the orchestra, speaking directly to the soul, and bringing, so often, the heart to tears.' It is certainly one of the most beautiful and expressive of instruments, but it is difficult to make a really good sound on the oboe, and all too easy to sound dreadful, 'bringing the heart to tears' for quite different reasons. The tone you make is important—there is no point in making a sound that no one will want to listen to, or which will give no pleasure (the reason for playing music). The oboe has a 'splendid expressive range of sound'. Let's keep it that way!

As a primary incentive to produce an attractive sound listen to good players, even if only on recordings. 'Listening to, and imitating one's betters encourages musical skill.' 'Hearing' their sound in your head when you play, and wanting to sound like them, is the first step towards it happening. Teachers and pupils should play together—hopefully helpful for the pupil!—to encourage tone production initially.

As with vibrato don't play every note with the same tone. Learn to vary your sound to suit the music you are playing (see 'Languages', Chapter 16). For tone practice play slow melodies, listening exclusively to your sound and consciously trying to relax your embouchure, remembering the 'OOOO' shape ('open' your throat, as in yawning), and using firm breath control. Slow studies are precious and few, but the slow exercises in Ferling's *48* (see 'Recommended Publications') are excellent (my copy has disintegrated with use), covering a wide range of notes and dynamics. Pretend these are orchestral solos when you play them, not 'just' exercises, and make them as expressive as possible. Bach excerpts are ideal too (see 'Recommended Publications'). They are so beautiful it would be terrible to render them other than beautifully! A real inspiration.

In Marcel Moyse's flute studies *Tone Development Through Interpretation,* he suggests transposing well-known expressive slow tunes, working through all keys. I recommend these for oboists, too (see 'Recommended Publications'). It is wonderful tone practice—*and* a good study for tuning. The gorgeous melodies should inspire you to make a beautiful sound, and to play in tune in every key, despite the different feel, sound and problems of each. (How different D♭ and C♯ seem for example!)

Don't be afraid of top C''' which can sound particularly thin and 'tinny'—the worst note on the oboe—(though C♯''' is usually worst to get). Relax, and listen even more. It will only sound bright, sharp or 'nasty' if you pinch or tense up (which usually the mere sight of one makes you do). 'OOOO' again—and *keep calm!*

Try to hit the 'middle' of each note, which enourages a 'plummier', 'warmer' tone. This also helps intonation. 'Hear' a good sound in your head as you play; imagine how you would really like to sound. It works.

Don't ever rely on being lucky enough to have that rare and cherished thing—'a good reed' (to misquote the title of a Radio 4 book review programme). Ninety-nine per cent of the time we have to make do with a less than ideal one, often making a good tone hard to produce (sometimes a good *anything*) so we must compensate with our playing for its shortcomings. (For the effect of different reeds on tone see chapters 9 and 12.)

Basically YOU must make your sound. Don't be lazy and expect your reed—or instrument—to make it for you. Good 'tools' help, of course, but tone production is largely governed by *you,* —your embouchure, breath control, use of diaphragm and posture, and by listening and 'wanting' to sound good.

I recently met a six-year-old who had 'tried out' his auntie's clarinet. "I blowed it and it made a noise," he told me excitedly. "Was it a *nice* noise?" I asked. "Yeees!" he said, proudly. (I hope everyone else thought so, too.)

Why is the oboe so rudely referred to as 'an ill wind that nobody blows good'? Or unkindly likened to a duck? (Because it represents the duck in Prokoviev's 'Peter and the Wolf'? Or because this is the sort of sound some

41

oboists make?) Americans even call the oboe 'the English Bum' from 'hobo' (tramp). No! Let us preserve the oboe's deserved reputation as the 'loveliest woodwind voice' and 'queen of orchestral instruments'. It must *never* be allowed to sound like a duck...

Chapter 4

Practice...or Lack of it!

Using a work pattern; When time is short; Suggestions for how and what to practise

Sound technique once learned, like riding a bicycle or a language spoken fluently, will never be forgotten (though may need occasional revision) BUT— so will bad habits.

Efficient study is, therefore, an excellent investment. Plan carefully how to use your practice time, however scarce, most effectively.

'Little and often' is recommended for beginners (while the embouchure muscles develop)—I would add 'little and concentrated'. It's easy to feel virtuous after two or three hours' practice, but the chances are that it was not all 100 per cent meticulous, therefore not only a waste of time, but possibly even harmful if inaccuracies were overlooked. So—stop if you find your concentration going. If practising for more than an hour take little breaks. 'Switch off' for a few minutes, then return to it refreshed. Don't always practise in the evening, or when you're tired. Vary the times and use your freshest period sometimes, at least.

Avoid practising when you have other things on your mind, or distractions, spoiling concentration. Half-hearted practice can be worse than none.

Using a work pattern

Have a definite practice plan so that everything gets covered and nothing left out however little time you may have. I suggest something on these lines:

Slow work first—long notes beginning pp, crescendoing to ff and back again to pp etc. (see 'Embouchure', Chapter 1) and slow scales, without vibrato, concentrating on breathing control, intonation and an even overall sound.

Then fingerwork—scales, straight and in thirds, fourths etc., in different patterns and rhythms (see 'Legato', Chapter 2).

Next, staccato and tonguing—one note in different rhythms, scales, or exercises, but always rhythmic, clean and controlled, with fingers and tongue co-ordinated, slow and short until clean, then in *gradually* faster tempi, as with legato practice. For example:

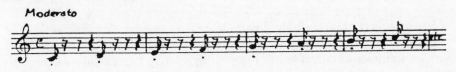

then:

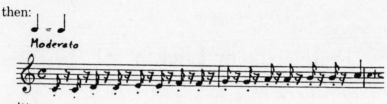

written:

on to:

and finally:

Follow this with a study. Work at it in sections, using a metronome to keep a steady tempo at first, only setting gradually faster speeds when it's ALL completely secure at the slower one.

Practise pieces and orchestral parts last. They're more fun than scales and exercises—don't be tempted to skip the 'donkey-work'! Try to include some sight-reading, especially if you're not getting reading practice elsewhere. Borrow flute or violin as well as oboe music from friends or the library, and invest in new studies and pieces occasionally. Use music written for instruments with a wider range; reading passages up or down an octave improves sight-reading, as does transposing at sight (as in Marcel Moyse's studies, see 'Tone', Chapter 3, and 'Recommended Publications').

Finally, try reading something without stopping—even if you make mistakes—keeping going without hesitating. This is useful preparation for playing with others.

This is a suggested practice routine only. *You* must plan *your* work pattern according to *your* needs and time available…and stamina. Don't try to overdo it, especially if you're a relative novice, or 'kill yourself' to get through an overoptimistic schedule. Leave some work until you're rested, another time—*or* simply spend a little less time on each item, but make sure nothing gets left out altogether, especially slow and scale practice.

You may choose to take a scale each week and cover all rhythms and patterns in that key—or major scales one day, melodic minor the next—or thirds on Monday, fourths on Tuesday, chromatic scales and dominant sevenths on Thursday, and work from a study book(s), 'x' pages or exercises (or parts of studies) per day or week…

Make practice notes if this helps you, allocating time for everything, or noting anything that got omitted. There must be NO excuse not to practise the boring or difficult things!

Keeping to a routine like this avoids the habit of always starting with the same scale (e.g. C) and never reaching others more difficult, always being tired and lacking concentration for the same things, or repeating exercises or studies at the expense of others.

For a sound technique *everything* must be practised, which means organised planning.

When time is short

Don't worry. Few of us have time to practise as much as we'd like to—with the exception of full-time music students. We just have to fit it in as and when possible. Twenty minutes per day, or twice a week even, can be plenty *if* the time is used intelligently—quality not quantity—but try to avoid long stretches with *no* practice. It's still important to cover everything however, if in smaller doses—perhaps five minutes on long notes and a couple of slow scales, two contrasting scales in thirds or fourths—(e.g. C and D*b*)—but NOT the same two each time!—two or three staccato scales in patterns or a short tonguing exercise, and a study (or part of one) one day, work on a new piece another.

Never skip slow practice though. It's tempting to 'rush' if time is limited, thus defeating the object. One might feel one has 'covered more ground' after playing a lot of notes, but the same time spent on slow work, listening and breathing well, is probably more beneficial, especially once you've acquired a reasonable finger technique.

I find the best use of short time, or when coming back to playing, say after a holiday, is to play *very slow* scales (each note 8, 12 or 16 *slow* beats) with sharp accents, crescendos and diminuendos, from ppp to fff (see 'Tone', Chapter 3, and 'Embouchure' Chapter 1). This will keep your lip 'in' when you're unable to practise much, or revive it after a break. (When very short of time play arpeggios like this instead of whole scales.) It's 'killing'... but worth it! Be cautious though, and stop *before* your lip is sore.

Tonguing agility (like sight-reading) goes quickly (more than fingers) when you don't practise or play regularly, but with a little concentrated work will soon 'wake up', so don't despair.

Add to this a few legato scales in thirds etc. to 'loosen the fingers' and you have a good 'refresher course'.

Suggestions for how and what to practise

How to practise

Always be hyper-critical; let nothing pass until it's perfect. Repeat it a few times *after* you've played it 'perfectly'—it was probably a fluke the first time!

Practise everything SLOWLY, increasing the tempo *gradually,* but never up to speed till secure at a steady pace. Tempo is governed by the hardest bit. Don't fall into the trap of setting off too fast and slowing down when you reach a difficult part, or always coming a cropper at the same place (see 'Bad Habits', Chapter 5).

One hears rushed practice all too often, players whizzing through pieces or orchestral solos when they realise they should have looked at the notes at home. This does more harm than good and is a sure way of getting into a panic. 'Slow and steady wins the race' is certainly true in oboe practice.

Never play aimlessly or clumsily—always work at something specific, and concentrate on 'correct' playing. Don't rush through exercises to impress yourself with fast—but not 100 per cent accurate—fingers—not really impressive at all.

Always listen for breaks or untidy intervals caused by clumsy fingering, and 'clean them up' before continuing.

Pick out awkward passages from studies or pieces. Practise these separately, slowly, in various patterns and rhythms, then again, as written. They'll suddenly seem easy! (Gillets' *Studies for the Advanced Teaching of the Oboe,* see 'Recommended Publications', includes a Practice Method, showing perfect examples of how to do this.)

It is a far better and quicker way to learn than repeatedly playing something the same way. Don't play the *whole* exercise or piece through until all tricky bits are 'under the fingers'.

Use different accents (or time signatures) too, viz:

or:

For example, take Luft's exercise number 16 (see 'Recommended Publications'):

and practise it in $\frac{6}{8}$:

One good way to learn a hard passage is to begin at the end! Work at the last bar, say bar 23, till 'safe'. Then play bars 22 and 23 a few times. Add bar 21, play 21-23, and so on. Finally play the entire phrase or section.

Find the root of a problem before it's ingrained. If you make the same slip or squeak twice find out why. Once you've established the cause you're halfway there. Stop at the fault, work at it to stamp it out, then repeat it correctly, as written, once or twice. Always start a bar or so *before* the slip, i.e. 'make the join' to smooth it out properly. Don't make the same mistake *three* times. If for every inaccuracy you play it correctly ten times I'm prepared to bet you won't make the same mistake again, so it saves time in the long run!

Use a mirror to see which finger is making an interval untidy. Concentrate on a lazy or weak finger as you use it—usually the third (ring) finger, or little finger. A mirror is also useful to check for flapping fingers or sticking out little fingers (see 'Bad Habits', Chapter 5), as well as the amount of the reed in your mouth and the angle of the instrument etc.

Use a pencil to mark any pitfalls—(breaths, left-hand fingerings, trill keys, rhythmically complicated passages, time or key signatures, tempo or dynamic changes or repeats which may catch you out, etc. see 'Mixed Bag', Chapter 18, page 188). Never practise (or rehearse) without a pencil.

Practising without music is useful. If you find memorising pieces or studies hard, play scales (straight and in patterns) from memory (see 'Using Your Ears', Chapter 3).

Practise in different rooms and acoustics too (see 'Listening', Chapter 3, and 'Mixed Bag', Chapter 18).

You can even 'practice' without playing your oboe, fingering notes silently (have you seen players doing this in rehearsals while the rest are playing something else?) or using a mirror to spot untidy fingering. This can be useful when your lip has 'gone' (i.e. is tired or sore) or when others might be disturbed.

After a spell without playing return to it with short (fifteen or twenty minute) sessions, stopping if your lip/embouchure tires and control starts to go. Your playing will soon come back with gentle perseverance and you'll notice a daily improvement. So—take heart if you're forced to give up for a while. A teacher of mine who didn't see an oboe for five years during the war claimed that, apart from initial lip tiredness, his playing had not deteriorated. Indeed he felt it had improved!

The object of practice is to make progress. Even a short session is satisfying if you have put right, improved, or 'perfected' something. If, however, as occasionally happens, you *can't* concentrate or play *anything* right, it's sometimes best to stop, and return to it fresh, another day. Otherwise you may tend to play clumsily and inaccurately, which might do your playing more harm than good.

Finally, even if you're not doing any playing and it's hard to find the incentive, *do* still keep up your practice, at least enough to keep your lip and fingers working. You never know when playing opportunities will arise, and, though an effort at the time, I promise you won't regret it.

What to practise
Concentrate your practice on anything which feels 'rusty' or below your usual standard, or which needs particular improvement.

For embouchure control and lip 'strengthening' slur from high to low notes, or play long notes with crescendos and diminuendos, in all registers, with *no* wobbles. Start ppp and 'creep' in with no bulge and an inaudible start:

(or begin ff, and diminuendo to pp.)

48

Or start with loud accents, *immediately* returning to ppp (see 'Embouchure', Chapter 1):

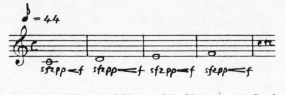

but don't overdo it (see 'Physical Hazards', Chapter 6). Such exercises can be found in Bleuzet's first volume (see 'Recommended Publications').

Can you diminuendo to pp on low B♭ without 'bubbling'? This is a hard test of control.

(Wide intervals are also useful tuning and legato training).

For smooth legato playing, co-ordinated fingering and agile finger technique, practise slurred thirds, fourths, fifths etc., or any phrase or motif in all keys—and exercises based on scale or arpeggio patterns, such as Luft, or Langey's 'exercises for working the keys' (see 'Recommended Publications'). Here is a taste of two of these:

Later Gillet's *Studies for the Advanced Teaching of the Oboe,* with Practice Method, should promote superior finger technique and fluency in playing, if studied properly. Avoid the temptation to tackle these before you're ready though (don't let pride come before a fall!).

For controlled trills repeat *each* interval slowly and evenly, in every key, before progressing to faster tempi—also in Bleuzet's method (see 'Legato', Chapter 2, and 'Recommended Publications'). For example, Bleuzet, volume 1, based on No 11, page 18:

To improve sight-reading, transpose tunes or exercises to all keys—helpful for intonation, tone and fingerwork too.

For staccato and an agile tongue, stop as well as start notes with your tongue, as crisply as possible, with daylight between each (see 'Technique', Chapter 2), concentrating on clean rhythm and co-ordinated tongue and fingers.

For breath control and tone improvement sustain slow 'dolce' melodies or exercises, with special attention to expression, dynamics and phrasing (e.g. Ferling's slow studies, Bach excerpts, or Moyse's selection, see 'Recommended Publications').

For vibrato control, play long notes, starting (pp) vibrato-less, and then introducing slow shallow vibrato, increasing its speed and depth (and volume) using your diaphragm, then vice versa.

Practise *any* awkward passages, whether from studies, exercises, pieces or orchestral parts, in different rhythms, articulations and patterns. Ravel's 'Daphnis and Chloë' for example, which is full of awkward intervals and travels through many keys, must be smooth to create the desired effect (though not a solo), see opposite.

It may help to 'think' it in 6:

Practice suggestions:

(If you ever play this work you'll be glad you practised thirds and fourths in all keys—or bitterly regret not having done so...)

Gillet, in his study number 12, takes a passage from Rossini's 'Barber of Seville' and bases a whole study on it:

Try doing this sort of thing for yourself.

Use a metronome a) when practising something slowly, then in gradually increasing tempi, b) to stop you rushing, especially in fast music (or losing tempo in slow pieces), c) for relating tempi in, say, sets of variations, or when 'Tempo I' is reverted to, and d) when a composer's metronome marking is given, or as a tempo indication (most metronomes include rough guides, e.g. 'march' tempo = crotchet = 120 or 'Colonel Bogey'!). Don't use one all the time.

Living in a house with uneven floors, my problem is finding somewhere where my 'tick-tock' metronome will not beat unevenly, making duple rhythm *almost* triple—exasperating to practise to...

I can't over-emphasise the value of thorough practice, as outlined in this and preceding chapters.

Though not always exciting, it's well worth the satisfaction—and resulting confidence—of knowing you have a technique secure in every respect.

We wind players, unlike individual string players within a section, can always be heard, so we must not only keep awake but keep our standard up.

Finally, don't be tempted to sacrifice practice time in order to try to solve the eternal 'reed crisis'. Allocate time to each—practise *before* reed-making.

The Bad News

Common bad habits; Musical pitfalls

Common bad habits

1) Breathing in without first breathing out, becoming redder and redder, eventually feeling dizzy and having to stop to gasp for breath (see 'Breathing', Chapter 1).

2) Shallow breathing, practising in an over-heated or stuffy room, or 'overdoing' playing, especially on new or hard reeds—all causes of dizziness and inferior playing.

3) Breathing late and not being ready to come in on time (see 'Breathing', Chapter 1 and 'You the Musician', Chapter 7).

4) Playing with the oboe too low (see 'Posture', Chapter 1). Imagine you're playing—and projecting your sound—to the audience in the back row of a big hall, *not* to somebody lying on the floor at your feet.

5) Slouching, resting the oboe on your knee while playing (*don't* tell me you've seen pros do this!)—or sitting/standing to play, with crossed legs. Generally poor posture.

6) Laying your oboe down keys downwards after playing, allowing moisture into the holes, which dampens the pads making them stick, besides probably damaging the mechanism.

7) Putting your oboe away without drying the bore, or with damp pads. *Always* remove moisture from both after playing.

8) Using a mop with exposed wire, risking scratching the oboe's bore, especially the narrow top joint (see 'Nursing Care', Chapter 15).

9) Spitting into your reed/oboe. Swallow and *always* suck any moisture from your reed *quietly* before you play (see 'Mixed Bag', Chapter 18). Avoid hissy bubbly notes.

10) Eating before playing and risking blocking the octave holes with soggy biscuit or fish and chips. Clean your teeth first.

11) Bulging cheeks. This may cause lack of playing control (you must be able to use the corner muscles of your mouth) and can be painful, besides looking silly.

12) 'Finger-flapping', a very common fault, producing untidy playing and noisy slapping and rattling. The *least possible* finger movement

facilitates playing. Oboe mechanism requires *no* pressure. Your fingers should be close to the keys ready for use, not two or three inches away! Use a mirror to check and correct this habit (see Legato', Chapter 2).

13) Thumb or fingers not ready for action. On a thumbplate oboe keep your left thumb on or positioned over the thumbplate, never on the wood. Don't let fingers curl under the instrument, or stick your little fingers in the air. You may think it elegant to drink tea this way but it's not a good way of playing the oboe.

14) Sliding/moving the C″ key (left index) finger too far, or lifting it. A minute *rolling* action to uncover the tiny hole in the key is all the movement necessary.

15) Jabbing the instrument against your shoulder, breaking the reed, while trying to look closely at your fingers.

16) Putting too much reed in your mouth, resulting in a generally bad 'noisy' sound, and sharp pitch, especially on middle C″ and G″.

17) Using the wrong octave key. The C″ key (left index finger) should be open (or half-closed) for 'middle' C#″ to D#″, the first octave key (left thumb) used for E″ to G#″, though G#″/Ab″ can usually be played with either , and the second octave key (left forefinger) for top A″ to C‴.

N.B. Using wrong octave keys on purpose produces a 'harmonic', effective for soft distant sounding controlled entries. The oboe has eight harmonics, notated thus, see Gillet's study number 22:

(small notes and their octave key indicate fingerings to be used).

18) Using the Eb key unnecessarily for forked F (second fingering for F—necessary in certain passages) making the note sharp and bright, if you change from an oboe without a forked F vent to one with one.

19) Leaving the left-hand D# key on for E, F or forked F after a D# producing nasty sharp notes.

20) Untidy fingering, especially involving a slide (e.g. low C′ to C#′ or B′ to Bb′) or movement of several fingers (e.g. middle B″ or C″ to C#″ or D″) or an awkward move (e.g. middle Bb″ to B ♮ ″ on a thumbplate oboe). Identify the problem, e.g. a lazy finger or excess finger movement (even faulty mechanics—but don't blame your instrument unfairly) then *practise* to correct it (see 'Practice', Chapter 4).

21) Catching a side key (e.g. right-hand G#) accidentally, producing a squawk.

22) Lazy third (ring) fingers not covering an open hole or ring key properly and causing squeaks or unco-ordinated playing. This finger is weak, having a shared tendon, so needs extra care and practice (e.g. forked F to E, as in Langey's 'exercises for working the keys', page 61):

An ideal third finger strengthener is Gillet's study number 3. Here is a small extract:

(He even suggests screwing the F key down allowing forked F fingering only!)

23) 'Cracking' low notes. These require a more open or relaxed 'OOOO' or 'OORR' shape embouchure than the upper register, extra diaphragm support and firmer use of the tongue on attack (cheat by adding a *tiny* accent). It's better to be a *little* too loud than for the note to be late, not there at all, or a loud squawk. An 'easier' reed helps too (see chapters 9 and 12). Try not to be put off by a conductor 'shusssshing' you on a quiet low entry, making your embouchure automatically tighten up nervously—fatal. (Conductors N.B.) Don't pinch, but relax if *possible,* except for your diaphragm/stomach muscles (see 'Confidence', Chapter 7). (There was once, I'm told, a horn player named Willy Crackit...but he could have been an oboist.)

24) Sharp 'pinched' top notes, especially C‴, and flat bottom notes. Make sure the instrument is thoroughly warmed up (not just the top joint), listen to the low, least flexible, notes, and tune the rest accordingly, checking your basic pitch first with a tuning-fork and adjusting the reed if necessary (see chapters 9 and 12).

25) Dropping an octave from top C#‴. This may happen if your reed's scrape is too long or its aperture too open. Otherwise try adjusting your E key to open more. It's a bad note on many instruments. Blow it firmly and confidently with plenty of diaphragm support.

26) 'Stirring pudding'. This seemingly habitual practice of many oboists makes audiences dizzy and distracts them from the music. Movement is natural during playing and I'm not suggesting you stand like a lifeless statue, but a continuous circular motion of the instrument is most unmusical and can be very irritating.

27) Playing an oboe d'amore (or cor anglais) 'like an oboe' (see 'The Oboe's Relatives', Chapter 17).

28) Blowing 'into' rather than 'through' the oboe, i.e. playing without firm steady breath, diaphragm control and taut stomach muscles (see 'Breathing',

Chapter 1 and 'Legato', Chapter 2). One teacher I heard of puts a coin on a chair in front of his pupils telling them to try to 'blow it away' while playing! This isn't as daft as it sounds, but encourages a fuller, more controlled sound, ease of phrasing, and helps avoid tentative or 'jerky' playing.

29) Counting aloud in the orchestra, an annoying habit. Devise a way of counting bars silently to yourself (see 'You the Musician', Chapter 7).

30) 'Foot tapping'—something else which can spoil the enjoyment, concentration and tempers of your colleagues (and which culprits rarely do in time, anyway). Don't become a foot-tapper...

Common musical pitfalls. (Not just oboists.)

1) Lazy rhythm, e.g.

 becoming

2) Slack dotted rhythm, e.g.

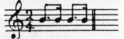 becoming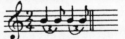

(Triplet interpretation of dotted rhythm is used in some baroque music, but that's another story, see 'Languages', Chapter 16).

3) Double dots becoming single dots, e.g.

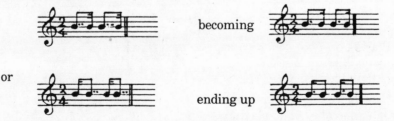

It's sloppy, inaccurate playing, changing/spoiling the intended effect.

4)

 becoming

or  i.e., uneven and irregular,

or  becoming

or

5) Accented notes becoming 'all forte'. (An accent means returning *immediately* to the original dynamic),

e.g. becoming

or fzpsub played as f.

Practise loud *short* accents (see 'Practice', Chapter 4):

6) Accenting grace notes (*acciaccaturas*)

i.e. interpreting them as passing notes (*appogiaturas* or leaning notes)

in post eighteenth-century music. These grace notes are short and played *before* the beat, added embellishments *not* important notes. Passing notes, played on the beat, equal half the length of the note following:

(Arrows indicate beat)

Grace note.   Passing note.

Play the tune without the grace note, then slip it in unobtrusively, e.g. Strauss' 'Radetsky March':

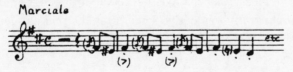

Marciale

(>)   (>)

Don't play it like this:

I've even heard it played almost as a triplet!

N.B. In pre-nineteenth century music grace notes are *correctly* played before the beat (see 'Different Interpretations', Chapter 16).

7) Vibrato and tone always the same. Variety is essential for an interesting performance (see 'Vibrato', Chapter 2 and 'You the Musician', Chapter 7).

8) Starting crescendos too loud and diminuendos too soft. 'Cresc' in effect means 'quiet'—something to crescendo *from*. The usual mistake is, seeing 'cresc', to play loud straight away. 'Dim' means 'loud', something to decrease *from*. Look ahead and 'budget' for a long crescendo by starting even quieter (and vice versa). Build (or decrease) slower, getting louder (or softer) right to the end without running out of crescendo power before the climax, or dimming to *nowt* before the end (see 'Practice', Chapter 4).

9) Anticipating a crescendo, new dynamic, rit., etc. Don't get loud immediately you see a crescendo or forte approaching, slow down too early when you see a rit. or pause, or speed up *before* reaching an accel. Imagine if you did that while driving, on seeing a bend coming...

10) The peak of a crescendo reached too soon, e.g.

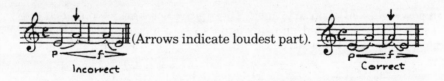

(Arrows indicate loudest part).

The first beat of the bar is the most important.

11) A forte bar or phrase in a quiet line of music not returning to p but continuing forte (or vice versa). If in doubt glance back to the general dynamic indication.

12) Getting louder at key changes, especially into a higher key.

13) Playing generally too loudly. 'Look after the pianos—let the fortes look after themselves'.

14) Careless or unrhythmic practice, e.g. starting too fast and slowing down at a difficult passage; generally practising too fast; omitting slow practice and being impatient; or making the same mistake repeatedly (see 'Practice', Chapter 4).

15) Rushing, especially in fast 'notey' or staccato passages. Practise these parts at home, slowly, in a controlled fashion using a metronome. Sometimes the metronome really does seem to be getting slower when, actually, you are rushing! I recommend 'rushers' looking for one which will eventually, very gradually slow down! (If such a thing doesn't already exist perhaps it should be invented...) In the orchestra, watch the conductor like a hawk (don't you always?), listen to the bass line, often a straightforward 'um-cha' or 'on beat' rhythm, and aim for the first beat of each bar. A teacher once advised me never to attempt to practise something like the 'Silken Ladder' overture 'up to tempo', but *very* slowly and staccato:

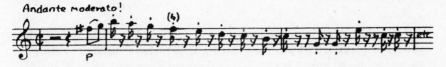

But it's wise to prepare different tempi. You don't know what the conductor may do on the night!

It's a natural reaction to panic at the sight of a lot of 'black looking' notes. Try to analyse the rhythm *calmly*—it's often not as fast as it looks—listening and watching carefully. Miss out a few notes if necessary, not nearly as noticeable as if you 'win', finishing before everyone else! (Mark the part ← or 👓 to remind you):

16) Losing tempo, though less common, is most likely during slow music or notes tied over bar lines:

Try to 'feel the pulse' all the time. Again, use a metronome to learn such passages 'a tempo' at home. Most of us are prone to rushing, especially when nervous, or to getting slower. Know which is your weakness and beware accordingly.

17) Playing quiet music slowly, e.g. a phrase repeated pp slower the second time. This is a frequent mistake.

18) Shortening rests, especially when they're on the beat, thereby rushing the tempo, for example in Suppé's overture, 'Light Cavalry':

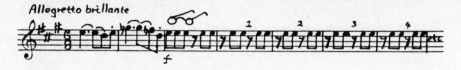

Another instance where 'hurried' rests might prove disastrous, considering what follows, is in the Rondo of Mozart's oboe quartet:

Here counting (- - 3456) carefully is essential. If notes are played when you have rests wait for them, but if silent rests, as here, counting (or watching) is the only answer.

19) Not looking ahead. Don't get caught out by key or time changes, accidentals, left-hand or forked F fingerings, or missed breathing places. Look out for (and mark) such traps, especially over the end of a line or page, or where octave jumps are involved.

20) Notes 'clipped' short. Shape *every* note. 'Clipping' notes is extremely unmusical (see 'You the Musician', Chapter 7). Each note continues until the start of the next note, beat or rest, unless marked staccato, i.e. a note lasting four beats must continue until the fifth:

This is easier to explain with vocal music. A consonant ending a word should be pronounced at the start of the next beat (even if that's a consonant too). For example, from Handel's 'Messiah':

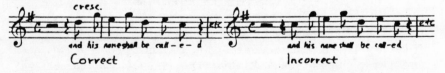

(The 'd' of 'callèd' sounds on the fourth beat). Even when an unavoidable breath *slightly* shortens a note it must still be phrased musically, 'rounded' not 'cut' off.

21) Music spoiled by badly chosen breathing places. Choose (and mark ✓0) the most unobtrusive and *musically sensible* places to breathe when there are no rests. Avoid interrupting the music more than absolutely necessary. Staggered breathing (see 'Breathing', Chapter 1) is useful in busy music, or where a solo is preceded by extended continuous playing (to avoid missing any notes) as in the last movement of Haydn's Symphony number 101, 'The Clock':

It's best, most natural, and least noticeable, to breathe after a tied note, a staccato note, a pause, or at the end of a phrase. *Never* break a phrase (see 'You the Musician', Chapter 7) or note. A note shortened for a breath must continue over onto the next beat or part beat, i.e. don't omit a whole note or beat:

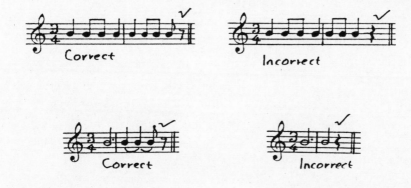

Look ahead for breathing places. Don't, for instance, take a breath in an unmusical spot, when there is a rest a few bars later, or run out of breath at the end of a piece, or phrase, if it ends on a pause note!

Physical Hazards

Risks and disasters to avoid

Physical hazards—Causes; preventions; cures.
Don't be alarmed, oboe-playing isn't really a dangerous occupation. However embarrassing or uncomfortable situations can often be avoided, such as the consequences of performing in clothes with overtight waistbands (see 'Breathing', Chapter 1 and 'The Pro Bit', Chapter 19). Any tight clothing is uncomfortable and restricting, and it sometimes takes only one accented bottom note to burst a zip or buttons, letting skirt or trousers fall to the ground! (Men can, at least, resort to braces—but loose, roomy clothes are best. Or a strong belt!).

Ladies—do avoid wearing lipstick when playing as this clogs up the reed.

Eating a heavy meal before playing can be disastrous. Breathing becomes uncomfortable and impossible to control, and salivation can lead to bubbly sounds and water in keys. I will never forget finishing a large Indian curry at 7.25 pm (choice of restaurants was limited and service slow) then rushing to perform, of all things, Bach's 'St.Matthew Passion'. An experience I'm *not* anxious to repeat. However, I *don't* advise performing on an empty stomach either. Nerves will feel more jittery and sustenance is essential if you're to have the physical and mental stamina to play well. Have some milk or yoghurt at least, which are nourishing, if you feel you can't swallow anything solid before a concert.

When touring music clubs playing recitals I find that landladies who've put musicians up before, usually know to offer a light snack only before the concert, and a meal (and a drink!) afterwards...but find out what suits *you* best.

A hazard not affecting us all is hair getting in the reed. If you have long hair fasten it out of the way during performances. I had one 'hair-raising' experience during a lunchtime recital at St. Martin-in-the-Fields in London. At the start of the busy last movement of Vivaldi's C minor sonata, which has little breathing space, I breathed in a mouthful of hair and had to play the *whole* movement praying it wouldn't get into my reed (one hair is enough to block a reed completely, silencing you). I was lucky that time, but it wasn't good for my nerves—or concentration.

Men who have moustaches should keep them trimmed, for safety, though a beard (I'm told!) acts as useful 'padding', preventing sore lips...

The *tiniest* particle of food will block a reed, too. Always clean your teeth after eating—*certainly* don't munch crisps or peanuts while playing. Deposits of rotting food inside the holes will *not* improve your oboe, or its performance (see 'Nursing Care', Chapter 15). (If you're a would-be slimmer use this as an incentive to skip the biscuit with that interval cup of tea.) Saliva alone leaves substantial deposits in your reed (see 'First Aid', Chapter 13).

A player I know got something in his cor anglais reed during the show 'Fiddler on the Roof' at a point where his part was a vital cue to the cast. The unexpected silence, albeit momentary, resulted in chaos and panic on stage. A bit dropped out of my cor reed, typically just before an unaccompanied passage, in the Royal Ballet—the brief silence, again 'throwing' the dancers. (It was bad for my nerves too, being the first week in my first job.)

Remember, the cor anglais is longer than the oboe, when you're playing in a pit with low headroom! My predecessor in the Royal Ballet 'murdered' her reed on the ceiling, missing the whole of the solo in 'Sleeping Beauty'—I got the job. Low-headroomed pits are themselves a hazard. One second oboe player, having several 'tacet' (silent) numbers, was bored during an opera performance. He yawned, stretching, his oboe (plus reed) in his hand...

Beware flying insects, disastrous if 'taken'. (A singer friend of mine breathed one in during a recital, causing an embarrassing coughing fit.)

An oboist in Bournemouth, meeting a friend at the stage door after a ballet performance, said "Quick, I must rush to the pub". They did, where he hastily downed a pint. When his friend asked the matter, he replied, "I've just yawned in the pit. I think I swallowed a fly and I wanted to drown it..."

Small hands, short or long—even malformed or arthritic—fingers are usually surmountable problems. Keys can often be adapted to individual needs. You can alter your right-hand position yourself by sticking a piece of wood or cork (of a thickness to your taste) to the oboe, below the right thumb rest, and placing your thumb on it, thus positioning it further from the instrument and compensating for a larger hand/longer thumb. Resting your thumb *below* this eases your hand position if the thumb rest feels too high. Experiment until you find what is comfortable.

Keys can be extended, as for a friend of mine who had lost part of two of her fingers, or if a side key (especially on the cor anglais) is out of reach for a small hand. I know a saxophonist who still plays professionally, although his right hand has been amputated at the wrist! He's successfully adapted the mechanics on his own instrument—showing determination can win.

I was recently asked if left-handed oboes exist. Before 1750 3-keyed instruments left the options open, then the third key disappeared and 'left hand above right' became accepted. As both hands play almost equal parts there would seem little point.

Extreme temperatures cause physical problems. In hot conditions, common in theatre pits or studios, breathing becomes difficult—sometimes more like panting! Intense cold, experienced in many church venues, seizes up the fingers, making fast or elaborate playing impossible. Personally I prefer cold to hot playing conditions as I tend to get hot when I play, especially when nervous. (I've had strange looks when I've arrived at winter auditions wearing summer clothes in efforts to 'keep cool'.)

There are *musical* problems, too. Temperature affects pitch, making instruments sharp or flat (the *opposite* for strings and wind!).

Cold creates 'plumbing' problems for wind players—condensation in octave or other keys, which must be removed (see 'Nursing Care', Chapter 15). Heat causes sweaty hands. I've experienced fingers actually slipping off keys, producing wrong notes, during performances in a glass-roofed hall during a heat wave. Perspiration also damages the silver-plating on keywork.

On a recital tour I once had to play in an unbearably over-heated hall in Minehead, when my rehearsed 'controlled', and usually confident breathing 'went for a Burton' and I thought I'd flake out. I felt myself getting ever redder as I gasped my way through the baroque programme (surely the worst music for hot conditions), hoping the audience wasn't too aware of my agony. The following evening we played in a totally unheated hall in Penzance (this was in mid-winter) and my fingers became so numb I couldn't feel any of the ornamentation in the music. Mittens could have solved the problem, but they might have looked strange with evening dress...

Another time, playing oboe d'amore and harpsichord music at a city bankers' dinner (my accompanist carefully tuning the harpsichord beforehand), by the end of the dinner, when we were to play, the heat had made it so out of tune I couldn't begin to match its pitch. It was one of those occasions when we just had to battle on, trying not to giggle, praying the bankers were enjoying plenty of liqueur and not being too discriminating. We tried to put on that 'confident' look, hoping they might be convinced, or think their ears were deceiving them.

At a wind quintet concert I remember well, in a north London park, the elements caused the problem, and we didn't carry it off with such aplomb (being students we were less experienced). Our programme included the rather tricky Damase 'Variations', with small parts necessitating many quick page turns (impossible to use wind irons, even if we'd had any). A breeze got up and pages kept flying across the gardens into the audience, members of which kindly retrieved one for us every so often. The performance finally collapsed amid giggles. For once I was glad my name had been mis-spelt on the programme!

At a summer lake-side concert at Kenwood, in London, after earlier rain, a sudden gust of wind dislodged gallons of water onto the oboist during the overture. He had to play, soaked, throughout the concert—but we mustn't let such inconveniences interfere with our performance.

Different climates and humidity can be hazardous for musicians. Florida is so humid that, apparently, oboists there find it unnecessary to wet their reeds before use, whereas New York is so dry that oboes have seized up completely there, due to bore shrinkage.

Illness is a real worry for wind players. It's not easy to drop out at the last minute—as everybody knows, we're indispensable...

One day when giving two recitals—an afternoon lecture concert at a large Midlands school followed by an evening recital at the local music club—I awoke feeling groggy to find myself covered in a rash. A call at my doctor's on the way to the first concert produced the diagnosis of German measles. I had to struggle on rather than let down two audiences at such short notice, but the day was an ordeal, and I felt very self-conscious as the rash spread to my face and arms during the evening's recital.

An early professional—and still vivid—personal experience was playing nightly 'double bills' at Sadler's Wells Theatre with an abscess on my front tooth. The agony reduced me to tears every night, but I carried on.

On a more recent 'Summer Season' engagement, the entire twelve-piece orchestra went down simultaneously with a tummy bug, having to leave the stage in turn. (It was rather like Haydn's 'Farewell Symphony'.) However, in true musicians' spirit the concert continued. In the interval a lady from the audience fetched a bottle of Kaolin and Morphine from her car, which was hurried to the bandroom and passed round. A slightly unusual coffee break!

Musicians generally do try to ensure 'the show going on' whatever happens. I heard of one who allegedly ran out of petrol on his way to a recording and, having a half bottle of Scotch in the car, tipped this into the petrol tank and just reached the studio in time...

If you wire your reeds—a more mundane subject—(see 'Reeds Again', Chapter 12) tuck the ends of the wire neatly under the binding to avoid painfully jagging your lip.

Other causes of sore mouths, an oboist's dread, are:

Front teeth cutting the inside of your lip, usually when you're 'pinching' or

66

playing with too tight an embouchure (see 'Embouchure', Chapter 1), using an over hard or too open reed, or trying half scraped ones, or just over-practising. Preventions: *not* pinching or overdoing practice on new reeds. *Stop* as *soon* as you feel the symptoms. A cigarette-paper folded in four, or piece of cellophane or plastic, placed over the offending front teeth during playing, will take the sharpness away. This makes further playing more comfortable, too, when you already have soreness. If this is a bad problem, or you have unusually sharp teeth, *don't* get them filed down like that proverbial 'gift horse'. A 'wind expert' dentist (see 'Useful Addresses') can make you a special plastic guard to wear while playing. (If you wear a brace or plate on your teeth though, you'll probably have to remove it to play.) Many players use *Bonjela,* a special ointment available from chemists, for mouth sores. Or swill spirit over the sore place. It will sting initially but numb it effectively—an excuse for a 'wee dram' anyway. Less pleasant, though equally effective, is surgical spirit, but it's inadvisable to drink it.

Sore lips hinder playing, too. Protect them in cold or windy weather with cream, Lipsyl or Vaseline, or 'Chapstick' which doesn't *soften* lips. Take equal care in *hot* weather. If you sunbathe, *don't* get your lips burned. Use plenty of protective cream.

Oboists' teeth are all-important—*do* look after them carefully. Avoid damage to front teeth at all costs. One of the worst such accidents happened to oboist Léon Goossens (when he was already sixty-five). His determination to overcome what, to lesser mortals, would have seemed an insurmountable problem, should be an inspiration to us all, and is described in a fascinating book by Barry Wynne (see 'Recommended Publications').

If you're a professional player you might consider getting moulds of your teeth made by your dentist, simple and inexpensive, to act as models in the event of emergency or major treatment. Replacements can then be matched to your present teeth, affecting your playing as little as possible (however much you may long to replace your overcrowded or crooked teeth with more attractive ones). Playing is more important than beauty, especially if it's your livelihood. Carry a note of the whereabouts of these moulds—be prepared for every eventuality. Tell your dentist you play a 'mouth instrument', too, so he'll know your teeth are especially important.

Avoid 'punch-ups'…and head-on collisions…as I experienced the day before a concert in Iceland, on the ski slopes, badly hurting my mouth but, mercifully, damaging no teeth. It was one of the worst moments of my life when the other skier, discovering I was English and, of course, not knowing my profession, asked, "Your teeth—is they all right?" and I gingerly felt with my tongue expecting to find a mouthful of loose ones, as Léon Goossens did. Cigarette-paper protection certainly 'saved my life' at that very painful concert.

If you ride a motorbike, or partake in other potentially dangerous-to-your-teeth activities, you might consider it sensible to wear a wrestler's gum protector.

Practising loud sharp accents is an excellent exercise (see 'Practice', Chapter 4), but don't rupture yourself. This has occasionally happened to oboists, so be prudent. Don't make it that 'first fine careless *rupture*'.

While on such cheerful topics, look after your heart, too. Not only must it be in reasonable working order for the exertion of oboe-playing, but apparently any teeth with neglected fillings are extracted before heart surgery...

An apt moment to mention Dutch courage perhaps? Many musicians find 'the odd drink' before a concert creates a feeling of confidence, counteracts 'nerves' and helps them relax. Treat it with respect though, and 'if in doubt, don't'. Wind players must remember that even *one* drink will affect tonguing control, so it's unwise to risk *any* alcohol before playing exposed staccato passages. (Try saying a tongue-twister fast after a few drinks and you'll begin to get the picture.) I speak from bitter experience here. As a young student I took part in what I believe was this country's first performance of Rossini's complete opera, 'The Silken Ladder' with its notorious overture. All term I practised my tonguing in preparation, but the build up was such that when the opening night arrived I panicked, making the mistake of going to the pub before the performance, thinking it would calm me down.

Disastrous! The rest of the week's performances went well, but the critics were only there on the *first* night. I avoid alcohol now until *after* a concert, when I enjoy relaxing and socialising in the pub, celebrating, drowning sorrows, unwinding, or just quenching my thirst.

Alcohol can 'loosen the tongue' in other ways, too. Alec Whittaker, a well-known player of his day, was much admired by Hamilton Harty. At one time, depressed at receiving no encouragement from the distinguished conductor, he and the flautist went 'on the booze'. They had an 'arrangement' with the local publican, who'd leave his back door open and two double Scotches on the bar, which they'd pay for later. One day, returning to the rehearsal rather inebriated, Whittaker was playing badly. The conductor stopped the orchestra and asked, "What would your old friend Hamilton Harty say if he could hear you now?" To which Whittaker replied, "I don't b...well care, but I know what he thinks of your conducting. He told me so himself."

There was one memorable 'performance' of the rather difficult wind quintet by Ibert. The players rehearsed until noon, and the live broadcast was scheduled to begin at 2.30 pm. You can imagine what happened. After two and a half hours in the pub they were none too sober, and even the opening wasn't together. It got progressively worse until, mercifully, the broadcast was faded out. The announcer said, "We regret that due to atmospheric conditions in the studio we are unable to continue this broadcast."

Dizziness has other causes besides alcohol. The most common is the body becoming short of oxygen during playing, through faulty breathing, especially breathing in without breathing out first, or shallow breathing (see 'Breathing', Chapter 1), or by practising in stuffy, unventilated or overheated rooms. Open the window and take deep breaths of fresh air first (if that's what is outside your window), then *close* it again before playing, if you respect your neighbours. Try a jog or swim before you practise (how many of us do this I wonder?). You'd be surprised how it helps breathing.

The only time I've ever fainted was in an oboe lesson, during my first term at college, where the room was small, hot and stuffy, and the window couldn't be opened because of noise problems. Later I was teaching at a Cambridge girls' school, in similar conditions. My pupil blacked out momentarily, her oboe going flying. (Both instances occurred during the same study! Coincidence I'm sure.)

And here is a 'precautionary tale'. During a rehearsal of 'Der Freischutz' at the Theatre Royal in 1825, a German baron appeared saying that he'd been authorised by his 'friend' Weber to restore a section previously omitted. It included a very long note for the flautist, who declared it impossible. When asked why, he replied, "Sir, it is so long that I would not attempt it unless you would have a surgeon by, that in case I rupture a blood vessel he may be ready to stop the haemorrhage." Earlier, a famous German bassoonist, trying to sustain a note for several bars stopped to breathe in the middle of it—he obviously hadn't learned circular breathing. On the conductor calling out, "Hold that note", he replied, quietly, "It's easy for you to say that, but who is to find der vind?"

Remember that you can't smile—even less laugh—when playing the oboe—sometimes a real handicap. We must exercise control, and look away when the conductor tells a joke or pulls a funny face, or an amusing 'disaster' occurs while we're playing.

The inability to speak and play can be frustrating too, like when you want to scream to your dentist to be more gentle, or even answer his questions, but can't because his fist is in your mouth.

Numb fingers are certainly a problem if you have to play the oboe with them. If, for instance, you ride a motorbike to play an evening show in winter, allow for 'thawing out' time on arrival. A cold sea-bathe before a morning concert improves breathing and is a good 'waker-upper', but it can certainly be interesting, and not much fun, having to face, say, a Rossini overture with 'insensible' fingers. Time is needed to thaw, in the absence of hot water. When at school I had my oboe lesson immediately after swimming, in the summer term, but eventually I had to change this as so much of my lesson was wasted before my fingers were warm enough to play. Perhaps your circulation is better than mine?

'Oboists' thumb'. Many players will, after a time, develop a lump on their right thumb from supporting the oboe and, especially, the heavier cor anglais—'how to recognise an oboist'. (A small price, perhaps, for playing such a beautiful instrument?) Most instruments seem to have some such hazard—violinists' 'lovebites' on their necks (only hidden by beard growth, not available to us all), 'cellists' 'groovy' finger tips, guitarists' overlong right-hand finger-nails, horn players' red rings on their mouths...etc.

Playing with coughs or bronchitis is Hell, or with a cold (which *can* 'blow' into your sinuses) and especially cold sores. Trying to avoid these symptoms is all I can suggest, though for asthma sufferers I understand playing a wind in-strument can be a real therapy. (Some good news at last!)

Take good care of your hands. If you're a DIY enthusiast—but inexpert, like me—you'll know that playing the oboe with hammered, sawn, cut, or 'sanded' fingers can be difficult! Somebody's got to do the jobs around the house, but be cautious, i.e. don't drink before carpentry, or attempt carpentry before a con-cert.

Smoking is certainly something that won't help your playing, but try telling many oboists this and they'll say reed-making drove them to it!

Eye-strain is often a danger for musicians. Legibility of music, and the standard of lighting, especially in churches or halls not normally used as con-cert halls, is often poor. (A pity, perhaps, there are no MU rules about this as there are for minimum temperatures we may work in.) At least be sure to prac-tise and 'reed-make' in good light at home. Eyesight is important for any musician, especially orchestral (whether amateur or pro). During a perfor-mance by the Hallé Orchestra, when both oboe parts were printed together, the second oboist came in with a beautifully controlled breve A', wondering why the first player wasn't playing his C", printed above. He, in turn, looked round at his colleague, who valiantly continued, afterwards discovering that what he'd read as breves C" and A' was, in fact, eight bars rest...

An army conductor once stopped a band rehearsal and asked the oboist, "What have you got in your part?" "Gs sir," he replied. "You b...f...!" stormed the conductor. "That's the side-drum cue!"

Poor hearing is a hazard often overlooked. Yes, seriously, years of sitting 'bang' in front of percussion—or brass—players eventually has a detrimental effect! Similar, I suppose, to working a lifetime in a noisy factory. (Perhaps musicians in front of us eventually develop 'oboe'-deafness?)

Most common *medical* problems for oboists, the experts say, are: os-teoarthritis in the base of the thumb, lip/teeth problems, hand lesions, and 'reed-makers' elbow' (a recognised condition).

Yet oboe-playing is generally *beneficial* to health. It's good physical exercise, and excellent for breathing—improving circulation and relaxing you, besides being an activity from which to derive —and give—much pleasure (good for mental well-being).

All in all a far 'safer' instrument than many!

Insurance of your body as an oboist? Where to begin? Heart, lungs, brain, eyesight, hearing, teeth (*teeth*—who will insure teeth? Well, somebody will, at a price), fingers, hands, arms. Legs are about the only non-essential part of you. Insurance? Something to look into, perhaps. Meanwhile, take care, and keep fingers crossed. Except, perhaps, while playing…

You the Musician

*Performance/Musicianship; Relaxing/Control;
Confidence—or pretence at it*

Performance/Musicianship

'Being a musician' is a very different subject from just playing an instrument—indeed, it's really all about 'making music' rather than 'playing notes'. It's not technique that's important, but the emotion one puts into—and gets out of—music. To quote: 'You are speaking through your instrument, it becomes your voice,' and: 'One sings with the instrument which one plays with the mouth.' We express ourselves through our playing; it is our fulfilment. The finest musicians are slaves to the music, not their instrument.

More important even than the sound you make, is to be able to give pleasure through your *performance*. As a musician, in whatever capacity, it's your job to interpret the notes on the page, and make them music—interesting, exciting or expressive—your performance, convincing, exhilarating, even 'electric' —*never* boring or 'machine-like', involving the audience and holding their attention...Whoever they are!

Tackle music which you may feel at first you don't understand, as a challenge to your *musical* skill and imagination, not as a technical exercise. Musical performance and overall atmosphere is far more important than squeaking or cracking a note (though, naturally, one tries to avoid 'fluffs').

Orchestral Playing

1) *Blend*. Blending with other musicians is one test of your musicianship. As second oboe, for instance, don't try to out-play or play louder than the first, unless it's especially required. It's important, particularly in a

chamber orchestra or small ensemble, to match the other player's tone as far as possible, too, as you'll be very audible playing together 'as a pair' (easier if you know beforehand who they will be and are familiar with their playing). Try to match the flute, as well, if you're playing first oboe (or any other player with whom you have exposed passages), by compensating with your vibrato, tone and phrasing. This makes it more interesting for you, as well as for the listener.

2) *Adapt*. Consider the venue and its acoustics. Your sound will carry more in, say, a church, than in a deep theatre pit or out of doors, and if you play in a small hall, or drawing room, you might be very close to the audience. Adapt your playing, reed and volume appropriately. (For reed adjustment see chapters 9 and 12.) Don't play too pp, for instance, even if it's the printed marking, if you have 'the tune' against brass accompaniment, or in a pit if it's vital you're heard by those on stage. Use your musicianship, ears and intelligence (and follow the conductor's instructions). A 'solo p' may need projecting or playing out more than a 'tutti p'. A good conductor should guide you here. Again, don't blast out ff, even if it is what is printed, if you know there should be six brass players in the orchestra, but there aren't, or when there are only six violins instead of sixteen (which might well happen in these days of cutting down). *Listen* to the balance all the time and adjust your playing accordingly.

Solo Playing

1) *Phrasing*. Use breathing to break music into natural phrases. Don't let a breath interrupt a phrase or spoil the musical sense, and never 'clip' notes short (see 'Musical Pitfalls', Chapter 5 and 'Breathing', Chapter 1). We oboists have the advantage of being able to play far longer phrases than our colleagues, without breathing, because of the small amount of air used compared with other wind instruments. Make the most of this, especially when playing the slow expressive music to which the oboe is consequently so suited.

Phrase and 'shape' artistically and imaginatively. For instance, notes slurred in twos:

will be more musical with a *slight* leaning towards the first of each than if all played exactly the same, viz:

and:

will surely be more interesting if played:

Two very simple examples to give food for thought.

2) *Rubato.* Use rubato (slight pulling around of the music *within* the tempo) in moderation, for added interest, especially in solo pieces. For example, a feeling of 'pulling back' into a recapitulation, or at the end of a piece or movement, will help the listener to understand and enjoy the music. It should be obvious, even to those unfamiliar with the piece, when it is the recap., repeat, new subject—or the end! Rubato is one useful way of 'explaining' such things. The audience should know when to clap—and when not to!

3) *Memorising.* I recommend memorising pieces you're going to play publicly, not necessarily to perform without music, but to aid real concentration in practice, and allow you to focus on the *music* rather than the notes—also, to quote a teacher of mine, 'in case the clouds of oblivion come down'. Yes, believe me, it's useful to feel that one's fingers will carry on despite 'blackouts'. (This applies to orchestral playing, too. Learn the notes of *any* important solo to play them 'safe', freeing your mind from technical matters to concentrate on a musical performance.)

4) *Relate and contrast.* When faced with unfamiliar music (or a sight-reading test), glance through, not only for difficult passages and traps, but for the fastest, slowest, loudest and quietest parts, so as to relate and contrast to make as much interest as you can, even on a first reading. For instance, if the loudest dynamic is f and the quietest p you can afford to exaggerate these by thinking 'ff' and 'pp'—even 'fff' and 'ppp' for more exciting contrast. As there are no fixed 'measurements' for dynamics, as there are with pitch, the actual loudness is not important, but rather the relation and comparison.

Dynamics must always be clear. Don't play a soft passage only slightly quieter than the forte passage preceding it—it'll only sound as though you're getting tired! It must be convincing. *Very* quiet 'pianos' can be most effective in solo playing. (In one of Tchaikowsky's symphonies, dynamics range from pppp to ffff in one movement—subtle contrast needed here in order to differentiate between them all—even more so in solo playing.)

Altering the position of your oboe temporarily can help to convey dynamic contrast. In the last movement of Mahler's symphony number 7 (among others) he instructs the oboes to play with 'bells up' (schalltrichter auf!) for added projection (this was originally to compensate for the softer sound of the Viennese instruments (see 'The Oboe's Relatives', Chapter 17) though it's hard, in practice, to do this and read the music at the same time.

Accents mean dynamic contrast, too. For example, in this variation from Theodore Lalliet's 'Prelude and Variations on Carnival of Venice' the non-accented notes are embellishments only. The tune (accented notes) must be louder than the rest, as if played on its own, to bring it out:

Look for other distinctions, too, besides dynamic ones. Contrast a smooth, flowing legato passage with a spiky staccato one—a heavy, sombre or melancholy (often minor) section with a light-hearted dance-like (major) one…or other mood changes.

A vivid example is the contrast between the first (sweet and gentle) movement of Poulenc's oboe sonata with the second (spiky) Scherzo movement:

What an exciting switch from one mood to another! It would be letting the composer down badly—as well as the audience—to make it anything other than the abrupt contrast intended.

Always use your ingenuity and imagination (qualities *every* artist needs) to make *all* music you play—even the 'dullest'—exciting and stimulating. Can music ever be dull? (I won't answer that!) A musical player should be able to make even 'dull' music 'come alive'. Nobody would choose to listen to a story-teller or reader reciting every word in a monotone. Neither will anybody enjoy boring or monotonously played music.

Professional musicians have to play whatever is put in front of them, whether they like it or not, and make something of it. (Some unpopular chamber music, considered unpleasant both to play and listen to, has even been labelled 'torture chamber music'.) It's your task, as a musician, to put as much emotion and expression as you can into everything you play—pieces, orchestral solos, even studies—sometimes a real challenge! Even exercises mustn't ever be treated as 'just notes'. (Chopin's beautiful 'So Deep is the Night' was, after all, written as a study.) In other words, don't be lazy.

Never just repeat a line—make *more* of it.

General Playing

1) *Freshness.* Your performance must never sound stale, even if you've played the same notes every night for five years! Try to approach each performance as if playing the music for the first time, to make it 'feel' different and sound 'new'—certainly a true test of your musicianship. Remember, the audience has probably not heard it before. There comes a stage when your fingers carry on in these circumstances, even if you've lost your place in the music! I experienced a performance of 'The Gondoliers' with D'Oyly Carte Opera Company during which there was a power cut. The orchestra carried on in darkness for some time before finally grinding to a halt.

One talented musician, forced as a boy by his father (a dentist) to practise every day where he could hear his son while working, soon learned to read a book and play scales, etc. at the same time, utterly fooling him. It's not uncommon for bassoonists playing a show for a long spell to play their entire part while reading a book, never opening the music.

As a one-time regular 'dep' in the show 'Jesus Christ Superstar', in London, I would just manage to fit in a game of Scrabble with the two flautists and clarinettist during the two hour show. The regular players didn't have to look at their music, certainly not count bars. I, however, being less familiar with the notes (and *not* mathematically minded), had difficulty adding up potential Scrabble scores while counting bars, especially containing five or seven beats each!

2) *Look ahead, observe.* It's imperative to read ahead in music, not only for practicalities—breathing places, left-hand fingerings, etc. (see 'Practice', Chapter 4), but for musical danger spots such as very high or low passages, solos, articulation and phrasing, dynamic and tempo markings, and key and time changes. Often 'details' such as dynamics get

overlooked at first, but there's no excuse for this. They're as important a part of the music, or effect, the composer wants, as the notes themselves—sometimes even more so!

Try to work out complicated looking rhythms before you reach them (more later). Cast an eye over 'chromatic looking' passages. Sometimes they're not quite—though you'll soon get to know the 'look' of a chromatic or scale passage. Don't be caught out, or end up on the wrong note!

Above all, where is the musical climax, or most important part or note of the piece or phrase? Look for this before you start.

Looking ahead avoids unnecessary mistakes interrupting the flow of the music, and encourages a musical and meaningful performance without a dozen 'goes through'. Even elementary players should be able to make musical sense of a piece on the first reading, if they're observant.

'Hark back' too, a memory test—like remembering what cards may have been played in whist—to recall complicated bars passed with many accidentals, and to remind yourself of the key and general dynamic of the moment.

3) *Read well, keep awake.* Being able to observe and take in as many points as possible (such as those mentioned above) on sight is an important asset to any player who enjoys playing chamber music, and particularly to professional musicians, especially 'freelancers' in Britain, where it's common to play a concert on one rehearsal (less than most other countries), when every note certainly won't be rehearsed. So, keep your wits—and a pencil—about you to ensure nothing's missed, even when there's little time to look at or learn a part.

At a rehearsal I was once in with a London orchestra, 5.30 pm came, the scheduled end of the session, and we still hadn't touched the Mozart symphony in the programme. The conductor merely announced, "The symphony this evening, Gentlemen, is number 40, not number 41." That was all the rehearsal we had on that. (Everybody knows Mozart 40, but we had not all played it recently.) It still had to be a 'performance'! Keeping awake and alert is even more important when the work you're maybe performing for the first time on one rehearsal is Britten's 'War Requiem' or Stravinsky's 'Fire Bird' or 'Petroushka'—or something more avant-garde perhaps!

Accurate, as well as musical playing, depends, of course, on your complete involvement and concentration. Do not let yourself be distracted or you might come a noticeable cropper...

Sometimes, the 'if in doubt leave it out' motto needs to be put into practice. It's not *always* possible to play *every note* the first time you see the music, and the art of leaving notes out here and there to give an otherwise

accurate performance is worth study and thought. 'Prune' hard passages *craftily* and the omissions will barely be noticeable, the general effect unspoiled. It's much worse (and very amateur) to play *every* note, but inaccurately. Your overall performance matters more than the notes.

4) *Counting*. Something we woodwind players have to do plenty of is counting bars. Develop a system to make this easy and automatic for yourself, so you can sit back and enjoy the music when you're not playing, rather than it becoming a mathematical exercise, with you sitting there going 'Seventeen, 2, 3, 4,—Eighteen, 2, 3, 4,…'etc. (the 'official' way of counting bars to yourself).

My own counting method, like many others', is on my fingers. I always start with my right thumb, through to little finger, then left fingers in the same order. Thus, I know automatically, for example, that left index finger means 7, 17, 27 etc. bars gone. In most conventional music (i.e. with the same number of beats per bar) it's easy to 'feel' when 8, 16, 32 etc. bars have passed as it usually falls easily into 8 bar phrases. So, in a long spell of counting, even if you've lost track of how many 'hands' worth' have passed, it's easy to guess intelligently and accurately when to come in, if you haven't been totally asleep, and if you're at all musical. It's *very unmusical* to come in, for instance, 1, 2, or 7½ bars early or late—worse than being 8 or 16 bars out—but the right place is best.

I often find, especially if I'm not relaxed, that I count bars quite unnecessarily, such as when listening to a concert. It's become so automatic. (I usually realise when I get to about 100!) I suppose it's like counting sheep—or 'counting baahs'! A different matter, however, counting silent bars (or beats) in music with constantly changing time-signatures. Then you must keep *wide awake* and count *every one*. NO need to count aloud or become a foot-tapper though…*please* (see 'Bad Habits', Chapter 5).

Opera or ballet parts, with long 'tacet' numbers—or even acts—when one is not playing, are often marked with such useful guides as 'time for a quick pint'. (Some of the 'D'Oyly Carte flute parts may still have markings for my benefit, like 'wake oboe'?) Players can help each other out, indicating bar or rehearsal numbers to each other by holding up fingers, or silent 'mouthing'—but watch out for jokers who'll purposely tell you the *wrong* one to cause themselves amusement at your expense.

Should you lose your place, use your musical instinct—listen out for landmarks, such as a silent bar, pause, sudden forte or piano, key or time change, or repeat.If you have a solo approaching, the conductor should, at least, glance at you to bring you in, so be poised for his signal. (If you get a glare instead, you'll know you've missed it.) Watch him all the time, of *course*—you *always* do—don't you?…

78

An oboist meeting a friend in the pub one evening apologised: "Sorry I'm late. I had a concert." "Oh," asked his friend, "Who was conducting?" "I don't know, I didn't look..."

It's better to be in the right place, even with the wrong notes, than to play the right notes in the wrong place. And make sure you don't do 'overtime'—i.e. finish after everybody else!

Accurate playing is so important, especially in the orchestra. It only takes *one* person playing short or staccato notes too long, using lazy rhythm, or playing too loudly (see 'Musical Pitfalls', Chapter 5) to ruin the whole effect and everyone else's work.

To unravel an approaching rhythmically complicated bar, 'think' it over a simpler bar just played, in the same pulse and tempo—a trick which helps sort it into beats in one's mind. It's also helpful to 'think' an impending solo during the introduction as it's played, to establish the exact tempo and 'feel' of it in one's head (for instance, Rossini's overture 'The Italian Girl in Algiers', or Dvořák's 'New World Largo'). In practice at home, or rehearsal, mark the beats with a pencil (lightly if not your own music) to facilitate counting next time, for example (Stravinsky's 'Orpheus'):

It looks alarmingly difficult—until you work it out.

Mark passages which might tend to 'run away' similarly. For example (Prokoviev's 'Classical Symphony'):

(see 'Practice', Chapter 4).

5) *Fluffs*. One missed note or squawk will *not* ruin a performance. We all worry far too much about such things, which, admittedly, feel *terrible* to us, but are hardly noticeable to an audience absorbed in the general enjoyment of the music. Squeaks, slips or wrong notes are over so quickly that 90 per cent of the audience won't have noticed, or be quite sure afterwards if they've happened at all. I long to carry out a survey after making a mistake, to prove this to myself. Fortunately, only students, critics, a few score-followers and audition panels come to listen *for* mistakes. An in tune *musical* performance is the most important thing, as I've tried to emphasise (and 'fluffs' in recordings can be 'cleaned off'!).

Be bold and daring in your playing. Let yourself go—take risks— let it all SING out. These are the ingredients for a dynamic, thrilling and memorable performance—hard for most of us who are too busy worrying whether we're going to squeak or not! A 'played safe' performance may be technically un-faultable and 'correct', but boring (therefore pointless).

For a convincing performance, musicians must be totally absorbed, preferably within a happy, relaxed atmosphere. Tensions within an orchestra or ensemble will nearly always show in its playing. An American statesman is quoted as saying, 'If we could only persuade our political leaders to join in music-making…there would be no more unrest in the world. Perhaps Mrs Thatcher could play the oboe, and President Reagan the bassoon?' I've also heard it said that 'playing a waltz stops a fight' by creating 'infectious joy'.

Music can certainly arouse many emotions. It can sadden, soothe, anger, amuse, cheer and excite, provoke fear or suspense and, of course, please. It should *never* bore. This rests as much with the performer as with the composer. If you *enjoy* your playing it will show in your performance and 'infect' your audience, who will enjoy it too. Bored musicians will give a dull performance, resulting in a bored audience.

Do not play like a machine. There are too many of them about already taking over our jobs. Hopefully, performing music is one thing humans can still do better than computers. Let's keep it that way.

'Keep music live'.

Relaxing/Control; Confidence—or pretence at it.

I think confidence, for oboists, must be knowing (or thinking you know!) that your reed will react *exactly* as you wish—a rare feeling—resulting in beautiful, relaxed playing; and lack of confidence, fearing (or *knowing*) it will not—an all too common feeling—resulting in nervous, tentative, 'accident-prone' playing—unmusical, too, as you're too preoccupied with technicalities to think much about your performance. So, *know your reed*. Don't use a brand new 'unfamiliar' one for a concert (especially if you're prone to nerves), but do plenty of practice and 'warming up' on the one you'll use, to know exactly how it'll respond to what you have to play. Know that *you're the boss*. Confidence, then, is being so in control of your playing that you can concentrate entirely on the music.

Most of us would admit to wishing we felt more confident more often. I know of no secrets or instant recipes, and can only advise safety precautions, namely: ensuring that you're 'in practice', have reliable reeds, and that your instruments—and you—are in working order. Then it's 'merely' a question of courage and convincing yourself you've nothing to worry about. If necessary, put on an 'air of confidence' and *pretend* everything's alright. It's astonishing how many people are taken in if you *appear* satisfied with your performance. They won't guess what you're feeling underneath if you act well enough! Don't give yourself away, though, by beginning, 'Good evening, jadies and lentlemen' (it's surprisingly difficult to say 'ladies and gentlemen' in an authoritative manner while quaking at the knees!). If you don't *feel* confident, how can you *play* confidently—or convincingly? 'If in doubt leave it out'—that well-known motto of musicians—could well be 'if in doubt don't', *or* 'if in doubt, make it up', depending on your degree of confidence.

Don't be fooled into a false sense of superiority because you can move your fingers fast and 'impress' a few non-musicians. Playing simple, but exposed, notes accurately and precisely (often in second oboe parts) can be much harder than 'rattling off' a lot of notes you've learned (see 'Mixed Bag', Chapter 18).

Feeling confident will be easier if you are feeling relaxed. Deep breathing is an accepted and recognised 'relaxer' (but you should be doing that anyway). Exercise can 'work off' surplus nervous energy, making you feel physically, if not mentally, more at ease, so try a run, swim, or other not too strenuous activity on the day of a concert (but save enough energy for the performance). A hot bath also relaxes.

Psychological attitude is most important, too. For instance, however large an audience is, it will seem less daunting if you think of 'it' as one individual. Each listener is, after all, just that.

Nervousness is a form of vanity, brought on by the worry of what people will think if you make a fool of yourself in front of them. Try, therefore, to imagine you're playing in your own home. Don't be diffident in your playing, but take your courage in both hands. After all, if you're going to make a mistake it might as well be heard! A tentative, or 'unconfident' entry will more likely 'split' or be late, besides sounding unconvincing. You have to take risks for your performance to be at all exciting to listen to.

'Throw care to the winds' with a nerve-racking entry—it's no good being hesitant. Remember all you've learned about diaphragm support and breath control—use it to create confidence—and blow firmly, to come in boldly, but not too loudly. Thorough, *unhurried* preparation at home of parts needing particular control, should also help build up confidence.

Weber's overture 'Der Freischutz' has a nasty 'cold' opening, two unison oboes on a quiet bottom C' (though I suppose if you 'crack' it you can always pretend it was your partner! or cheat by not coming in at the beginning, but joining in the crescendo).

Another danger spot is the second oboe solo in the slow movement of Dvořák's 'cello concerto—a nasty trick on the composer's part (and a typical audition piece!):

It appears simple, but, being so exposed, is nerve-racking in context. (A 'cheat' with this one is to play it transposed, on the cor anglais— a possibly more authentic sound, anyway.)

Another second oboe 'trap' comes in Rachmaninov's second piano concerto. Again, though so simple, it's the kind of entry to split if you let yourself be frightened of it:

N.B. Second oboe parts are often harder than first.

Don't lose confidence if a conductor glares at you, or 'shussshes' before, say, a difficult quiet low entry (see 'Bad Habits', Chapter 5). Take a deep breath, summon up your courage, and *CONCENTRATE*. You *can* do it (or cheat by 'muting' the bell of your oboe with a hanky!)

It's hard to relax your embouchure when *you* are not relaxed, but a tense embouchure will cause cracked or sharp notes and harsh tone (see 'Embouchure', Chapter 1). Cracked or out of tune notes are so much worse on an oboe than on less penetrating instruments; all the more reason to avoid them. (Forked F is a note that can 'blow sharp' if one is tense as you'll find out if you ever have to play the cor anglais solo in the 'New World Largo', transposed on the oboe.)

High exposed entries can be frightening, too, and need assertiveness and control, for example, the opening of Mendelssohn's overture 'Fingal's Cave', which begins (for the first oboe) on a quiet exposed high C#'''—a tricky note—(though, hopefully supported by the second oboe an octave lower). This needs firm support, plus pitching the note carefully from the preceding clarinet entry.

The beginning of the first part of Ravel's suite, 'Daphnis and Chloë', opens with a solo oboe entry starting on a sustained 'piano' top F''' again requiring calm nerves to sound positive, be free from shakes, and create the desired atmosphere:

Often just coming in with the first note of a frightening solo is the hardest part.

A simple looking passage for two oboes, which many find hard, comes in the slow movement of Beethoven's 'Emperor Concerto' (soli, except for the piano). This should *not* be difficult if you've practised long notes and embouchure control seriously (see 'Tone', Chapter 3, and 'Practice', Chapter 4), but without *confident* control you'll very likely 'wobble' or even peter out halfway through:

Again it looks so easy—out of context.

A last example is Mahler's fourth symphony, ending with solo cor anglais, dying away to ppp. It's extremely easy to die away, literally, too soon, or wobble, if you succumb to fear:

These 'simple' things are often the most difficult.

Only 'fake' as a last resort (though it's important to do even *that* confidently for it to be convincing!). I have been congratulated by colleagues for managing a pp low note despite a leaking pad, when, in fact, I'd made no sound at all, but merely pretended to play it! (For more 'fakes' and 'cheats' see 'Mixed Bag', Chapter 18—but you'd never sink to that sort of thing...would you?)

83

Choosing a suitable reed and testing all worrying or difficult passages on it thoroughly will go a long way towards that feeling of confidence (see chapters 9 and 12).

Very basically, a 'thinner' reed will make quiet low notes easier, so help allay the fear of splitting them (though its tone may be less good on top notes), and a 'thicker' one will help to avoid the fear of perhaps 'sounding horrid' on high solos (even if it's less 'safe' on soft bottom notes). You will feel better, knowing it will be 'safe' or sound 'good', and so give a more relaxed, therefore musical—performance. (If you have exposed high solos AND low quiet ones in the same programme—well, Good luck!)

I recommend, for your peace of mind, choosing and 'warming up' a reserve reed for *every* occasion, removing that fear of an 'accident'. This is certainly essential when preparing for an audition or recital, which is invariably when your 'good' reed will split or 'die', decidedly bad for nerves—and confidence—if it's your *only* good one. As a very *last* resort 'betablocker' tablets are available, on prescription, *not* for daily false confidence, but to help musicians who suffer from real shakes which actually spoil their performance. *BUT* take care (see 'Mixed Bag', Chapter 18).

Often one plays best and gets most absorbed in music when emotionally upset, or under stress. Music itself, and its performance, should be a therapy and form of mental relaxation—even if it is one's job.

Reeds—Reeds—Reeds

Introduction; What is a reed? Choosing a reed; Recanes

Introduction

Now to the dreaded subject of reeds—the oboist's bugbear, and an all too often frustrating problem.

Oboe reeds are not only critical, but *extremely* fragile—therefore temporary, as well as temperamental. So, beautiful as the oboe is, we all sometimes wish we'd taken up the flute instead, and didn't have the worries and problems reeds cause (which can also become very time-consuming if you make or adjust them yourself). String players and others are usually unsympathetic. You only have to mention the word 'reed' to get shouted down for moaning! It's almost become a 'dirty' word.

No one but an oboist can understand the frustration of having beautiful music to play but only a 'duff' reed to play it on— of knowing that your hard-earned standard of playing (and quality instrument) will sound inferior when notes 'crack', are out of tune or pack up altogether, squawks or other extraneous noises occur, or your tone sounds unattractive—because of your reed! How this can spoil the enjoyment of playing, sometimes making you feel like giving up altogether! The mere worry of unreliable reeds can cause tense, faulty playing—a vicious circle—and often very psychological, too.

Every oboist dreads breaking his reed at a critical moment, or not finding one good enough for an occasion...

It must be said, though, that it's often easy to blame the reed unfairly, using it as an excuse for bad playing. One must endeavour to get things in perspective. The problem begins as your playing progresses, getting worse the more particular and 'perfectionist' you become, always searching for the 'ideal' reed instead of getting on with practice. The headache sometimes seems so insoluble that it's enough to lead to a nervous breakdown! But cheer up! Look around at the high standard of oboe-playing, and the vast numbers of oboists (I sometimes wish competition wasn't *quite* so fierce). 'They' all seem to have overcome the problem (I wish I knew their secret)—or at least learned to cope satisfactorily. If this weren't so, we oboists would be a dying breed, not a thriving one.

The first thing to accept is that you'll rarely have a reed you're happy with (about 1 per cent of the time for most of us!), so it's important to learn to cope with, and hopefully overcome, its shortcomings, either by adjusting/improving your playing, or adjusting/improving the reed, or a compromise. Did I say it was often psychological? What an understatement! If a reed *feels* 'wrong', we're rarely convinced by kindly colleagues reassuring us it's 'sounding great'. "Only you can tell," they say, but there's no escaping from the fact that the quality of the reed makes *all* the difference to the quality, and enjoyment, of our playing. Reeds affect tone, dynamic range, attack, agility, pitch and intonation, sometimes even whether notes are there at all. Your instrument is only as good as your reed—a horrifying thought! The world's certainly a rosy place if one has a 'good' reed—it can be a depressing place when one has not!

If you let yourself get into a panic, *every* one you try seems terrible; when you're more relaxed (perhaps after a holiday) you'll be surprised how good you can make many sound which you'd previously discarded! A relaxed *mental* attitude encourages a relaxed embouchure (see 'Embouchure', Chapter 1), improving playing as well as making the reed 'feel' better.

Avoid 'going through' reeds when your mood makes every one seem 'useless'. Don't destroy them all in frenzied depression, but wait until a 'better day'. Remember, too, the importance of 'knowing your reed'—so, give it time. Here's how psychological it can be: If you get a bad reed out thinking it's your 'winner' it's astonishing how good you make it sound—until you realise your mistake!

Whatever the reed (or instrument) though, and *however* it feels *you* will still basically sound like *you*. Playing on a reed you're unhappy with is a test of your playing skill and musicianship. A good player should still be able to sound good even on a poor reed. He has to! It's one of the essential skills of being a good player. You can identify different oboists on radio, for instance, regardless of their reed, as you can recognise somebody speaking, even with a cold.

First, then, try to find as good a source of reeds as you can, which suit *you*, to minimise the problem. They're a very individual thing, varying enormously from player to player and maker to maker, so look for makers whose reeds are to *your* taste (whatever anybody else thinks of them!). Or if, but not until, you're a reasonably accomplished player, consider learning to make your own, as nearly all professional players and many amateurs do (much more later, see 'Making Your Own', Chapter 9).

As you become more discerning, you'll discover what you're looking for in a reed; the better player you become, the more choosy, so there'll come a time when you're no longer satisfied with those you buy, and decide to make them, to your own taste.

Always look after and store reeds sensibly. Buy a good reedcase (only improvise one with *extreme* care), and carry them tips uppermost to be safe. Don't leave the reed in your oboe if you put it down with other people around, and avoid neighbours leaning across, say, to look at your part in a rehearsal, and 'murdering' your best one. Never lay the

instrument across your knees with the reed sticking out vulnerably, an early experience of mine at a school concert which I've never forgotten. Avoid premature death by accident!

What is a reed?

The short answer to this question could be a 'big problem'. But, to basics:

The oboe's reed, or mouthpiece, is the most important part of the instrument; it's the reed, or its two blades vibrating together, which activates the sound. Without a reed the most expensive instrument, or finest player, is useless. 'The reed of the oboe is what the larynx is to the human voice.' It is, in effect, a fourth joint of the instrument—the cane, scraped paper-thin at the tip, is bound tightly on to a *staple* (a short metal tube which is an exact continuation of the oboe's conical bore, with cork around its lower half) which fits into the top joint.

Oboe   Oboe
reed   staple

A reed may last only a few days—sometimes even

87

less—or perhaps weeks, depending upon use and conditions, and barring accidents, which *easily* occur, hence can be a perpetual worry. So the more you understand about them the better.

The oboe's reed is called a 'double' reed, not—as you might think—because it's double the problem and more than double the price of a 'single' clarinet reed, but because it has two blades. (A bassoon also uses a double reed, though much larger and stronger than the oboe's. A clarinet reed is a single blade which vibrates, more safely, against the mouthpiece to create sound.)

The oboe reed is made from a length of 'bamboo', first split into three, then gouged and shaped to very precise measurements, and folded in half to produce two blades as identical as possible. These are bound onto the staple, the tip trimmed to form an aperture, and scraped thin so as to vibrate freely when blown. (Each of these stages is described in detail in chapters 9 and 10.)

The special cane comes from the Mediterranean area (see 'Cane', Chapter 11). Man-made substitutes such as fibreglass, plastic—even metal—though used, have not, regrettably, yet proved to be *the answer*. So, although man can get to the moon, he's not yet found a solution to this surely *much* more important problem.

Choosing a reed

Some shops which sell reeds allow you to try them and choose from a wide selection, providing water for moistening them, and a solution to sterilise unwanted reeds afterwards. So you'll need to know what to test and look for. Here are some suggestions:

Plenty can be told about a reed just by looking at it. You can see whether the tip is straight and 'clean', or 'nicked', the binding secure, the 'scrape' smooth and even on both sides, the reed cracked or split, its blades crossed, or the aperture too open or closed (which you'll soon learn to recognise). It's easier to detect a split if you hold the reed up to the light—or, wet it, insert a *plaque* (see 'Apparatus', page 127), and move each blade gently (don't do this dry!). Avoid buying reeds with any of these symptoms.

Too open a reed will often make middle G#″ wild, top C#‴ likely to drop an octave, and top notes hard to get. Too closed a reed will have a small sound and may squawk on low notes.

Look for cane with a shiny surface and smooth, not coarse, grain (see 'Cane', Chapter 11). Hold a reed, preferably upside down, to the light to see this more easily.

Test for leaks by blowing into a reed firmly while stopping the other end with your finger. See if air escapes. Find where a leak is by sealing the sides with your forefinger and thumb (still blocking the end) and, blowing hard, moving your finger and thumb down the reed, or pushing the reed gradually further into your mouth, until you cover or uncover the spot. Alternatively, suck water up the reed and, with end sealed, blow it out through the (leaky) side. *Minor* side leaks can be sealed with *goldbeater's skin*, plumber's tape (cheap and effective) or Clingfilm (see 'Apparatus', Chapter 13), but serious 'draughty' leaks can cause insoluble problems. Well-made 'professional' reeds should *not* leak. Avoid any which do.

Much can be learned by a reed's 'croak' (different from 'squeaking' a reed, see 'How to Start', Chapter 1). To croak a reed, wet it, then, putting more into your mouth than normal, blow loosely, with very slack embouchure and no articulation.

If a hoarse croak, like that of a crow, is produced easily, the reed is promising.

Reeds which won't 'crow' can sometimes still work, but when choosing to buy, they're perhaps best avoided.

A reed's *squeak* is usually around B″ or C″ (without 'lipping'). Be suspicious if it's *miles* away from this.

When testing a reed in your instrument, check the following:

1) Pitch. (Have your tuning-fork with you if you don't have perfect pitch). Check notes over the entire range, not just 'A'.

2) General responsiveness and ease of playing. Allow for new reeds to feel slightly stiffer at first, they'll become easier once 'blown in'.

3) Tonguing. Try a few staccato notes to see how the reed responds. Some are agile—good for tonguing fast—others hard work, and 'lethargic', especially if made from 'soggy' cane.

4) Test tone and general 'feel' on a few easy notes, such as Ds, or better still by 'test playing' a piece or tune you've played often and know the 'feel' of.

5) Try the worst notes on your oboe, accident-prone or out of tune ones, e.g. top C#‴ or forked F. If the reed's scrape is too long to suit your oboe, top C#‴ may drop an octave, Ebs become 'wild', or high notes difficult to play.

6) Test the reed's 'sound' on middle C″ the 'barest', most revealing note (using least fingers). This can also be a flat note on some reeds, especially on thumbplate oboes.

7) Range and control. Try some quiet low notes to see how controllable and 'easy' they feel, then a few high notes, e.g. top E‴ or F‴. Do they feel 'safe' and 'speak' easily?

8) Attack. Play some short loud notes. A leaking reed, or one with too long a tip (the very tip thinned too far) sometimes produces squeaks, especially on high or accented notes.

9) Dynamics. test the reed's loudest and softest. It's no good, however beautiful it sounds, if it won't play quietly, or cannot get above pp. Discard any which start to lose their tone or grow feeble after a few minutes' playing. They're possibly made from under-ripe or over-soaked cane, or are too closed.

You can use wire to regulate a reed's aperture, and make numerous alterations to correct many of these faults (see 'Reeds Again', Chapter 12), but do *NOT* attempt adjustments without proper tools and guidance—for instance, never try to 'trim' a 'chipped' reed with scissors! Meanwhile, buy reeds needing *no* alteration—after all, they cost enough.

You'll soon learn to tell quickly whether you like a reed or not, or if it's promising, by its feel, and whether it seems responsive and feels comfortable.

There may not be an opportunity for lengthy reed testing in a busy shop, but I hope these guidelines suggest what to look for, and, later, prove useful tests when you alter or make reeds.

Perhaps the truest test of all is whether you want to go on playing on the reed...

Recanes

Staples are re-usable, so don't throw the whole reed away when the cane part is broken or finished with. New cane is bound onto the old staple, and scraped, to make a new reed. This is called a recane. Once you have several reeds you can send spare staples away to a reed-maker (see 'Useful Addresses') to be recaned—cheaper than buying a whole new reed. N.B. Not all reed-makers do recanes, or accept your old staples in part exchange, but if you find one who does, please send them in a tin, or hard box—not an envelope, to arrive flat! Although you won't be able to try or select them yourself, you can specify 'hard', 'medium', 'soft', 'medium hard', etc. There are, of course, no set 'measurements' here, so (as with ordering 'hot' or 'medium' curry) you must take a chance. But if you go repeatedly to the same reed-maker you'll get used to his standards, assuming his reeds are reasonably consistent. I advise asking for 'soft' reeds if you're a beginner. They're easier to control and kinder to an inexperienced embouchure.

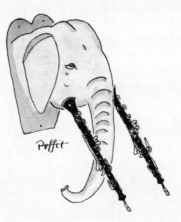

Proffet

Chapter 9

Basic Reed-Making

Making your own; Gouged and shaped cane; Tying or binding; Scraping

Making your own

I call it 'reed-breaking' not reed-making, as that's what it turns out to be when I do it, more often than not.

My first advice to anyone contemplating making their own reeds is *don't* try it too soon. If you embark on reed-making when you're still learning the rudiments of oboe-playing, you won't know whether difficulties you experience are caused by faulty reeds or faulty playing. One will hinder the other, probably slowing up progress in both.

However, when, as a busy player, you begin to get through a lot of reeds, and find yourself becoming dissatisfied with those you buy, it's well worth learning to make them (or at least to alter bought ones). Not only will you save money (ready-made reeds are expensive), but, more important, you will be able to make them to your own taste. Commercial reeds are produced mainly for beginners, so, though usually 'easy' to play, often lack tone.

Reed-making is an 'exact science'—'one stroke of the knife can change the entire tone of the instrument', i.e. it must be taken seriously. You'll need to buy proper tools, which are important. (A list of apparatus needed for making and altering reeds will be found on page 127) ; see also 'Useful Addresses'.) Learn all you can before experimenting, to eliminate trial and error and frustration— but don't let reed-making take you over…

Take advice from somebody competent before you start. Choosing a good *scraping knife*, for instance, may save many headaches and wasted reeds later. Practical tuition is the best teacher, but study books too, and compare different methods. A good book or manual is useful for thorough stage-by-stage direction (see 'Recommended Publications').

Evelyn Rothwell's *Guide to Reed-Making* offers invaluable and detailed guidance, with many photographs. *The Art of Oboe-Playing* by Robert Sprenkle also gives precise instruction and includes excellent large photographs of every stage (often more helpful than lengthy descriptions)—a handy reference, even if the American sound/style may not entirely be to your taste (see 'Languages', Chapter 16).

A workshop or 'reeding room' is a useful luxury, where you can keep your equipment, make a mess, and work in comfort. If you haven't a spare room to donate to reed-making you must improvise, and be organised. In my small flat my 'reedery' is a wooden 'case' about a metre wide, half a metre high and 10cm deep, fixed unobtrusively to a wall below a window, so hidden behind long curtains when they're drawn.It's divided into many 'compartments' inside. In the largest I've fixed hooks and nails on which to hang tools, knives, etc.

The shelves nicely fit reed tins (tobacco tins) or rows of reeds, plus housing feathers, nail-varnish, oil, twine, etc.—everything has its place. The front hinges down providing a 'table' to work on. I suggest your rigging up something similar if you're short of space.

My 'Reedery'

Before beginning complete reed-making, experiment with 'part scraped' reeds, available from some reed-makers, a sort of 'inbetween' stage, using the scraped part as a guide. Start gently.

G and S cane

'G and S' (gouged and shaped) cane (*no* connection with the Savoy operas) is what most oboists use. Few bother with the business of gouging and shaping the cane themselves, so I'll describe these procedures later (see 'The Nitty-Gritty', Chapter 10). G & S cane only (*only*—did I say?) needs to be tied or bound onto the staples and scraped. I must add here that at recent 'reed seminars', where oboists of every calibre meet and compare notes, I learned too much to include here, but, above all, that there are as many reed-making methods as players! Advice from several respected 'experts' was contradictory! The following chapters are, therefore, suggestions for your guidance, not laws, as methods vary at every stage.

Tying or Binding

First soak the G & S cane for about half an hour in room temperature water, or until it sinks. Some advocate three minutes only in boiling water (saying the least soaking is best for the reed), others four hours.

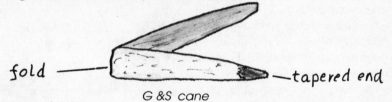

fold ———— ————tapered end

G &S cane

Remove the old cane if re-using a staple, using an all-purpose knife. Push the staple on to a *mandrel* (a tool which fits the slightly oval staple end, giving the reed a 'handle' to support it when scraping or tying), squeezing it into shape with *pliers* if necessary.

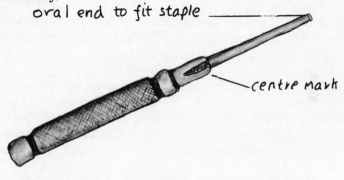

oral end to fit staple ——————

——centre mark

Mandrel

'Re-groove' it by making diagonal cuts or grooves in the metal part (see illustration page 87). This will prevent the cane slipping after binding. Use a non-precious knife for this very blunting process, preferably one with replaceable blades, such as a *Stanley*.

Different staples affect the binding process as well as the finished reed. (A wider staple—which the average mandrel pokes right through—will make a flatter pitched reed, a longer staple a wider aperture in the reed, etc.) To experiment with other factors, such as 'shapes', or diameters or gouges of cane, it will be easier to judge the results if your staples are as similar as possible—preferably identical.

Use strong, thin thread, such as fisherman's twine, nylon or silk, for binding, or buy special twine from a shop selling reed-making equipment (see 'Useful Addresses'). Dental floss is ideal, and is non-slip if bought ready waxed, though expensive (some condemn it!). Avoid anything elastic or hairy!

Anchor one end of the thread to something stable (*not* the best antique furniture or anything precious). A window catch is perfect (I've even seen twine ends preserved 'for posterity' behind double glazing!), or a door handle, or the handle of a clamp, which can be fixed anywhere convenient, or a metal music stand—so you can tie reeds on by the fire-side (but steady it with your feet).

You can even use your own thigh which you've always got handy (as my—male—teacher advised at my first reed-making lesson, when I happened to be wearing a mini-skirt!). But, the thinner the item, the less twine you waste. Or tie a string around a large 'anchor' and your twine to this, for the most economical solution.

Hold the mandrel/staple in your left hand (if you're righthanded). Place the folded cane on the staple, its blades parallel to the flatter sides, and hold it firmly with your left forefinger and thumb—at the sides, rather than top and bottom, to prevent the blades crossing. The cane should come one third to halfway down the uncorked part of the staple, so that it extends 25 to 27mm beyond the top and the whole reed measures 72 to 74mm. One way of getting this right is to measure the cane against something constant, e.g. marks on a work bench, marking 27mm from the centre fold (match this mark to the end of the staple when tying), or position the cane on the staple, then mark the staple end on it. (A flat-handled mandrel is most practical. Mark a round handle with a file, or nail-varnish, on the flat side of the oval end, and align the cane with this when tying, see illustration, page 93.)

Wind the twine once around the cane to hold it firm, meanwhile, holding the cane in position with your left hand and keeping the twine taut, 'juggle' the cane from side to side with your finger or thumbnail until the gaps either side are equal, checking that it's straight.

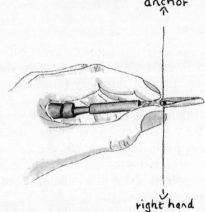

'anchor'

right hand

(To conserve twine slide the reed towards the 'anchor' at this point, still holding it firmly in position.) Bind the cane firmly, but not *too* tightly, up to the (marked) top of the staple. Don't bind it beyond this point or you'll inhibit the cane's vital vibrations. If the sides close before or after this, 'back-pedal', or unwind the twine to the first turn, and adjust the position of the cane on the staple, before re-binding, always keeping the sides parallel. Pushing the cane further onto the staple closes the sides earlier, making the finished reed shorter, sharper in pitch, and its aperture more closed. Putting less cane on the staple closes the sides later, making a longer, flatter pitched, more open reed. If you tie reeds on

94

longer, i.e. the cane is narrower at the binding, the reed will vibrate more freely. You'll soon learn where to place the cane on the staple, but as staples, and cane, vary, exact rules cannot be laid down. A *very* rough guide is the mark where the last reed came to, but you should really be more precise than that. The finished reed's length is your best governing factor.

After reaching the top of the staple, cross the twine over itself and bind back down, beyond the bottom of the cane, or even to the cork. Some people bind up again a third time for extra security. The twine must always be taught, but don't let it cut into your hand. Move it around on your fingers to 'hurt' different places! Tighter thread makes a more open reed—looser allows more vibration.

Finally, knot the twine firmly, using three loop knots, or similar (many knottings are used) and trim the ends. I heard of one player who would deliberately leave a loose thread hanging from his reed's binding. If he mucked up a solo he'd pull the reed untied, using this as an excuse...

Paint the binding with nail-varnish, especially the knot (unless you're like the player just referred to) particularly if you use non-waxed, or slippery thread. This secures the binding, helps prevent leaks, and smartens reeds (important if you sell them).

Let the varnish dry before putting the reeds away or they'll stick together; and *don't* varnish the cane, which will hinder its vibrations. Different shades of nail-varnish, or binding threads, are useful for distinguishing between batches, when you're using different canes, shapes, etc. (Note which to avoid or repeat next time.) Labels can get lost or mixed up.

Now the reed is ready for

Scraping

Again, the cane must be soaked first, to prevent splitting during scraping (unless you scrape the reed straight after binding it, when it'll still be damp) Immerse the reed's tip in half an inch of cold water for 10—15 minutes.

Meanwhile, sharpen your knife, which must always be razor sharp. A blunt knife takes extra pressure, which will probably split the cane, and almost certainly guarantee 'nicks' out of the reed's tip and an uneven surface. Smooth, even scraping is vital for the reed to respond well and play easily.

Buy a good scraping knife with one flat side (available left as well as right-handed) and a *sharpening stone*, and some *honing oil* (see 'Apparatus', page 127.)

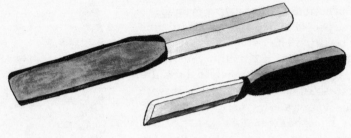

Scraping knife (righthanded)

Learn how to sharpen your knife efficiently (Sprenkle and Evelyn Rothwell give detailed instructions, see 'Recommended Publications'), using a figure-of-eight or X-movement, *or*, making a few strokes on the flat side, then drawing the other side towards you, using pressure (two of many methods used). Sharpen it before scraping each reed. (Make a 'burr' after sharpening, either on the stone, or by running a hard, rounded polished steel object, a special *'ticketer'*, or the back of another knife—along the bevelled edge towards the flat side of the knife, giving a 'biting' scraping edge. Take care not to cut yourself.)

Blow any excess water out of the reed, and place it on your mandrel (which I find makes scraping and binding easier, though some players prefer not to use one). Hold it in your left hand and the knife in your right (if you're righthanded), supporting the reed with your left forefinger. Remove the bark or shiny surface, thinly, smoothly and evenly from the top 4mm or so at the sides, in an arc shape. This area is the 'lay'.

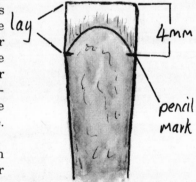

Bark must be removed equally on both sides. Mark the first side with a pencil after scraping, round to the other, and match it up.

Scrape the very tip (about 1mm) both sides, until it's quite thin. Next, remove bark, thinly, down to the required length of scrape, each side (roughly 8mm) in a U shape (some prefer a V or W shape—more later, see 'Reeds Again', Chapter 12). Remember, if you start with a shorter scrape you can lengthen it later, not the other way round. Use the tip of the knife for scraping the reed's tip, the lower part for removing bark. Many take the bark off the whole scraping area while the cane is still wet from binding, completing scraping later; this saves your knife.

After this initial 'rough' (*smooth*, of course) scraping, I find fine sandpaper useful to smooth off what's been scraped, though a few frown on this—be careful not to lengthen the scrape though. This produces an even surface more easily and quickly than using a knife. Use emery paper, wet-and-dry, or any fine sandpaper. Some reed-makers (and players) use a *'sanding machine'* or *'profiler'* for part of the scraping process for speed during mass production. (This removes the outside cane to the required contour, but doesn't complete the job.)

It's important not to thin the 'heart' or 'back' (centre and lower scrape) too much, taking away from the tone. Bark *can* even be left up the reed's centre, making it last longer.

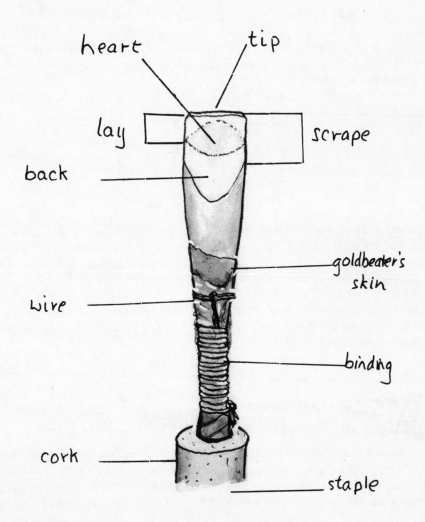

When the tip's well thinned take a *'plaque'* or *'tongue'* (a small flat oval piece of metal used to separate and support the reed's blades during scraping), and slip it between the blades from one side (fig. a):

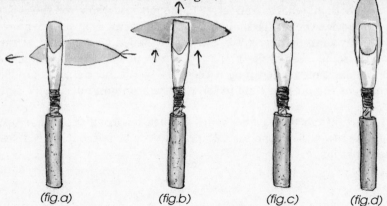

| (fig.a) | (fig.b) | (fig.c) | (fig.d) |

Then slide it upwards, separating the blades (fig.b). The tip may now appear ragged (fig.c). Turn the plaque parallel to the reed (fig.d) and thin the reed's tip gently, with your knife.

Some players start in a point (fig. e), then revert to an arc (fig. f):

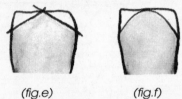

| (fig.e) | (fig.f) |

Always scrape equally on both sides. Scrape the tip (1-2mm) very thin now—as one oboist said to me 'until you no longer hear any click when the knife moves from the cane onto the (metal) plaque'. Convex plaques, which fit the reed's curve—available in wood or metal—are better for scraping; they don't blunt the knife, and avoid scraping 'at the wrong angle', continually 'shutting' the reed. Don't exert pressure or cut into the reed during scraping. Use a gentle circular motion of the knife, from the wrist (you'll soon get the knack), to ensure a smooth surface:

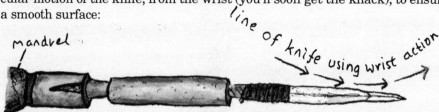

mandrel

line of knife using wrist action

If, by careless or hurried scraping, you get a 'bump' on the reed's surface, scrape it from *different* angles, otherwise it'll become more exaggerated. If you push a garden roller repeatedly over a 'hump' on the lawn from the same direction you will exaggerate it and make a hole the other side. As with reed-scraping, it would be 'ironed out' if rolled from different sides. (Or use sandpaper.) To ensure not getting carried away and removing too much wood at once, try making a pencil mark on the cane, scraping *only* until it disappears.

trimmed corners

Trim the tip next. Place the end of the reed on a small wooden *block* with a convex surface and, with your *cutting knife* or *cut-throat razor,* trim just enough to 'clean' the tip, using one firm action. Press the knife down with both hands, while steadying the reed, taking care to cut it straight. Then trim the corners.

This helps prevent damage or 'tearing', some say making top notes easier, too. (Many, though not all players do this.) It can also close the reed a little, but neatens its appearance. Some cut the tip earlier, to separate the blades, instead of using a plaque, which is, perhaps, safer.

Next, whether or not the reed is leaking—but especially if it is—wrap *goldbeater's skin* around the reed's base, from the lower scrape to the cork (nowadays, many oboists use Clingfilm or plumber's tape instead.) Cut a strip about 1cm wide and 5cm long, with scissors. Wet one side to make it adhesive, wrap it round the reed firmly, and allow to dry. (N.B. Clingfilm and plumber's tape do *not* need wetting.)

If the reed still leaks, re-varnish the binding and 're-skin' it until airtight. (To check for leaks see 'Choosing a Reed', Chapter 8.) It's hopeless trying to play on a reed with even the smallest leak.

The reed is now ready for its first crude test, and should 'crow', even at this early stage (see 'Choosing a Reed', Chapter 8), though it'll still be very tough, so don't 'bust your gut' or rupture yourself trying to produce a sound too early. Instead, thin the tip *fractionally*—the whole reed even—and test again. When it eventually crows easily you'll get an idea of whether it's going to work or not (you'll learn to tell this with experience, and by 'feel'). Until then, keep removing *small* amounts of cane from different areas, testing after each alteration.

My system is to scrape about four reeds at a time, getting them to this 'crow' stage, then leave them until another day. Do it in stages. Reeds will feel different on each blowing until they settle down. I find that after scraping four or five I begin to lose concentration and become careless, but I tie on

99

larger batches at a time, waiting till I've fifteen or twenty redundant staples. You'll form your own routine.

It's a good idea to have reeds at every stage all the time and to keep a rota going, like home-made wine, so there's always a 'mature vintage' and— others 'maturing'.

When the reed crows easily, it's time to test it on your oboe.—'The moment of truth'. It'll probably sound loud and uncontrolled and be hard work at first. *Don't* panic and scrape it too thin too early, ruining its tone and shortening its life, to get it to feel easy. Keep making *minute* adjustments, testing between each, blowing and scraping until it becomes easier to play. Experience will soon tell you what to alter to obtain the required improvements (see also 'Miscellaneous Tips in Reed-Making', Chapter 12)—a question of trial and error at first, guidance and study.

When a new reed will play—after a fashion—check its pitch and adjust accordingly. Trim the tip a little to sharpen it, lengthen the scrape a little to flatten it. Then make the tests described in 'Choosing a Reed', Chapter 8. When you think a reed shows promise, 'blow it in' thoroughly before further alteration. Reeds change with time and use and may need further adjusting to keep them working well (see 'Miscellaneous Tips in Reed-Making', Chapter 12, and 'First Aid', Chapter 13). Make sure you give every reed a fair 'blowing in', and yourself a chance to become familiar with it. Remember, cane removed cannot be put back, so only alter a reed a *soupçon* at a time, then give it a jolly good blow, testing *both* sides (they always differ). If it's improved give it a little more of the same treatment; if not, try something else. Make only one alteration at a time, so you'll know whether it's made an improvement or not.

Be patient! Don't rush reed-making or try several remedies at once on a 'sick' reed, or you'll end up confused—and probably reedless.

The length and type of scrape, aperture (wire can be used to alter this, more later), and length of reed, varies between players, as do tastes in sounds and styles of playing (see 'Languages', Chapter 16). Sprenkle gives interesting, and sometimes surprising, statistics, from the reeds of well-known players around the world (see 'Recommended Publications'). No two pieces of cane are identical—quality, density and diameters vary, as well as gouges and shapes; every instrument—and above all every player—is individual, thank goodness! So, study and investigate as many methods of every stage of reed-making as you can, and experiment with canes, staples, scrapes, lengths, gouges, shapes, etc., till experience tells you what suits you, and your oboe, best.

Aim for a reed that is as free as possible, but *with control*. It must be agile as well as having a good sound; one of these qualities is not much good without the other.

It's possible to gouge, shape, tie, scrape and play a reed all in one day, but it is best done in stages, certainly at the scraping stage, allowing time—preferably days—between scraping and testing sessions, while reeds settle and dry out, when they'll alter by themselves. Some players choose to do it all at once, or have no option through lack of time. This saves re-soaking at each stage, so, since many believe a lot of soaking has a detrimental effect on the cane, it is a point worth considering.

I find that reeds (like wine) improve—up to a point—if left to 'mature', so besides making them in stages I like to make them a little in advance of when I'll need them, if at all possible (see 'Mixed Bag', Chapter 18). I don't know about you, but I feel a lot happier, and more relaxed, when using a reed I'm *really* familiar with (an 'old friend') *even* if it's 'on the way out', than one I don't know well, even if it's 'on the way in' (see 'Confidence', Chapter 7), although new reeds *do* have a 'fresh', almost 'bouncy' sound and feel, that old ones have lost for ever—like new sheets.

Don't get carried away, as one RCM student did one day, sitting in the canteen scraping reeds and smoking a cigarette. Her cigarette came to an end and she absentmindedly 'stubbed out' her reed in the ash-tray.

Finally, don't annoy conductors by scraping reeds in rehearsals— performances even—as in one famous incident (of which I've heard several versions). This player (who had a wooden leg) unnerved and irritated a new conductor by constantly doing this, often just before a solo, eventually making him so agitated that he asked him to stop. The oboist, in retort, jabbed the reed knife into his wooden leg and continued to play. The conductor, not knowing the leg was false, fainted.

The Nitty-Gritty

*Pros and cons of gouging your own cane; Preparing the cane;
Gouging; Shaping*

Pros and cons of gouging your own cane

The first obvious advantage (but not necessarily the most important) is cost. It is, of course, the cheapest way to get reeds, a fraction of the price of ready-made ones (or even G and S cane). So, if you do a lot of playing, this is one very real consideration. Second, and more important, you have the opportunity of experimenting, not only with sources of cane, but gouges and shapes (besides tying and scraping methods) while keeping some stability by changing only one factor at a time—hopefully eventually finding the best combination for your 'perfect' reeds. For example, you can try different canes, or shapes, whilst keeping a consistent gouge (till you reset the blade on your gouging machine). On the other hand, if you do it all yourself, it's not only time-consuming, but there are more opportunities for accidents or bad workmanship. If you buy G and S cane you *hope* you can assume that its preparation (and quality) is satisfactory (*only* leaving scope for errors during tying and scraping). If you prepare cane from scratch, breakages can, of course, occur at every stage (but you'll be able to afford a few). You may take the opposite attitude, however, that your handiwork is more reliable than that of others. One thing is certain, *any* stage badly done leads to poor end results, and frustration—(but so can reeds you buy). The cane must be gouged to exact proportions and shaped with precision. These are not, therefore, things to tackle, except seriously and carefully.

The chief drawback to gouging and shaping is, of course, the work involved, but I find the extra time spent, for my own needs, well worthwhile. It also avoids the necessity of relying on others. I gouge and shape a big batch every few years, and always keep a 'stock' of different canes. A different story if you undertake to supply prepared cane to all your pupils!

The very reduced cost of each reed, if self prepared, makes breakages less of a worry, inducing a more relaxed approach to reed-making, which, I find, helps me make better reeds—(though it could, I suppose, encourage carelessness). Even G and S cane, though *much* cheaper than ready-made reeds, is still relatively expensive.

Another consideration is the initial outlay on your *gouging machine* and other tools (seldom justified for cor anglais or oboe d'amore, unless you sell reeds), but you needn't buy the most expensive or sophisticated machine. Mine is a simple model which I bought cheaply in Germany while studying there (see 'Useful Addresses'), and so far it's served me well for over twenty years with no further costs. A machine, once bought, should last, given normal use and treatment. Blades, and other parts which may wear out, are replaceable. (All tools required are listed on page 127.)

You can buy 'gouged only' cane, to shape yourself, which saves buying a gouging machine—another compromise or middle route—worth trying first, perhaps.

Preparing the cane

Several processes are necessary before cane is ready to gouge. First, 'splitting' and 'pre-gouging' (the only time we 'split' cane intentionally!). Wear protective gloves for these two operations.

The tube cane is split with a *three-bladed tool*:

Tube cane   Tube cane (end view)

Three-bladed tool for splitting tube cane

(Look for the 'sunny' side, see 'Cane', Chapter 11.)

Hold the splitting tool, blades upwards, between your feet, the tube cane straight (very important) on it with your left hand, then 'hammer' it downwards, using a *mallet* (or your Carborundum, but don't break it), or, again with the cane placed on the tool's end, thrust it downwards onto a table, a board, or the floor. Put down newspaper first to make sweeping up easier (and don't do it above your downstairs neighbour's bedroom late at night!).

Each tube thus becomes three segments:

Split cane

Split cane (end view)

It is then 'pre-gouged' or levelled off:

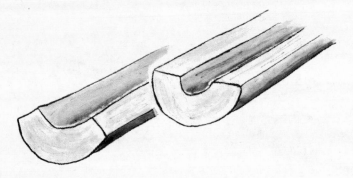

(before pre-gouging)   *(after pre-gouging)*

Split tube cane

Pre-gouged cane (end view)

104

Do this by 'hammering' it, as for splitting, through a *pre-gouger*, a straight tough blade fixed across a small block of wood whose centre is 'grooved out' to fit the tube cane:

Pre-gouger (end view)

Fix this to the edge of a table or work bench with a clamp or vice. Press the cane against the pre-gouger with your left thumb (a glove is essential to prevent your thumb being cut to ribbons by the cane's sharp edges), and 'hammer' with a mallet or similar implement in your right hand, pulling the cane through from below (like slicing runner beans!)—A warming exercise, depending how blunt your blade is and how crude a gadget your pre-gouger!

You *can* simply trim the cane 'free-hand' with a pen-knife instead. (A metal *'half-hole,'* or *'gauge'* is useful to measure diameters of cane; if it sticks up from the 'bed'—again, trim it with a pen-knife.)

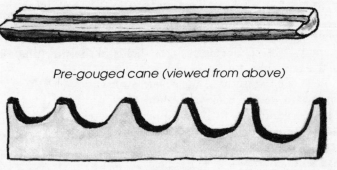

Pre-gouged cane (viewed from above)

Half-hole

Cut the pre-gouged cane into required lengths (80mm approximately). Most gouging machines provide for this process. On mine, a small saw operates through a fixed slot, the cane resting on two shaped supports. The distance between these fittings, governing the cane's finished length, can be altered (another factor to experiment with.) 'Posher' machines incorporate a *guillotine*, making cutting much quicker and easier.

Select the straightest lengths. Bent cane is useless and will be rejected by the machine during gouging. Cut off both ends and use the middle section if it is the straightest part—worth the extra work. It's a false economy getting two lengths from one piece of cane, unless they're straight. Taper the cane's ends, using a *razor* or *Stanley knife,* about 5mm, viz.:

Cane with tapered ends

Some do this after gouging. There'll be less risk of breakage if it's done now when the cane's thicker and stronger, but possibly more breakages during gouging because the pointed ends may make the cane slip off the machine. Don't taper too much; you only need to take the corners off to aid binding. (You can get into quite a rhythm—two strokes each end. Try doing this to music.)

Gouging

First, soak the cane in warm water for several hours. You *can* gouge dry giving a smoother finish (though the fibres will swell differently when wetted), but it'll wear out your gouger blade more quickly. Don't soak too much at once—either now, or prior to shaping—but prepare small batches, in relays, to avoid over-soaking if gouging (or shaping) takes time. If gouging and shaping at once, on one soaking, soak only very small amounts—(don't bite off more than you can chew).

Set up your machine on a non-precious table, or work bench, where you have good light and will be comfortable. Screw-holes in the machine allow you to secure it to the table if you wish.

Place a piece of cane in the gouger bed, lower the blade onto it, and gouge backwards and forwards firmly, pushing *downwards* rather than forwards, to keep the cane firmly 'in bed'. Use firm, even pressure lifting on return strokes; don't 'jab'. Bent canes will slip off the machine and break. The cane must fit the bed; trim the edges with a razor until it does. If it's too wide the centre will gouge too thin.

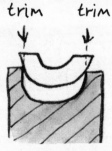

*Cane
(too wide
for bed)*

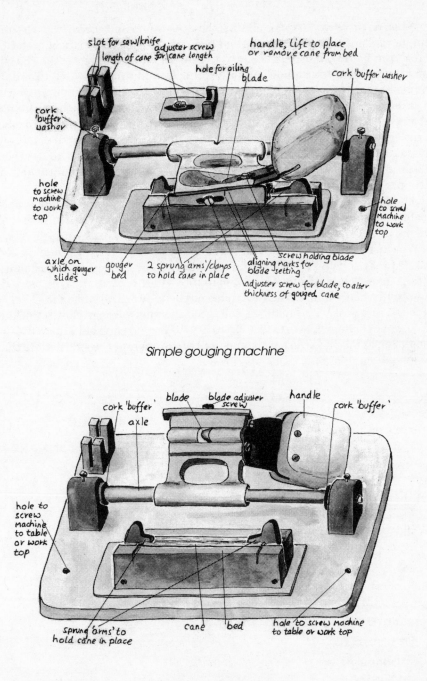

slot for saw/knife
length of cane for
adjuster screw
for cane length
hole for oiling
blade
handle, lift to place
or remove cane from bed
cork 'buffer' washer

cork 'buffer' washer

hole to screw machine to work top

hole to screw machine to work top

axle on which gouger slides
gouger bed
2 sprung 'arms'/clamps to hold cane in place
aligning marks for blade setting
screw holding blade
adjuster screw for blade, to alter thickness of gouged cane

Simple gouging machine

cork 'buffer'
axle
blade
blade adjuster screw
handle
cork 'buffer'

hole to screw machine to table or work top

sprung 'arms' to hold cane in place
cane
bed
hole to screw machine to table or work top

Gouging machine 'open'
(cane 'in bed')

When no more wood comes off turn the cane round and gouge from the other end, to make the gouge as exact and even as possible. It's critical to get this right. Don't stop too soon, leaving it too thick. The thickness of the shavings can tell you that your blade is blunt, if they're too thick—over 0.07mm. The gouger blade, which resembles a miniature plane the size of a small fingernail, is precisely shaped to produce cane thicker at the centre than the sides (about .57mm to .59mm in the centre, tapering to between .40mm and .45mm at the edges). Sprenkle (see 'Recommended Publications') compares measurements used, and their results. The gouger blade can be reset to degrees of hundredths of a millimetre, allowing for detailed experimentation, and ultimate consistency.

Simpler machines run on greased runners (keep well greased); more sophisticated models on ball bearings. Oil your machine frequently during use (holes are provided) and grease the blade with Vaseline afterwards.

You can measure the cane's thickness at any point on it with a *micrometer*—a useful gadget if you're looking for any kind of consistency or experimenting with gouges. A micrometer measures to thousandths of an inch, converted to hundredths of a millimetre (conversions are usually on the gadget itself, or can be found in a book). For instance, the recommended average centre thickness of .57mm to .59mm converts to .022" to .023". Gouged cane held up to the light should appear dark in the centre and lighter (thinner) at the sides. More thickly gouged cane makes more open reeds.

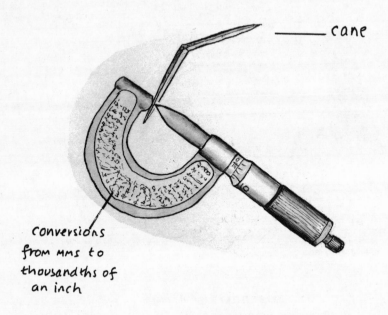

cane

conversions
from mms to
thousandths of
an inch

A simple micrometer
('Dial' models are much more accurate—but very expensive)

Now score the cane's centre. Place it on an *'easel'*—a wooden or hard plastic rest the diameter and length of the cane, with 'buffer' ends to secure it, and the centre marked (not unlike a mascara container, which is what I actually used for years!). Or get a piece of dowelling the right size, marking it yourself.

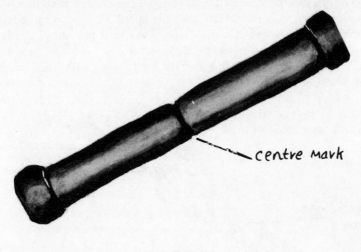

Easel

Score the cane carefully, so it'll fold easily without splitting. Run your (Stanley or similar) knife blade over it gently, several times, at the easel's centre mark. Cut into the very edge of each side but *NOT* right through the cane. Rotate your wrist with the curve of the wood for even scoring. Taper the ends if you've not done this already (see above), then thin the bottom 5mm or so of the ends, like sharpening a pencil. (Thinner cane 'under the binding', i.e. in this area, allows more vibrations.) These last two processes also help prevent the cane from splitting when it's bound onto the (narrow) staple.

Scored and tapered cane.

Fold the cane in half—easier if you hold a knife blade underneath the scored centre, placing your finger and thumb either side, on the cane, and gently press downwards. The cane is now ready for

Shaping

Again, the cane must be soaked (unless you carry on while it's still wet from gouging). Immerse in cold water for three-quarters of an hour to one hour, or until it sinks (in small batches if you're slow). Another method is for one minute in boiling water. A *'shape'* is a hard metal 'model' the exact dimensions of the required finished reed, against which the cane is cut. Shapes vary considerably (another thing to experiment with). Keep two or three shaping blades for producing different styles of reeds for different music (see 'You the Musician', Chapter 7, also 'Languages', Chapter 16), or for use with cane of differing diameters or gouges.

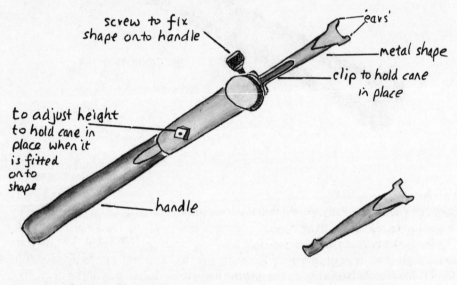

Shape with handle   Shaping blade

Shaping blades are fitted to a handle which has screws or clips to secure the cane, and are easily changed. Some have 'ears' at the top, as in my illustration, to hold the cane straight. You may need to trim the corners for it to fit between these, or it will split. Place the folded cane on the shape, making very sure the grain is parallel to it, i.e. that it's straight and exactly centred, and screw or clamp it in place. Use a *sharp*, non-precious knife, preferably one with a replaceable blade (change the blade frequently) or a razor (and keep sharpening it), as it's another very blunting job. Trim the cane *firmly*, following the edge of the shape exactly. Use *one positive stroke* down each side for a clean edge—don't 'carve at it' with little knife strokes. Take care also to cut it *level*, i.e. take equal wood from each side, otherwise the sides of your finished reed won't close properly and it will leak. If you shape in the 'wrong' direction (i.e. upwards) it'll end up straight, with the grain—not shaped!

Remove the cane from the shape and trim its 'ears' if necessary. Grease the blade with Vaseline before putting it away. Leave the cane to dry thoroughly (preferably overnight) before storing—especially if using airtight containers (see 'Mixed Bag', Chapter 18), unless you carry on while it's wet (avoiding re-soaking) with the next step which is, of course, tying (see 'Basic Reed-Making', Chapter 9).

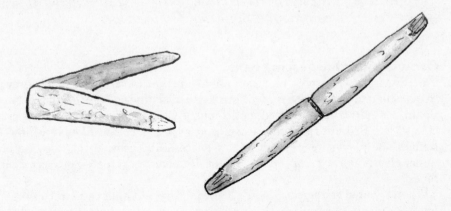

G and S cane

As a rough guide, eight ounces of tube cane produce approximately two hundred pieces of G and S cane (allowing for breakages). It is usually sold by the kilo, in short lengths. One kilo approximately fills a shoe box.

Chapter 11

Cane

Growing and harvesting cane; Choosing and general comments; Soaking; Conclusion

Growing and harvesting cane

The cane from which oboe reeds are made (*arundo donax*) is especially grown in marshlands bordering the Mediterranean in southern France and northern Spain. It's cultivated and dried meticulously. Climate and conditions are crucial—Great Britain is generally unsuitable as, like me, cane likes sunshine!—though one player in Scotland is now successfully growing his own supply under glass. Like any crop, quality varies. Bad harvests create *worse* problems for us.

When I visited Francisco Médir's 'cane factory' at Palamos, near Gerona in northern Spain (where these pictures were taken), he assured me there was nothing secret about his methods but that he used plenty of fertiliser. Wild canes, growing profusely along local road-sides, are, sadly, mostly too soft to use.

It is grown in rows and carefully measured while growing. Diameter is all-important for the various reeds it makes. Larger cane is used for saxophone, clarinet and bassoon reeds, smaller for oboe (oboe d'amore and cor anglais) and bagpipe reeds.

Oboe cane is a small part of Signor Médir's business, but when I met him he had fifty outlets in Scotland for bagpipe cane, and every forty-five days was sending *four tons* of sax and clarinet cane to *one* USA dealer.

The cane is harvested after two years' growth, in January/February, dried slowly, and sold the following year (sometimes later). Note good or bad 'seasons' or 'vintages'. At one time it was dried over a period of three years, but now demand forbids this. (Occasionally even 'oven drying' is used.) The cut stems—five to six metres long—are stacked outside to dry. (There's no fear of rain spoiling it at this stage.) Outside leaves are removed.

The cane is laid on racks, and turned every five days in August, every fifteen days in September, and the amount of sun measured, to dry to an exact degree—obviously critical.

By October drying is complete, and the cane is stored inside, above floor level, in well ventilated buildings. Cane not good enough for reed-making is used for matting and fencing.

Choosing and general comments

The quality of cane varies hugely. Not only the care of the grower, but soil quality and weather conditions affect harvests crucially. Much reed trouble and many headaches would be saved if only more inferior quality cane was

Cane stacked up to dry

Francisco Médir explains his growing
methods, beside a stack of cane

Inside, part of a 4½ ton batch ready for
shipment to U.S.A. 'No Smoking' essential!

Dried cane cut into short lengths for oboe reeds

Cane in various stages of drying, also
growing wild outside the fence

Signor Médir demonstrates how he lays
the cane on special racks and turns it
regularly, to dry it perfectly

Wild cane, a common sight in the area

thrown away earlier! It's sometimes marketed green and bendy, i.e. unripe. I know no cure, though I've heard of 'green' tube cane being usable after *nine years* in store.

One interesting point, which most of us overlook, is that, while growing, one side of the cane only will get sun. The cells on this side grow faster, are larger (making its diameter slightly asymmetrical), and the *other* side is, therefore, denser. Look for this when splitting the cane (see 'The Nitty-Gritty', Chapter 10). The question is, which side makes the reeds you prefer?—Something to investigate.

When buying tube cane we rarely have the opportunity to choose individual pieces or examine it in detail, except perhaps to glance at its general condition and appearance, but if opportunity allows, observe these guidelines (some of which also apply to finished reeds and G and S cane):

The appearance of the cane is important. Look for a shiny, hard looking surface, preferably 'barky' (i.e. showing brown patterns) rather than all white. Dark stripes all through are also a good sign. Shallower bark is often preferred. Avoid very pale, or yellow-all-over cane. Browner or purplish cane will be softer—white, harder. Green or split tube cane means water has run down its bark; it'll be weak. Your thumbnail should not make an impression in good cane. Knots further apart means it's been 'searching sun'—a *bad* sign.

Ensure tubes are parallel as well as straight, i.e. not wider one end. Inspect carefully for dust, either flying out when you break/cut cane, or at the bottom of a boxful—signs of woodworm, which, unchecked, will spread to your house and furniture. Don't mix new cane with old without examining and 'de-worming' it if necessary. Soak it to drown them. One batch I bought arrived full of maggots! I had to cut and pre-gouge it (and some of them too, I'm afraid) very quickly.

If you buy cane in bulk but lack space, pre-gouge and chop it into 'reed-lengths'—it'll occupy much less room (these processes lose a lot of wood) though it matures better in tube form. Or hang it up decoratively (more later).

Cane's diameter varies, greatly affecting the finished reed. In Britain oboists favour cane with a 10 to 11mm diameter; German players prefer narrower 8 to 9½mm diameter cane—I've made reeds from this (see 'Languages', Chapter 16). Narrower cane makes more open reeds, wider cane more closed reeds, affecting sound and pitch. Different staples, shapes, lengths and gouges are used to compensate.

Hardness or softness of cane affects tone, attack and general response. Reeds made from hard cane usually last longer, are better for staccato playing, and though may sound bright and 'tinny' initially, often mellow beautifully. Reeds made from over soft cane sometimes sound good briefly, but won't project or last, soon losing tone and becoming weak and woolly, with no 'guts' (body) or power (volume). It's a bad sign if a reed sounds too good too soon—it probably won't last. Don't raise your hopes prematurely.

Store cane in a dry place—but avoid central heating, which can wreck it. I've found that threading tube cane on strings (with coloured beads) makes effective ornamental 'Chinese curtains' (with a difference) besides being a good and space saving storage idea.

It worries me to think of the multitude of reed instrument players there are today using cane. How terrible it would be if supplies ran out, especially before any satisfactory man-made substitute can be found!

An oboist, once, noticing old discarded anemone baskets among theatre rubbish, thought the cane looked good, so took them

'Cane curtain'

home. Sure enough, they produced some excellent reeds! He told a colleague, who quickly ordered similar baskets from his greengrocer, which he stored in his garage—his new Rover car meanwhile parked in the street. But alas! *he* had no success.

Necessity being invention's mother, I've heard, first-hand, that some wartime musicians managed to make reeds from matchboxes (sometimes all they had) which would just 'get them through' one concert! During the war cane was used for camouflage and the story goes that Hitler used wood hung and matured for making into instruments, for pit props . Many fields of cultivated cane were also bombed, a burst dam later flooding yet more fields, around Fréjus, causing a terrible shortage of good quality cane for some years after the war ended. I'm thankful I wasn't an oboist then. Once, early in my career, I thought I'd 'mastered' reed-making *at last*, but found my temporary confidence was due, not to any skill, but to a batch of exceptionally good cane. Realising this, I rushed to the supplier for more. "Everybody's been asking for that," he said, "I wish I'd never parted with any of it." When I asked its source he replied, "They're building houses on the fields where that was grown." I could have wept!

Soaking

There are many theories about soaking cane, but it's generally agreed best to avoid oversoaking. Softening, however, lessens the risk of splitting, and wearing out your gouger blade and knives.

Whatever vital pigment or oils are lost during soaking, the water certainly becomes 'yellowish'. Oversoaking may cause symptoms similar to those of unripe cane (see above). N.B. *Never* try to 'dry out' a reed made from unripe or oversoaked cane by, for instance, holding it over a convector heater! The blades will simply curl outwards and the reed be ruined (no loss anyway). Instead, choose ripe 'shiny' cane, discard unripe or green cane and avoid oversoaking. Cane has even been soaked in whisky in efforts to produce 'better' reeds—doubtless making them very palatable, though salivation during playing is another problem (see 'Physical Hazards', Chapter 6)—in milk, and in milk and honey, besides different temperatures of water. You name it—it's been tried.

Conclusion

THE answer has not yet been found.

Personally, I'd rather practise to overcome problems—even, perhaps, those caused by reeds—with playing technique, than spend too much time tinkering with them (or with the instrument's mechanism), but I find playing easier than 'reeding' or mechanics. Find out what *you're* best at—but try to learn about everything.

Some years ago we thought reed problems were solved when woodwind members of the LSO returned from Florida with the latest 'reed-making machine', or *'Reedual'*, which, at the time, created excitement in the oboe world. These copied exactly one blade of a reed (necessitating sacrificing your 'best'…ouch!) producing two blades 'identical' to the original. But alas! they didn't prove accurate enough. Another shattered dream. Experiments are, however, constantly being made. Profilers and small hand-machines are quite commonly used. Some (for example by Michel of Hanover—see 'Useful Addresses') work well. So we struggle on…

One compensatory thought, though—supposing 'perfect' reeds grew on trees…there might be over fifty million oboists in Britain alone instead of the 'mere' thousands there are today.

Perhaps it's best the way it is, headaches and all.

Chapter 12

Reeds Again

(Miscellaneous tips in reed-making)

General tips and reminders

Buy a good purpose made scraping knife from a reputable source (see 'Useful Addresses'). Protect knife blades with a plastic 'sheath', or make one from cardboard or cloth, and sticking-plaster. Always use sharp knives. Study sharpening methods, and use an 'Arkansas' stone, or the fine side of a two tone stone, with honing oil, for best results. Otherwise, finer oil is preferable (or you *can* use water). To avoid pouring excess oil onto the stone, tip the bottle against your (flat) knife blade instead. Clean your stone regularly with hot **water**, soap or washing-up liquid, and a nail brush.

Don't tilt or roll a knife when sharpening. You'll lose the bevel **and** they're difficult to get re-ground. Scraping reeds with a blunt knife is asking for trouble. (You *can* scrape with a Stanley knife, and sharpen it on your stone.)

Don't leave reed-making until the last minute. Making reeds hastily, or while in a panic, causes frayed nerves and unnecessary (reed) breakages. Find a time, if possible, when you're relaxed and 'impartial'.

Even when playing a four month 'Summer Season' (over two hundred concerts), I tried to avoid reed-making, beyond minimal repairs (see 'First Aid', Chapter 13) while 'on the job', but prepared them in advance, before panic set in—but maybe you're as cool as a cucumber about the whole business?

If I wasn't an oboist I feel I'd probably be a good reed-maker. Instead, I'm forever seeking the 'right' reed for every concert—striving for perfection and never satisfied. A colleague of mine, staying in digs where the landlady's small son became fascinated watching him scraping reeds, let the child have a go one day. He says the youngster produced one of the best reeds he'd ever had, which he used for many concerts!

Unfortunately, reeds won't keep *indefinitely*. Otherwise one could prepare a life-time's supply in advance, given a few months (or years...) to spare. As it is, busy players must seize any opportunity to make reeds, e.g. on the 'plane, travelling to a foreign tour...

A common sight is an oboist scraping last-minute reeds in rehearsals.During one Hallé Orchestra rehearsal, the second oboe, having little to play, was absorbed in reed-making obliviously, until Barbirolli called, "Will the reed-making factory kindly move to the left"

But be careful in theatre pits. I was once in a Royal Ballet rehearsal when a bassoonist dropped his reed knife on an electric cable. There was a loud bang, the lights fused, and his knife acquired a large hole in its blade! (I've even heard of this happening during a performance.)

Make reeds 'to the tuning-fork' (A=440), but be prepared for extreme temperatures, out of tune keyboard instruments (see 'Physical Hazards', Chapter 6) or 'continental pitch' (slightly sharper than ours, A=442—445) if playing abroad. The difference, albeit small, can throw you out completely and you'll have to use slightly shorter reeds to compensate. Variations as high as A=448 have apparently been recorded in Vienna.

A flat or sharp reed is a useful standby. It's easier to flatten your pitch slightly by pulling out the reed or even the instrument's bell, *fractionally*, but not too far (see ' Mixed Bag' Chapter 18), than to sharpen, without reed alteration. 'Pinching' kills the tone and your lip. Instead, a 'short sharp reed' can be invaluable. N.B. If pitch seems very flat during 'reed testing' ensure the reed's right in, before chopping it short. If it's a stiffer staple than the previous one, it might not be pushed in fully.

Don't be tempted to alter reeds too early; allow them to settle and change by themselves. Make *minimal* alterations *singly*, then give the reed a good 'blow test', and yourself a chance to get used to it. Beware sore lips if it's new, very open or hard (see 'Physical Hazards', Chapter 6).

You *can* combine 'blowing in' a new reed with study—fingerwork perhaps, or 'notebashing' (learning the notes of a new piece or part) but don't get put off the piece! Curb impatience. Remember, you can remove more cane but not put it back. Never try to 'beat the clock'.

When 'blowing in' or getting used to a new reed, play familiar tunes or studies—preferably something you've often performed on a 'good' reed—rather than miscellaneous notes. Slow music tests sound and 'feel' (comfort); faster music agility and response. Telemann's unaccompanied (flute) fantasias are excellent for proving a reed's capabilities; they combine expression with nimbleness.

Repeat each test on *both* sides of a reed after *any* alteration, listening closely for the result of any modification. Every reed has a good and bad side (don't we all?). Mark the best with a pencil, or always put them the same way up in your case, e.g. 'good' side up. If one side is more curved, putting this towards the bottom lip will make the sound brighter—curved side up, flatter. The 'sound' you hear is basically the reed's 'lower' side.

Use a rehearsal—performance even—and, of course, practice time, to 'size up' a reed and decide what, if any, alteration is needed to correct or improve it.

I like to start with longer, flattish reeds, as they tend to 'sharpen up' with playing (the aperture closing a little). So I blow them in to some extent before adjusting their pitch. You can shorten a reed more easily than you can lengthen it! Tips can be cut quickly using jeweller's cutters. Longer reeds allow for more minor 'accidents'—'chipping' the tip during scraping, or knocking it against your teeth—(*SO* easily done)— or when a bit drops out of the end for no reason except that you've a solo approaching (at least that's when it happens to me). Why does this *always* occur *just* when a reed is nicely blown in, and comfortable? Even the smallest 'chip' in a reed's tip dulls the tone, makes attack uncertain, and low notes, in particular, unreliable, so must be dealt with.

Fortunately, minor surgery can often prolong its life (see 'First Aid', Chapter 13). One army player, reputedly, used to bite the end off his reed whenever a solo loomed and hold it up, saying, "Look, my reed's broken, I can't play."

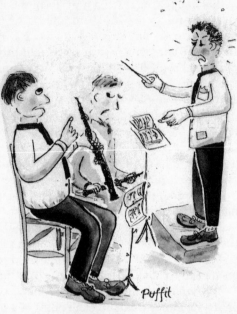

Puffit

Try to prepare varied reeds, for different circumstances, occasions and music (see 'You the Musician', Chapter 7, and 'Languages', Chapter 16) using different cane, shapes, gouges, lengths and scrapes (even staples). Variety is the spice of music, as well as of life! A 'thinner' reed, 'easier' to play— certainly on low notes and quiet dynamics—may have less tone, and less control on the upper register, therefore be more suitable for playing second oboe than first, especially in a small ensemble, where precision will be more important than a big sound. But an over long scrape can cause poor intonation, flat pitch (particularly middle C″), 'flying' middle F‴s and a 'bland' tone, notably if the 'heart has been taken out of it' (thinned too much, see 'Scraping', Chapter 9). A wider, 'thicker' reed will sound stronger and 'creamier'—especially on the high register—and (certainly if made from hard cane) hopefully last longer, too (though may be flat on top A″). It will be more suitable for playing first oboe in a large orchestra, particularly for the music of Brahms and Bach (see 'Languages', Chapter 16) or in 'dead' acoustics—or when 'competing against' brass or others—though may be harder to control on quiet low solos—unless you're 'ultra-confident' in these. A 'bright' reed will penetrate *and* be safer. If the cane is unripe or soft, a shorter scrape and thicker 'heart' and 'back' *can* help to compromise, but it's probably best thrown away. Too long and thin a tip can cause high pitched squeaks, especially on accented high notes. (Top C#‴ is the worst offender.)

To 'thicken' the tip, smooth the entire scrape with sandpaper (or, very carefully, with your knife) lengthening the scrape slightly, then trim it. The result? More wood on the tip.

Thinning the very edges of the reed makes hard reeds easier; all edges are 'sensitive' areas. Avoid removing cane unevenly. Examine the scrape, side view, for lumps, especially just below the tip. Thin the base of the scrape if the reed's not speaking on the bottom register. Trim the tip to stabilise top F''' and G'''. Lengthen the tip, or thin its sides, to flatten top A''. Shorten it to flatten Gs. Trim the sides of the lower scrape to stabilise F#''' and C#''' (i.e. make a V scrape into a U). Of the U, V and W scrapes, V is most commonly used. W = freedom without being flat, as a long U or V would be, and is softer than a U scrape.

If a reed starts to split from the binding, score the split, gently, to 'check' it (as painting nail-varnish or soap across a ladder in a silk stocking stops it running).

Reed splitting from the bottom, the split arrested by knife cuts

A woolly, 'cracked' or unclear sound, despite thinning the reed's tip, can mean it has a 'hair crack' in it—easier to see if you insert a plaque between the blades and *carefully* bend each towards you. Don't overdo this, and open, or even cause a split. The only remedy, if the split's *very* short, is to cut the tip and try to 'oust' it, lengthening the scrape and thinning the new tip to compensate and correct the pitch. Don't keep a split reed, even if it *seems* satisfactory; it might let you down at a crucial moment, perhaps when dry and open.

A weak 'hissy' sound may indicate that the cane's soaking up water. This will need constant sucking from the reed, probably getting into octave and other keys, too (see 'Nursing Care', Chapter 15). There's no cure, though it might be comforting to know this is usually less apparent to others than to you.

Weather and humidity affect reeds—dry (though not excessively hot) conditions improving all but over bright, hard reeds.

Always use goldbeater's skin, or a substitute, and seal the binding with nail-varnish (avoiding the cane). Carry spare strips of skin, or pinch some from another reed in an emergency. *Any* leak will cause unreliability and poor tone. Test that every reed is airtight, as described in 'Choosing a Reed', Chapter 8. *Or*, stopping the end with your finger, suck, creating a vacuum. The staple should 'stick' to your finger and 'plop' on removal; if not, and instead you hear a hiss, it's bad news. Habitually suck any water out of the reed before playing, to ensure a clean, not 'bubbly' entry.

Some players wire all their reeds, others never do. Wiring can open or close the reed's aperture. I feel it also stabilises it during its constant wettings and dryings, which open and close it during use (or when it closes a little with age, as some reeds do), having a strengthening effect and encouraging the reed to last longer.

Some feel wiring inhibits the cane's vibrations, deadening the sound. This could happen if it was wired too high, or too tightly—but the reed can then be 'freed' by thinning, to compensate. (One theory is that it doesn't matter how far onto the staple the cane is tied, as the aperture can thus be altered.) Keep testing a reed, tightening or moving the wire (or even removing it) until it feels comfortable. Use 10 amp fuse wire or similar, or fine copper wire, and small cutting pliers (see 'Apparatus', page 127). You *can* use thicker wire—but don't throttle the poor reed! Cut a 5-6cm length, wrap it twice around the base of the reed about 3mm above the binding, then twist the ends, four times by hand and once with pliers, not *too* tightly, and push it up to 4mm from the binding. Cut the ends close for neatness—and, to avoid torn lips, tuck them under the top of the binding. (Thicker, 15 amp, or doubled wire is more suitable for cor anglais reeds—or make three turns instead of two round the reed.) N.B. If you push the wire up to open the reed during a performance make sure you haven't pushed the reed up too, flattening your pitch suddenly, or the wire too far, opening the reed's sides—equally disastrous!

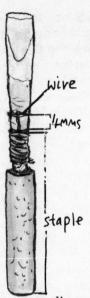

An alternative way of closing a reed is with a clothes peg or paper-clip, overnight. A too open reed can make top notes non-existent, wild, or at best flat, requiring greater lip pressure. If it's too open to control, it's no use. It can sometimes be made more controllable by trimming the sides, narrowing it or, in an emergency, cross the blades which will sharpen the pitch, make the aperture smaller and a woolly tone clearer, then trim the edges. (This *can* also have the opposite effect 'dulling' an over bright reed.) Watch out for leaks and poor attack.

Another way to alter a (finished) reed's aperture is to squeeze the end of the staple, i.e. the top of the binding, gently, with pliers. To open the reed, squeeze the front and back together:

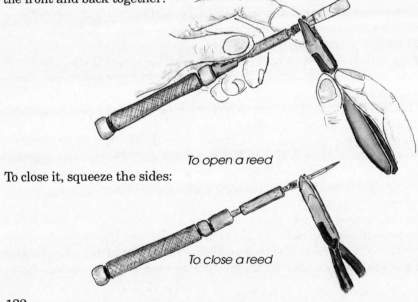

To open a reed

To close it, squeeze the sides:

To close a reed

Stop as soon as you see the aperture change. (This *can* ruin staples though, so wait until a reed's well blown in and settled before attempting it.) To undo this, push the mandrel into the reed firmly, 're-shaping' the staple (see 'Tying', Chapter 9).

For clarity and better response, thin the upper scrape of a reed. (Sandpaper's useful for this—it certainly saves time.)

The longer a reed (or instrument) the flatter, or lower-pitched it will be—the shorter, the sharper (laws of physics). Hence a piccolo is higher than a bassoon! Lengthening or shortening a reed, even minutely, flattens or sharpens its pitch. Lengthening the scrape (removing wood further down the reed, even to the binding itself) will flatten it considerably too; but remember the hazards of an over long scrape (see 'Scraping', Chapter 9, and above). It *must* be lengthened, however, after cutting the tip, for instance to 'mend' a 'nick', to compensate for shortening (sharpening) the reed. Even half a millimetre sharpens the pitch noticeably—so, trim cautiously.

After cutting the tip you'll need to thin it, so it can once again vibrate freely. To see if one side of the tip is thinner (bendier) than the other, run your finger-nail along each side, or waggle a plaque gently between the blades. Thin both equally. A thin tip is essential, and a question of knife technique. Scrape the tip with the knife at a 20° angle, barely to the *very* edge—'stroke' the dust off that. If it's too thick you'll get a very 'dead' response. A longer scrape is best with a shorter staple. (A shorter staple sharpens bottom C' area.) If, in desperation, you need to sharpen a *good* reed, shorten the staple by filing the bottom with an emery-board—an irreversible step.

The reed's 'heart' or centre is where tone (and control) is. The more wood you remove from here the less tone the reed will have, possibly even sounding coarse (though it may *feel* 'easier' to play). Don't thin the lower scrape or 'back' too much, if you want a reed with a fuller sound. This, too, will make it freer, but take care not to flatten its pitch. Thin the sides below the tip ('corners'). If the sides are too thick in relation to the back, top B''' and C''' may sound 'gritty'. The 'back' should be thicker than the 'heart'. Using a 'cliff' tip leaves a thick 'heart' and 'lay' avoiding thinning all over:

Reed's tip, side view

Most (mass-produced) commercial reeds are over thinned in these areas, making them 'easy' to play, and suitable for beginners who've not yet developed their embouchure muscles—but when you're more experienced, and in control of your playing, you'll want reeds with more tone. Professional reed-makers turning out large quantities quickly are, understandably, more concerned with them 'working' easily, than with their individual sounds. You will take more care than anybody who makes reeds for a living. I must say it *doesn't* appeal to me—but, fortunately, we're all different. I find it enough of a problem making my own reeds.

As a general rule, aim for a full sound as well as agility; don't sacrifice one for the other. Make sure a reed will do what you want, i.e. you're in control, by testing dynamics—especially 'ppp's—attack, diminuendos, etc., including 'singing out with gay abandon'. Keep adjusting till you achieve these results.

And compensate with your *playing* to make *every* reed sound as perfect as possible—*always*.

Chapter 13

First Aid

Rescuing and reviving old reeds;
Tools and accessories you need; reed-making and general

Rescuing and reviving old reeds

In chapters 8 and 12 I've described ways of testing for, and correcting faults in new reeds. Good 'has-beens' can often be 'resuscitated' also, or have their life prolonged, which is both desirable and worthwhile, as they're such rarities.

Old, dry reeds are more brittle than new ones, and so are prone to splitting (especially if given rough renovating treatment) and often open at the sides. Wet them thoroughly, 'blowing and soaking' until completely closed, before testing them properly. Reeds sometimes become out of tune with age, too, so beware.

If you 'chip' the tip of a reed, keep calm! It can usually be 'mended' by moving the scrape down, unless the reed is already short or scraped to the binding, and is quite a feasible operation. Don't try to complete this in one go, especially if the nick is deep. If you do it in small steps you should be able to retain the reed's original 'feel'. Trim the very tip, lengthen the scrape a little, and thin and lengthen the tip, to compensate. Then test it, keeping its old sound in your head. Repeat until the tip's 'clean', the pitch correct and the reed feels comfortable again and as near as possible to how it was before the accident. If you start with your reeds longish there'll be scope for this, not only once, but several times if necessary, before the scrape reaches the binding. After this, further shortening will make the reed sharp. As a last resort you can play with it pulled out a little. Alternatively, 'lengthen' the reed by unbinding it and re-tying it higher up the staple, then cut and thin the tip, and lengthen the scrape to obtain, roughly, what you had before (though it'll be slightly narrower). This is only really worthwhile with a good reed, as it's hard to get the blades absolutely straight, parallel, and opposite, once separated. However, if a reed is well 'skinned' (with goldbeater's skin or similar) and wired, it should hold while you slit the binding down the sides and slide the reed up or down the staple before re-tying.

Even without a breakage, lengthening the scrape and trimming and thinning the tip fractionally, can re-liven a reed when it begins to sound stuffy or tired. If one blade of a 'winner' splits, the reed can be saved by unbinding, removing the broken blade, and replacing it, if you can match it well enough—a drastic and delicate operation.

Often a tired, 'dead' sounding reed will revive simply with overnight soaking in cold water (the tip only). This has a brightening and rejuvenating effect. Don't leave it for more than twelve hours, or it may waterlog—or 'drown'.

Any improvement should have occurred by then. (Americans use a gadget called a 'high frequency oscillator cum sterilizer' for reviving and cleaning reeds.)

Cleaning the inside of a 'dying' reed often revitalises it. Immerse the tip in a glass of cold water and, carefully (remembering it's your good—or potentially good—reed) poke the tip of a feather through and move it gently up and down. You'll soon see a 'cloud' coming from the reed—deposits from saliva accumulated with playing...yuk! (see 'Physical Hazards', Chapter 6). Take great care not to damage the reed, or get bits of feather stuck in it. Alter-

Reed soaking in water

natively, clean a reed with neat hydrogen peroxide, leave it ten minutes, then rinse. Even if, like me, you're a fanatic teeth cleaner, never blowing solid food into your oboe, saliva alone—plus residue from cups of tea, etc. eventually produces this muck. If it's clogged, cleaning is often all that's needed, to give a middle-aged, hard-worked reed new life. (At first this 'gunge' has the opposite effect though, mellowing 'bright' new reeds and making them sound and feel 'blown in'.)

The *outside* of a reed can also eventually become 'choked' with dirt—even lipstick. Give it a light overall 'dusting' with fine sandpaper, or *gentle* scraping with your knife—not thinning or lengthening the scrape. Reeds often seem to 'thicken up' with playing, so *minute* thinning all over can be an effective 'freshener'. Ageing reeds frequently get sharper in pitch—then *do* lengthen the scrape *slightly* when 'cleaning' the outside. Don't forget to clean your staples, too, using a pipe cleaner, or feather dipped in hydrogen peroxide.

Sometimes, simply turning a reed after a time, and playing on the 'other' side, creates temporary 'newness'. Wiring an old 'good' reed to save or preserve it is often unwise. This can wreck it and it will possibly need re-scraping. A reed that has been unused for ages can sometimes sound pretty good without any treatment, for a limited time. I've heard of players forgetting their reeds, or taking the wrong ones to an audition or concert, who *had* to use an old 'cast-off', which rose to the occasion surprisingly well.

Always keep a spare reed in your instrument case, handbag, or dinner-jacket pocket (but don't send it to the cleaners). While I was in D'Oyly Carte Opera Company my handbag, containing all my decent reeds, was stolen and I had no alternative but to use rejects temporarily ('the show must go on'). Believe me, I was glad of them.

Play a bad, horrible-sounding reed (or spend all day teaching beginners) then play your 'tired' one. How good you sound! Perhaps it doesn't need renovating after all? A relaxed mental approach can often make even an old reed sound fine if you are fresh, or rested. By the end of a tiring four month 'Summer Season' of twice daily concerts, with no day off, I invariably found myself 'reedless'. Yet after a break, returning to playing refreshed, physically and mentally, I could usually get through most of the winter months, using the very reeds I'd rejected as being too poor even for open air concerts, when tense!

So remember, before you go altering or discarding old reeds prematurely, many of their faults may be 'only' in the mind!

Apparatus
Tools and accessories required for reed-making

A) What you need for scraping, or altering bought reeds:

1) Scraping knife (available right- or left-handed) with one flat and one angled side (see illustration page 96).

2) Cutting knife, sharp and tough. A converted cut-throat razor is ideal (but avoid one with a 'thick' top-side, which will prevent you from seeing the reed's tip over it).

3) Mandrel. A specially shaped tool or 'handle' which fits exactly into the staple, for holding the reed while working on it or re-shaping staples (see illustration page 93).

4) Plaque or tongue. A small, flat, oval shaped piece of metal, to support the reed's blades during scraping (also available 'convex' to fit the curve of the reed—better for scraping—in wood or nickel).

5) Block. A small hard wooden block with convex surface for trimming the reed's tip on.

6) Goldbeater's skin. Thin membrane, used to separate the sheets of gold during beating, made from cow's intestines (the darker, thicker variety is best), becoming adhesive when wetted one side, to wrap round the lower part of the reed, sealing leaks. (Available in small sheets, direct from goldbeaters, as well as music shops, see 'Useful Addresses'). Plumber's tape and Clingfilm make cheap effective substitutes. (Cut a 1cm 'slice' from the Clingfilm roll, which squashes flat, and use lengths from this.)

7) Small pair of scissors for cutting skin.

8) Fine sandpaper (emery or 'wet-and-dry') or emery-boards, for smoothing (or 'cleaning') the outside of the reed.

9) Thin soft wire, for altering the reed's aperture, 10 amp or similar, or 15 amp for cor anglais reeds.

10) Small wire cutting pliers, for cutting and applying wire, 're-shaping' staples, and instrument repairs.

11) Knife sharpening stone, a Carborundum, or, better, Arkansas stone.

12) Honing oil, or other fine oil, to use with the stone for effective sharpening.

13) Water. A glass or small bottle of water is handy during reed-making, or playing, for moistening reeds' tips, or 'rinsing' them after use, especially useful when doubling (see 'Cor Anglais', Chapter 17).

B) What you need if you use G and S cane (extra to above):

1) Measure, or ruler, in mms, to measure the reed's length, and how far to tie it onto the staple.

2) Twine. Strong thin twine, e.g. nylon thread, silk or dental floss, for binding the reed onto the staple.

3) Nail-varnish, to secure and seal the binding; the cheapest will do. (Different shades can be helpful.)

4) All purpose sharp knife, preferably with replaceable blades, such as a Stanley knife, for removing old reeds from staples, 're-grooving' staples, and shaping cane.

5) Pencil, to mark the position of the end of the staple on the cane, showing you how far to bind it, the 'best' side of a reed, and how far to scrape the tip or push in a staple or crook (besides markings in music).

6) Gouged and shaped cane, (see illustration page 111).

7) Staples, preferably identical, or as consistent as possible (see illustration page 87). (47mm Lorée or Glotin are recommended, see 'Useful Addresses'.)

C) What you need for gouging and shaping (extra to above):

1) Splitting tool. A three bladed tool to split the tube cane into three equal sections (see illustration page 103).

2) Pre-gouger. A sharp blade fixed across a small gouged out wooden block, for levelling off the sides of the split cane before gouging (see illustration page 105)—or use a knife, free-hand!

3) Mallet (or 'hammer') for splitting and pre-gouging.

4) Vice or clamp, for securing the pre-gouger to a table or worktop.

5) Chopper, guillotine or saw, to cut pre-gouged cane to correct lengths (usually supplied with gouging machine).

6) Gouging machine. A machine with precision shaped, adjustable blade, to gouge cane to exact dimensions, a shaped 'bed' for the cane to rest in, and, usually, with measure and guillotine (see illustration page 107)

7) Shape and handle. A hard metal model for shaping the cane, fitted to a handle. Different shapes can be fitted to the same handle; buy several! (see illustration page 110).

8) Easel. A wooden or plastic support the length and diameter of gouged cane, with wide ends to keep the cane in place, and marked centre, for scoring the centre of the cane for folding, and tapering the ends (see illustration page 109).

9) Micrometer, for measuring the exact thickness (to thousandths of an inch/hundredths of a millimetre) of gouged cane at any point on it. Simple ones (see illustration page 108) or more accurate, but expensive, dial (clock gauge) models are available (see 'Useful Addresses).

10) Half-hole. A metal sheet with graded semi-circular holes in its edge (like a knitting needle gauge), for measuring the diameter of tube cane (see illustration page 105).

11) Oil and grease (3-in-1 and Vaseline) for smooth running of your gouging machine. Vaseline is also useful for greasing the corks on your instruments, staples or crooks. 3-in-1 can be used with your sharpening stone.

12) Tube cane (see illustration page 103).

General tools and accessories (extra to above)

1) Small screwdriver(s). Always carry one in your instrument case for simple mechanical repairs (but carry the 'phone number of a repairer, too!).

2) Lubricating oil for instrument mechanism. Clock or sewing machine oil is best, or special 'key oil' from music shops.

3) Oil pen. Applicator for oiling keys (or use a fine needle tip).

4) Non-drying oil for the bore. Almond oil is recommended and available from chemists.

5) 'Shammy' leather, or polishing cloth, to wipe perspiration from your hands, and from the keys after playing, and for polishing the keywork.

6) Pheasants' tail-feathers, for drying out the bore after use (safer than mops).

7) Cigarette-papers, for 'blotting' water from under pads (specially octave keys). Never be without some.

8) Sheet of thin cork or leather, useful for adjusting mechanics, stopping rattles, or replacing lost corks (if you dare). Slivers from good quality wine corks can be substituted.

9) Stiff household paint-brush, for dusting instruments' keywork.

10) A needle, for unblocking small holes (such as in the C″ key), or to replace a broken spring in emergency.

11) Elastic bands. These make excellent 'temporary' springs, if one breaks or becomes weak. Always carry a couple, but replace them frequently—they perish quickly.

12) Spare set of pads, and glue (for emergency only, until you're a dab hand oboe 'DIYer').

13) A matchstick and small pen-knife. If your oboe loses a screw which secures a rod, a piece of matchwood makes a temporary replacement; be prepared for this.

14) Reedcase, a wise buy. (You can make your own by 'fitting-out' a slim cigar tin, or similar, with strips of draught excluder, but make sure reeds are properly protected.) Choose a slim case, to fit in your pocket or hand-bag, for six or twelve reeds (you always want to carry more than three, it's somehow good for the ego).

15) Instrument case. Again, you *can* improvise and adapt a hard brief-case using foam rubber or, better, polystyrene, but be *fastidious*. I would recommend buying the best case you can afford—your instrument merits it, surely.

16) Waterproof cover for your case—very advisable, not only as protection from the weather, but to keep the case safely closed (or use a strap or belt). You can make a cover using Rexine and strong, open end zips or Velcro—with pockets for your music or other paraphernalia. If you make it roomy enough you can line it with foam rubber or insulating material for extra protection against vibration or cold—a worthwhile extra. Don't carry too much weight in the pockets though, and strain or break the handle of your case. There are now good covers on the market with a shoulder-strap as well as handles, and useful pockets.

17) Tuning-fork. An essential gadget unless you have a 'built-in' one, i.e. perfect pitch, especially when reed-making or if you have to give 'A's (see 'Tuning', Chapter 3).

18) Metronome. Useful for practice (though not all) and reference. 'Tick-tock' metronomes, though attractive, are sadly becoming things of the past; modern technology has supplied us with neat and accurate substitutes, with many variations.

19) Music-stand. I recommend a proper one, to encourage good posture. Don't practise with your music on the floor (see 'Posture', Chapter 1) or balanced awkwardly on a piece of furniture.

20) Bonjela, or surgical (or other!) spirit, for mouth sores.

21) Lipsyl, Chapstick or Vaseline to protect lips from cold or drying conditions.

22) Octave-box remover. A tool for removing the metal 'cup' round each octave hole, enabling you to clean these out yourself (though this shouldn't need doing often if you follow my rules about teeth cleaning!).

23) Electric tuner. These come in different sizes, for measuring the sound-waves of individual notes (if you can't trust your ears).

24) Profiler. An expensive machine which removes the outside cane from

tied-on reeds to your specifications, but does not necessarily do the whole scraping job. Used by busy pros and reed-makers.

Additional requirements if you play the cor anglais or oboe d'amore:

1) Sling, for use with heavy cors anglais—a strap worn around the neck which hooks onto the instrument, to support it.

2) Double case (for oboe and cor anglais). Keep your oboe case too, as you won't want to carry your cor anglais all the time and will often need your oboe on its own.

3) Cor anglais or oboe d'amore reedcases (or use tobacco tins and fix the reeds to squares of card using paper-clips, possible with oboe reeds, too).

4) Instrument stand, for your second instrument when doubling, so it's handy for quick changes, and not balanced vulnerably on the floor, your lap, or a chair. Cut down a clarinet one to fit the oboe's bell and it'll travel inside the instrument in your case, if the base detaches, but DON'T forget to remove it before playing (see 'Mixed Bag', Chapter 18), or carry it in the pocket in your case cover. Cover the wood with soft cloth to protect the oboe's bore. When the cor anglais is standing on it (which is taller and heavier than the clarinet it was designed for) plant your foot on the base, take no risks! Or build your own stand to a safer and better balanced design. A double stand is useful when you're playing three instruments.

5) Pipe cleaners, to clean the inside of your cor anglais or oboe d'amore crooks—and all staples.

6) Bicycle-valve rubber tubing, to hold a reed firmly on a crook.

7) Cor anglais (or oboe d'amore) mandrel if you make cor (or d'amore) reeds (or cheat by using an oboe staple on its mandrel, instead, which fits a cor reed).

8) If you plan to gouge and shape cor anglais or oboe d'amore cane, you'll need the appropriate sizes of shape, pre-gouger, and gouging machine, too—only worthwhile if you're doing a *lot* of playing on those instruments, or selling cane or reeds to others.

All About Oboes

How an oboe is made; Choosing an instrument

How an oboe is made

Most people—even many oboists, I expect—would be amazed if they could watch an oboe being built, to realise how incredibly intricate it is, and see the amount of time and skill demanded. (It incorporates machine tool operating, woodworking, metal casting, plating, and precision engineering, besides musical skill in tuning.) A visit to an instrument factory is both fascinating and illuminating, and if more players had this experience they might treat their own instruments with a great deal more respect and care. Here is a synopsis of the many complex stages, with photographs:

1) The tree is cut down. African Blackwood (*dalbergia melanoxylon*)—surprisingly small 'bushy' trees—or Grenadilla—is generally used today (the same family as rosewood, used for some earlier oboes). The wood is cut into 'joint-sized' billets. (This is done before export, therefore there's no guarantee that each joint of an instrument comes from the same tree, area or even vintage!) It is very knotty, grained wood; care must be taken to avoid 'grainy' bits—unevenly grained pieces are rejected.

2) These billets are seasoned for several years.

3) A small primary hole is bored down the middle. This is done free-hand—a straight eye is essential (i.e. it is inadvisable after a few pints—curved bores are only for such instruments as shawms or serpents—or old cors anglais!).

4) The wood is now sometimes left for up to another year.

5) The primary hole is opened up and 'tapered' to the correct bore size.

6) The outside is 'turned' until it's the correct diameter. Tenon linings (metal reinforcements), if used, are fitted into the top of the bottom and bell joints.

7) Holes for pillars and tone holes are drilled. It's important to choose the 'front' or where to make the holes—to avoid unsuitably grained wood, and splits.

8) The bore is polished. 'Octave pipes' (metal surrounds) are fitted into the octave holes.

9) The pillars (supports onto which the keywork will be mounted) are fitted to the instrument.

10) Holes are drilled through them for springs and screws— an exacting job.

11) Pieces of barrel (or rods) are cut to fit each width between pillars. (This is known as 'cutting in the barrel'.)

12) Rough castings of the keys and parts of keys are made, using nickel-silver. These are filed and 'papered up' with emery-paper.

13) They are mounted onto the barrels.

14) The various bits of keywork are soldered together as necessary—a complicated process.

15) They are acid dipped to remove flux (a substance used to help fusion during soldering) and generally clean them.

16) All keywork is polished up, and silver- (or even gold-) plated (often necessitating sending it away).

17) The keys are corked.

18) Springs are fitted into the tiny spring holes in the pillars, each measured against the respective key and cut to the exact length— another fiddly operation.

19) Each key is fitted to the instrument. It is padded at the same time.

20) The oboe is tested thoroughly, and any necessary minor tuning adjustments carried out.

The 'Oboe Tree'

Billets of wood

Primary hole being bored

Enlarging the primary hole

The three joints, outsides turned
and polished

Outside being turned

Tone holes being bored

After the tone holes are drilled

After the pillars are added

Drilling holes in the pillars for springs and screws

Pillars with holes drilled

Rough key

'Cutting in the barrel'

Keys being mounted onto barrels

Key being filed and 'papered up'

Keys being soldered together

Cutting corks for keys

135

Smoothing a corked key

Keys after corking

A spring fitted into a pillar

Fitting keys to instruments

'Seating' a pad

Testing for leaks in a joint

Testing a key for leaks, using
cigarette-paper

Tuning the instrument, using
an electric tuner

Manufacturers' methods vary, of course, but I hope you now have some idea of the complexities, and intensity of skill and labour involved. At any stage errors or accidents can occur, even with the most highly skilled technicians. Whole joints are scrapped if a tone hole is incorrectly placed, or at any sign of a crack in the wood.

Perhaps now you're aware of the expertise, effort and time—hundreds of 'craft' hours—which go into making an oboe, you'll be inspired to care for yours as it deserves, and to play it as beautifully as possible, to justify its manufacture.

'FINAL SELECTION'

Choosing an instrument

Careful selection is important. Even if you are reasonably knowledgeable, do get a second opinion; take advice from a teacher or player whose opinion you trust. Buy the best instrument you can afford. As long as there's nothing radically wrong with it (hence being choosy) an oboe is an investment, the more so the better its quality, so you shouldn't have any difficulty in getting your money back if you decide to sell. However, it's often sensible for a beginner to hire an instrument at first, and not rush into buying one. Many shops offer hire schemes.

The 'better' the instrument the more beneficial to playing progress, too. Avoid the 'cheapest' (still a lot of money) which will almost certainly have out of tune notes, a crude sound, and lack many 'trill' and 'extra' keys (which facilitate awkward passages on better instruments), making playing harder—a definite *dis*couragement.

Oboes are expensive, but, unlike any other instrument in the orchestra, 'student' models are made. These are simplified versions, made affordable by omitting a few trill keys and other luxuries. A good 'student' oboe is an ideal first instrument. (The cost of an oboe is the intense labour involved.) School instruments are often cheap,'bad' and in a state of disrepair—unless the teacher is a competent 'mechanic'—making children *and* teachers struggle.

There are no half-sized oboes, as with stringed instruments, or small instruments for a child to learn on, such as a piccolo or E*b* or C clarinet—a limiting factor in the age/size a child can start. Many children begin on the recorder, progressing to the oboe later. (It's not uncommon, though, for eight-year-olds to play, unless they have very small hands.)

One child learning the French horn was asked, "Isn't that an unusual instrument for a little girl to play?" She replied, "I was going to learn the trombone, but my arm wasn't long enough."

Investigate the many options. Sometimes shops offer discounts on new or used oboes to music teachers or professional players (perhaps I should keep this quiet?) or allow you to hire different instruments over a period, prior to buying, and offer good terms for this arrangement. You may be able to find a good second-hand oboe.

Look for advertisements—in music magazines, Exchange and Mart, your local paper, music college notice boards, etc., or advertise yourself if you know what you want. Many music shops deal in used, as well as new instruments, so are worth approaching, too (see 'Useful Addresses'). A second-hand oboe will cost less than a new one, and be 'blown in'—(this applies to instruments as well as to reeds)—and free from 'teething' troubles such as stiff mechanism or settling pads and corks. One that's been used by a professional player should be of a good quality, and hopefully well selected by him initially, so a good buy—unless it's worn out.

Everything should be working easily, nothing sticking, rattling or clicking, and the action co-ordinated, not stiff or lazy, if an instrument's in good condition. If the mechanics are worn out, or loose on the rods, they'll rattle noisily, and the instrument may leak. The 'ease' of low notes should tell you if it's airtight, with all keys 'covering' nicely; they'll be 'sticky'—even impossible to play if any leak.

Check carefully that *any* instrument is airtight, by closing all keys on each joint, sealing the end with your hand and sucking to test for a vacuum (see photograph, page 136 also 'Mixed Bag', Chapter 18).

Avoid second-hand oboes that have been 'meddled with' by their owners, affecting intonation. Examine the bore and tone holes for scratches, or damage caused by excess cleaning or moisture. If unsuitable cleaners have been used, fluff and hairs might have accumulated in, or blocked, holes. These factors, and the general state of the silver-plating and pads, are important, and will tell you how well a second-hand oboe's been looked after. Be wary of buying a second-hand instrument more than fifty years old (you can check its age from the manufacturer's serial number)—unless it's had little use, and avoid it if it has automatic octaves! On a 'worn out' (or badly bored) oboe, notes from G″ downwards may be flat or 'gurgly', and top notes sharp. (The bore tends to shrink with age, possibly compensating for wear and cleaning?)

Oboes have improved greatly over the last twenty years with the stiff competition, so 'younger' second-hand (or new) instruments are better than ever now. Modern oboe makers go for precision—unlike the old 'craftsmen' who 'fiddled' to make the instruments work. A new oboe will carry a guarantee, and shouldn't need re-springing, re-padding or servicing for some time. It might be wise to get a quote for any such repairs necessary *before* purchasing a 'used' instrument. A re-conditioned second-hand oboe from a reputable dealer should be in guaranteed condition and 'safer', though perhaps more expensive, than one bought privately. A second-hand instrument in good condition should last adequately for any except a professional player (for whom a new instrument is surely a wiser buy) though oboes do wear out with use. Some professionals change their instruments as regularly as their cars—but treated properly, a new instrument should 'see you out'. Léon Goossens played the same oboe for over sixty years.

Don't assume that if you pay a lot, or buy an oboe by a well-known manufacturer, you'll automatically get a perfect instrument. Even the best 'professional' models may have imperfections, which is understandable considering what complex machines they are. So, try *any* oboe *thoroughly* before buying, testing for obvious faults and weaknesses, particularly on cheaper models, and examine the general condition and standard of craftsmanship. Sometimes even new oboes leak, or are in poor condition, as many shops have no resident 'technician'.

There are two basic fingering systems—*thumbplate* and *conservatoire*. Thumbplate models are more common in this country. Conservatoire fingering means the right hand index finger (F# key) is used instead of the left thumb (thumbplate key) when playing from A to Bb and B to C in the middle and upper registers. Middle B″ and C″ tend to be brighter on conservatoire instruments and flatter on thumbplate ones, so are notes to check.

You *can* have the system changed if you find the perfect oboe with the wrong one, but, though adding a thumbplate is simple, removing it is not, and such alterations are always costly. It's more sensible to look only at instruments with the fingering system you prefer. Some more advanced instruments have a thumbplate added to a conservatoire fingering—'Dual' system.

Most oboes are made of wood, with silver-plated keys, but some 'cheaper' ones are made from a type of plastic, or have nickel-plated keys (more slippery, especially when you've perspiration on your fingers, therefore harder to play than silver-plated ones). This is reflected in the price. Wood is used mainly because it machines well to a good finish—better than synthetic materials, which are also not cheap. It is resiny, and doesn't soak up water easily. (When tested in boiling water it only penetrated a fraction of a millimetre, then dried out rapidly.) Plastic instruments usually have a poorer sound, but are lighter and more durable, so perhaps more suitable for a child (though joints *can* break off as this material is rather brittle). They are machine made, hence cheaper, and in theory, identical, but individual testing is still advisable. A good plastic oboe will probably be a better buy (and the same price) than a cheap wooden one.

Avoid cheaper models which do not have a) a forked F vent, and b) an adjuster screw on the C″ key. No F vent means adding the E*b* key to play forked F—tiresome in many passages. The adjuster screw affects high notes, which will be hard to get if the C″ key opens too far; you may have to slide paper under the key to close it, or 'block it off'. Some cheaper instruments have no low B*b*, a sensible economy as it's expensive and not often needed. It's *possible* to add one, but uneconomical on a cheap oboe.

Look for cracks in the wood, especially between close together holes, e.g. C″ and B″, B″ to C#″ and C″ to D″ trill keys, or from the base of a 'pillar'. Cracks are most likely in the top joint, which has more keywork set into it and experiences the strongest force of air passing through its narrow bore and the most fluctuating temperatures (i.e. the roughest treatment and conditions), or in a larger area with more 'movement' (i.e. the bell). They're most usually caused by sudden temperature or climatic changes (if left in a showcase an oboe would never split)—or by central heating, unseasoned wood, or the wood's grain—but can nearly always be repaired.

Test top and bottom notes carefully. They can just be very hard to get on some oboes— perhaps due to an invisible bore defect? Can you get top F‴ easily? Don't panic if you can't get top notes straight away; there are many fingerings—I'm assured the notes are usually 'there' if adjusted for *you*.

It's important to buy a British standard pitch (A=440) instrument. Some oboes are flat, and to be avoided. Short reeds—*even* cut down staples—used in efforts to compensate, generally lead to endless problems. Modern German oboes tend to be sharp. Listen to intonation over the whole instrument, checking every note, including trill keys—preferably in normal room temperature — i.e. allow the instrument to warm up thoroughly in cold weather or, if the room's very hot, allow for a little sharpness. Be particular.

Certain notes are especially poor or unreliable on cheaper oboes. Middle C″ is often out of tune or wild, with a nasty sound, and 'bright' or flat depending if the oboe's thumbplate or conservatoire. Low E′ and G′ are often flat and, as with all lower notes, hard to alter by 'lipping' (see 'Embouchure', Chapter 1). Top C#‴ is frequently unstable or sharp, also some middle notes, e.g. forked F″, especially if not vented, F″, F#″ and G″. Experiment with fingerings for higher notes (e.g. C#‴) before you 'write off' an instrument. Middle C#″ may require 'half close' fingering (C″ key down, but the hole not covered) to flatten it.

Do not accept *any* instrument unless you're *absolutely* satisfied. Most notes can be 'tuned', but it's worth remembering that if *one* note is out of tune, i.e. the tone hole wrongly placed during manufacture, the whole joint is scrapped as the instrument won't sell. Bottom notes are often flatter than the rest, check these carefully. There's *nothing* more annoying than an out of tune note on an instrument.

Reeds affect individual notes (see chapters 9 and 12) so use as many different ones as possible when trying an oboe. When you have an instrument on trial you'll have plenty of opportunity to try different styles of reed with it—the only way to give it a fair and thorough test. (One player, asked to test an oboe, said honestly, "I couldn't get a note out of it"—not surprising since he'd forgotten his reeds!)

Different lengths of reed or scrape, widths, types of scrape, cane, gouges, apertures, etc. all affect notes differently on different instruments. Find the reed to suit the oboe. It's also important to get the right marriage of staple with the instrument's bore. It must be an exact continuation. This *can* be sorted out by mathematical calculation and measuring if it doesn't work at first.

Reeds, however, cannot cure a defective instrument. If you don't feel happy after some experimentation, try a different oboe.

When buying a new instrument, particularly an expensive or 'professional' model, if you're unhappy about *any* note (after trying different reeds) get a second—even third—respected opinion before returning it to the shop or manufacturer.

It might only need minor adjustment with a screwdriver, but if it needs radical tuning by removing wood from inside, etc. (see 'Nursing Care', Chapter 15) get it corrected *before* buying, in case it proves impossible or unsuccessful. Every dealer or manufacturer will assure you *their* oboes are perfect, and that *your* playing, or reed, is to blame—so it's worth being able to quote a name or two of respected

players who'll back you up to convince them—and you. I speak from experience. You *can* try tuning, yourself, but avoid a new instrument with any defective note. Keep taking it back until it's to your liking.

Many alterations are surprisingly simple—for example, extending a side key if it's out of reach for a small hand (see 'Physical Hazards', Chapter 6), but don't be deceived. One well-known player's spare oboe had no F vent, so he asked to have one added, and on getting the instrument back pronounced it much improved. Years later he took it to a repairer for servicing, who pointed out that though the vent *key* was there, there was no hole! The maker, believing it unnecessary, had added the key only, to fool the player, which it did (a 'placebo' key—Psychology doesn't only apply to reeds).

Many keys can be added to (even removed from) oboes. Some useful extras to consider or look for on an instrument include a low B' to C#' coupling (avoiding a bad slide), a 'long F' key (avoiding forked F fingering), a right-hand G# key, a G# to A# trill key, and a low C' to Db' trill key (see Ferling's study number 36, see 'Recommended Publications'), though this can sometimes get in the way. A third octave key is sometimes a doubtful asset but this really does depend on the oboe. Covered keys in place of open or ring keys make 'tidy' playing easier, and tone rounder, but adding them could adversely affect tuning (not worth risking, perhaps?), and automatic octave keys are, as far as I'm concerned, more trouble than they're worth (semi-automatics are preferable). Most of these keys should be found on professional oboes, though not on all 'student' models.

As with anything mechanical, the more mechanism you have the more there is to go wrong—especially automatic octaves!—and the heavier and less manageable the instrument becomes. So weigh up the pros and cons before buying the instrument with the most keys (or having a lot added), impressive though it might appear.

If there are particular 'extra' keys you've been used to or consider invaluable, look for an oboe which already has them, first. Most alterations are probably only worthwhile if the instrument's very special, or the modification relatively minor.

Sound varies between oboes, though it is largely governed by you and your reed (see 'Tone', Chapter 3). (A top player playing a cheap oboe sounds more like 'them' than 'it'.)

Probably by the time you come to invest in a top quality instrument you'll know the kind of sound you want, which may influence the make of oboe you choose. Even two 'identical' models by the same maker will vary, so you must just keep trying different ones till you find what's *exactly* right for *you*.

How lucky string players are! A child or beginner can learn, satisfactorily, on a really inexpensive (or small) instrument. For us the cheapest oboe isn't cheap at all (and sometimes a real handicap.) Reeds, too, are a big expense, till you make your own—then they're a big time consumer. The more string players can afford, the better instrument they can buy—the sky, literally, is the limit. It must be wonderful to make music on such a fine instrument as a Strad. There is, regrettably, no equivalent of a 'Strad.' oboe—even if money was no object. The 'tool of *our* trade' is only as good as our reed. (A sobering thought.)

The oboe's mechanism developed comparatively recently (see 'A Brief

History'). A little over two hundred years ago oboes had only one or two keys—thoroughly 'old-fashioned', one might say. Also, their life is limited. Stringed instruments, on the other hand, mature and improve with age, and their design has changed little in two and a half centuries. Quite literally, the uglier (or older) the fiddle the better the sound—not so with oboes!

In theory, modern mechanism could be added to an 'old' oboe, but this would ruin its antique value and entail re-building it, so the idea is a nonsense.

A few oboists choose to travel to the country of origin to buy an instrument of foreign make, visiting the factory in person, rather than choosing from a few imported models in this country (see 'Useful Addresses'). Imported instruments used to be liable to duty, but today—though VAT is payable—this only applies to countries outside the EEC, so is virtually irrelevant. (The instrument's serial number might have caught out a smuggled oboe, not only on arrival in this country, but when the owner came to insure, repair, or sell it later. Though unlikely to get caught, he had to watch out if taking it abroad again.) One way round this (it's said) was for a player to leave the country with a cheap instrument, declaring it at customs—chuck it in the Seine—and return with a new oboe, pretending it was the same one. I know of one British dealer (no names!) who regularly took instruments to musicians overseas. At the customs he would declare an extra half bottle of Scotch, meanwhile walking through with several smuggled instruments in his luggage. They never seemed to smell a rat (maybe he was lucky)...

Chapter 15

Nursing Care

How to look after your oboe

Care of your oboe

For any player a faulty instrument is frustrating; for a pro it's disastrous. The importance of proper instrument care cannot be over-emphasised, and should be stressed by every teacher of beginners. I explain this to pupils before showing them how to play their first note. The oboe's mechanism is particularly delicate, even 'simple' models (see 'How an Oboe is Made', Chapter 14), are *very* susceptible to damage. It seems possible to drop or knock over a flute or clarinet and it'll still work—but the *slightest* accident to an oboe usually means you're in real trouble. Keeping it in working order, therefore, means treating it with utmost consideration—always.

Assemble instruments gently, without pressure, easing each joint into place.

Lay an oboe down on the low B♭' key side, which has fewer holes for water to run into, dampening pads and making them stick—and less mechanism to damage, *never* on its right, or upside down *on the keys*.

Always dry the bore after playing. Don't put the instrument away wet, or leave it wet for long. If you must, temporarily, prop it up—e.g. against a cushion, so any moisture runs down, but never where it may fall or be overlooked. Use pheasants' tail-feathers to 'dry' the instrument, especially the narrow top joint. You can usually get them from your local poulterer. They don't really remove moisture, but distribute it to evaporate more quickly.

A mini-skirted oboist jumped, when, putting her oboe away after a rehearsal, her neighbour's feather had accidentally tickled her bottom...

Avoid cleaning mops with wire in them which can scratch the oboe's bore. Clarinettists and flautists use a 'pull through'—a cloth or shammy leather on the end of a rod or weight. These are now made for oboists; you can make your own by attaching a *very* thin strip of suitable material to a large darning-needle, but *don't* get it jammed in the narrow top joint.

Never put an oboe on or

144

near a radiator. Even vehicle floors can get too hot for their well-being; don't put yours at your feet during a long journey in the front seat. Avoid leaving your instrument, even in its case, on a table or chair in a crowded place as I experienced while in D'Oyly Carte Opera Company. My oboe case got knocked off the bandroom table in an Edinburgh theatre, *of course* falling upside down, damaging the oboe's mechanism so that only a few notes worked. I limped through that evening's performance of 'Iolanthe', helped out by the flautist—spent half the night transposing 'The Gondoliers' onto the cor anglais (for the next day's matinée)—and tore round Edinburgh next morning looking for a repairer, there being no specialist shop. I eventually got it mended—at 1.45 pm—in a bagpipe shop. A relief—though I'd been quite looking forward to playing 'The Gondoliers' on the cor! It was a nerve-racking experience.

It's even more inadvisable to leave assembled instruments unattended, e.g. on your chair or the floor during tea-breaks—though everybody seems to do it. I could recount many disasters here—it mightn't only be a *tea* break...

Oil the mechanism regularly—every few months or when the action becomes stiff or unco-ordinated—depending on use. Prolonged inaction may also result in the mechanism 'stiffening up'. Use very fine oil, e.g. sewing-machine or clock oil, or special key oil from music shops. Apply it sparingly, using a needle tip or 'oil pen', to every moving part, working the keys until it's sunk in. Avoid using too much, or getting *any* on the pads. Wipe away any excess before dust, etc. sticks to it, clogging up the action. Like any  other machine, wear and tear will result if the keys are not oiled frequently and are allowed to dry up. Never use thick, or bore oil, for the mechanism, as I once did when a student. All the keys on my oboe seized up, putting me in a real panic (until I understood the cause), and each had to be removed and cleaned—another example of treatment having the *opposite* effect from that intended!

If the keys on a long rod feel stiff, even after oiling, remove the rod, sliding it out carefully. Take off all the keys and lay them down on a dust free surface or clean sheet of paper, *in order* (with any luck you'll then be able to replace them correctly!). Wipe the rod with a clean, non-fluffy cloth, *gently* (they bend easily, and unless 100 per cent straight will *never* fit back again). Apply fresh key oil, and replace rod and keys, using tweezers or a small screwdriver (or crochet hook) to ease each spring back into place without straining or bending it. If still stiff repeat, but sand the rod a fraction, cleaning the filings away immediately, before re-oiling and replacing. If it's still not cured the rod's probably bent, and may need replacing.

A small household paint-brush is effective for dusting the mechanism (provided it's not moulting!). Even the *smallest* specks of débris can prevent keys working properly, or block holes, affecting tuning. (It doesn't take much to block a pin-hole—and that's about the size of it.)

Remove moisture from under keys—especially octave keys—holes nearest the top of the instrument so most prone to water trouble—after playing—and whenever necessary, by blotting with a clean cigarette-paper (always keep some in your case). Open the offending key, slide the paper under it (avoiding the gummed part which *won't* help the situation), close the key firmly and remove the paper. Repeat until *all* signs of dampness have disappeared. Do this automatically whenever you put away your oboe after use. Water not removed causes extraneous bubbly noises and gurglings, besides sticking pads. If you put your oboe away with damp pads they'll stick persistently. Stuck octave keys make notes sound an octave lower—others produce 'wrong' notes. The problem's worse in cold temperatures or humid atmospheres; don't encourage it by carelessness.

If a reed's soaking up water it provokes dampness getting onto pads. They can stick anywhere on the instrument; water has a strange way of travelling down 'channels' to odd places. I frequently get it under my C# key (making it sound C♮ !). If middle C″ sounds spluttery, there's probably water under the key itself.

An unfortunate principal oboist in Sydney, Australia (playing a conservatoire oboe) suffered this problem in a performance of Brahms' first symphony. During the first movement—in which the oboe part is largely based around C, water got into the key, producing Bs instead. He understandably became nervous, and kept fiddling, and, as he told me, maltreating his oboe in efforts to put it right—so that eventually the key stuck. He could now only get C not B! By this time they'd reached the slow movement—which features B. The experience shattered his nerves for some time.

A similar experience happened to a cor anglais player in that seemingly fated 'New World Largo' (or is it just that it's so exposed and famous?) His A♭ key stuck and he played the entire solo with (written) Gs sounding instead of Abs!—An interesting variation. (The first time I played cor anglais in Dvořák's eighth symphony—a few bars in all—I felt a fool when my first long awaited note came out as a 'wrong' one!)

If a pad sticks despite 'drying' with cigarette-papers, try a) 'powdering' it. Put a *little* powder (talcum or other) on a piece of stiffish paper, slide this under the pad, close the key firmly, and draw the paper out keeping the key closed (take care not to overdo the powder and 'bung' up the key), or b) doing the same using paper 'blacked' with soft lead pencil. Both these temporary remedies *can* lead to clogging, though. (Lead pencil eventually dirties pads; spilled powder can stick to oily springs, etc.) So first try using *clean* crisp paper—e.g. a new bank note—or, for speed during playing, a corner of your music (if it's not too ancient or 'soggy'). Alternatively, simply drawing the corner of a damp hanky under a sticking pad, then drying with a cigarette-paper, might help, especially if there was something sticky on it.

If water's a frequent problem in any key, rub Vaseline, silicone oil (WD40) or grease round the inside of the hole on a feather, to encourage the water to run straight down (oiling the bore helps too, more later).

Clean a very dirty pad with meths, applied on cotton wool. You'll probably have to remove the key to do this. As a *last* resort fit a new pad. If water persists in an octave key, remove the reed, 'dry' the instrument's top joint with a feather, then, blocking the joint's end with your right hand, close the keys (by fingering G″), keeping the offending key open. Place a cigarette-paper under it and blow hard down the joint, blowing the water out through the open key. Move the paper a little and repeat, until there's no sign of dampness. (Sometimes a cigarette-paper remains dry after 'blotting' yet symptoms of water continue—then if you try this you find 'bucketfuls'.)

Quick emergency remedies are: a) blowing sideways, sharply, across the hole, with the key open, to blow the water away. But choose your moment. Avoid a silent bar during a concert or live broadcast…preferably pick a fortissimo chord if there is one at an opportune moment. Or b) thumping the oboe (vertically) on your knee to shake the water down the instrument.

To cure a sticking cork which has become 'indented', slide fine sandpaper, or the smooth side of an emery-board, under it and lightly 'dust' the surface to clean it. Blow the dust away quickly. Don't try this too often on the same cork, and NEVER on skin covered pads. (Corks are less likely to stick than pads.)

Tiny pieces from a sheet of thin cork or leather are useful for replacing small corks if they drop off—affecting tuning, sometimes causing leaks, and often rattles. An instrument repairer I know goes to the home-brew shop for corks, where he's very choosy indeed.

Vibration (during transportation or general use) is detrimental. Always be gentle and careful with instruments and wrap them well for any rough ride, such as on a bike (see 'Mixed Bag', Chapter 18).

Keep an eye open for loosening rods or screws. By regularly running your eye over the mechanism (e.g. during lengthy bars' rest) you should notice any beginning to work loose and catch them before keys actually drop off, or screws get lost. (Always carry a screwdriver.)

Polish the keywork occasionally, gently, with a *clean* soft cloth or shammy leather, and wipe it over after every playing to preserve the silver-plating. Keep a shammy leather handy to wipe your hands—and keys. Acidity in perspiration soon destroys silver-plating, then the nickel-silver underneath becomes pitted, making keys more slippery, and eventually dangerously thin. Re-silvering is expensive, necessitating removal of all keys, pads, etc., so avoid it unless the instrument's being overhauled at the same time. Prevention is much cheaper than cure.

Don't handle your oboe with dirty hands; wash before playing.

If the instrument becomes stiff to assemble *don't* use force, risking damage to keywork, but apply Vaseline, sparingly, to the corks on each joint (most oboe cases incorporate a small grease pot). Sometimes the joints become so loose, through shrinkage, wear or over-greasing of the corks, that a joint of your oboe might even drop into your lap while you're playing (or worse, onto the floor)—or you'll wonder why your pitch is becoming progressively flatter. Then you'll need to *swell* them. Wet the cork, hold a lighted match a couple of inches below it, turning the joint slowly to warm the cork evenly. Take *great* care not to burn the cork, or hold the match too close and over-heat the wood, risking cracking it. You'll see the cork swell a little—a little is enough. Afterwards apply fresh grease.

A player in the Midland Light Orchestra actually suffered the embarrassment of his oboe's bell dropping off with a loud clatter during a performance. Luckily the metal band prevented it breaking.

Once, in the BBC Concert Orchestra, an oboe d'amore player's bell fell off during the solo in Ravel's 'Bolero' (in this case it was dangerously held on with cigarette-papers between the joints, Sellotape, etc. Cork swelling would have been a safer precaution).

On an even more embarrassing occasion this happened to a cor anglais player during a performance of Debussy's 'Les Nuages', in Australia, in a big hall with a tiered stage. The bell dropped off, bounced down the tiers and 'lobbed up' in front of the conductor noisily, during a quiet 'atmospheric' spot in the music, when the 'dreamy clouds were fading away', somewhat spoiling the 'atmosphere'...

Cork swelling or greasing can also be applied to corks on staples and crooks, if they become too tight or too loose. If an oboe staple or a crook is very loose, a temporary remedy is to stick stamp paper, or a folded cigarette-paper (which you always have handy of course) round the cork.

In my experience one alteration to mechanism affects a dozen other things. Make a careful note of *any* adjustment you make, so if it doesn't work you can, at least, undo it and start again. If you alter an adjuster screw for instance (if you DARE) note how many 'minutes' (or degrees) you tighten or loosen it (e.g. a forty-five degree turn = 'quarter of an hour').

Never 'doctor' your oboe's mechanism, however simple it may seem, unless you know what you're doing (not think you know). Speaking as one who, I'm sure you've guessed, is not a born mechanic, my advice is, if in doubt it's best to leave well alone, and get professional help. There's a psychological side to tinkering with the instrument, too, especially for 'non-repairers', such as mistrust of an alteration you've made, or *thinking* your oboe's leaking. (It's enough to make you split notes worrying about it.) Or when, after a fault's been corrected, you still produce the same symptoms from habit. Or 'effective' placebo keys (see 'Choosing an Instrument', Chapter 14).

It's certainly useful, however—and sometimes essential—to be able to carry out minor surgery and basic maintenance, safely, yourself. You can't always get specialist assistance when you need it, for instance when playing chamber music with friends on a Sunday afternoon, or on tour miles from any repairer—especially abroad.

One BBC cor anglais player had the theory that he could right any fault on his instrument if he removed every key, and replaced them all systematically, but when something went wrong with it before a concert in Portsmouth, he couldn't get the instrument back together again.

An elastic band makes a useful emergency substitute for a broken or weak spring, as proved necessary during a performance of Brahms' violin concerto by the London Symphony Orchestra at the Royal Festival Hall. The oboe-player had a good reed and it was going well. After the first movement the soloist

asked for an 'A' (the note the oboe solo begins on, enabling the oboist to 'test' it). The movement began, the oboe entering with a beautiful A″, but when he played the second note (F″) another A″ sounded. On the third note (C″) yet another A″ sounding, the soloist turned round anxiously, and the conductor was looking far from happy. A spring on the oboe had broken and the key 'stuck' open. The performance had to stop while the oboist rigged up an 'elastic band spring' then gave the instrument a chromatic 'test'—all in front of the RFH audience—before the concert could continue. (In such a situation one player might borrow the other's instrument, but on this occasion the two were different systems, making it impracticable.)

Have your instrument serviced professionally every four to five years, depending on use (don't leave it longer than ten), especially before going on tour, abroad or where emergency repairs might be hard to come by, or starting a long season or show, when you won't be able to spare the instrument. (It's advisable to have it looked at once a year, however much or little use it gets.) You'll know servicing is necessary when the mechanism becomes 'lazy' and unco-ordinated, notes squeak, keys rattle or stick, pads leak, and the instrument feels generally hard to play (especially on bottom notes). Don't put it off until too many things go wrong. Nowadays, fast and safe ways of sending instruments make quick repairs possible—sometimes by return— by reputable restorers, even outside your area (see 'Useful Addresses').

A long period without use may cause dried out, shrunk corks or swollen pads, preventing the mechanics working properly. If you keep an instrument unused for some time (especially in a dampish place) you may find the keywork somewhat 'green around the gills' when you next get it out. It's a shame to let this happen. Do give it a 'blow' occasionally, or sell it, lend it, or hire it out. An instrument of my own, after a while 'in store' turned out to have half a pad and parts of the corks missing. They had been eaten! (I'm told 'pad bugs' are not uncommon—a mosquito net might be the answer perhaps?)

I would oil the bore of a new instrument every six months, and occasionally thereafter if the oil appears to soak in quickly, or the bore looks dry. It's crucial NOT to get oil on the pads, so slip a small piece of (news)paper under *every* pad *before* applying oil. Use a 'non-drying' oil, such as almond oil—available from chemists—and apply thinly (enough to make the wood glisten, but not to run everywhere) on a feather. Dip the tip of the feather into the oil bottle and squeeze/spread the oil all over it with your fingers. Twist the feather around inside each joint of the instrument until the bore is evenly covered. Also rub a little onto the outside of the wood, avoiding pads and keywork. Wipe any excess off your fingers. Some players are against oiling the oboe's bore, even believing it has a detrimental effect on the tone; others just feel it's unnecessary. It might help prevent the wood cracking, especially on a brand new instrument (though other factors affect this, see 'Choosing an Instrument', Chapter 14), but I'm told that if the wood's going to split it will anyway (because of flaws in the grain?) *whatever* precautions you take (see 'Mixed Bag', Chapter 18). But, take heart! Cracks can usually be 'pinned' by a good repairer, who'll insert metal pins, closing the split, which becomes barely visible (like they mend broken legs these days).

I feel oiling must counteract dry roughness inside the bore, certainly help prevent your oboe smelling (of that garlic, nicotine, etc. you've blown through it), and definitely encourage water to run straight down inside, instead of getting onto pads. It seems to me that if the wood drinks up oil it must need it—

though at least one manufacturer claims to soak the wood in oil before making their instruments (in which case further oiling shouldn't be necessary). Another, after carrying out experiments, claimed this made little or no difference.

A much used oboe with constant wetting and drying, or exposure to hot dry conditions, must surely lose some of its natural oiliness in time? So oiling the bore occasionally should do it good, even when the instrument's no longer new. Consider the 'wettings', 'dryings' and 'cleanings' it gets if you've twice daily performances, each with an interval (when, of course, you'll clean and put away your oboe, safely), and you warm up or practise before each—or if you teach all day, alternately demonstrating, and packing your oboe up between umpteen schools or classes. Whatever you decide, rest assured—I have it on good authority that oiling the bore does it no harm.

One word of warning—*never* oil the bore straight after playing. Allow it to dry out completely first—otherwise you risk sealing *in* moisture and CAUSING splitting! Wait until you won't be using the instrument for a while. Leave it a few days to dry before oiling if you can, and, preferably, a few days afterwards for the oil to sink in, before playing it again (i.e. don't wash it away immediately). Ideally, all keys should be removed before bore-oiling, for a really thorough job.

Clean out your instrument case occasionally (it's surprising how much rubbish accumulates). Don't let fluff, dust, bits of feather, etc. jam up your oboe's mechanism. Completely empty the case and, holding it upside down, brush the inside with a stiff clothes-brush (preferably outside or over the bath to save sweeping up afterwards.) ALWAYS do this after oiling the keys or wood, or dirt will immediately stick, undoing half your 'servicing' work straight away.

Close your instrument case carefully after use, even at home. I heard of a bassoonist who, getting his instrument out after a longish break and finding it wouldn't play, discovered a dead bat inside. (The case hadn't been properly shut.)

You may find that the octave holes (nearest to the top of the instrument so the first to become blocked) need cleaning out occasionally, especially if you're careless about teeth cleaning. This necessitates removing the octave pipes (the metal 'cups' surrounding the holes) for which a special tool is required (see 'Apparatus', page 127. If you buy one of these you can do this relatively easy job yourself (but a toothbrush is *far* cheaper). After removing the octave pipe, clean it by drawing a needle threaded with cotton soaked in lighter fuel through the hole. Decaying food in your oboe won't rot the wood, as it will your teeth, but causes blockage and is unhygienic. The dimensions of the holes are critical. If partly blocked, notes become flat. (Don't make a compost heap in your oboe.)

Food can also collect in crooks and staples; use a pipe cleaner to clean these regularly. Unblock small 'pin-holes' (e.g. in the middle C″ key) with a needle.

Everything I've mentioned so far is a simple operation which every player should learn as general maintenance (even coming within *my* capabilities). The following are more complicated procedures which players can do themselves, but which 'non-mechanics' may feel are safer left to an expert:

Tuning notes. This is something I wouldn't advise novices tackling, and is best sorted out when you buy your oboe (see 'Choosing an Instrument', Chapter14), but need not be impossible. To flatten a note adjust the lowest open key when the note's fingered to open less, by altering the relevant adjuster screw, or applying thin cork or leather, or make the hole smaller by filling the side

nearest the top of the instrument with shellac or nail-varnish. Adjusting the key to open more, or enlarging the hole minutely—(using sandpaper wrapped around an orange stick) sharpens the note. To 'move' a tone hole, 'fill' one side and 'sand' the other.

Keep a spare set of pads in case you lose one (most likely to occur in hot or dry climates) and cannot get it seen to professionally, straight away. It's a dreadful sight to see a pad, or screw, from your oboe rolling away to be lost for ever…

Replacing a pad is deceptively hard, though, and is often done badly. It's surprisingly awkward to get it 'seating' evenly, so is best not attempted unless one actually falls out. An oboe with a pad missing isn't much use. Otherwise, experiment *only* when you're *not* using the instrument, so you've time to get it put right—if necessary—before your next concert. No cheating—use proper pads…

Before a pad is fitted all the old glue must be well cleaned away. (White sealing wax can be used instead of glue if preferred.) To 'seat' a pad hold the oboe—key downwards—over a small flame or lighted match to melt the glue (or wax)—then close the key firmly. Test for leaks.

To test a pad for leaks, insert a *tiny* strip of cigarette-paper under the edge of the key from different sides in turn, closing the key normally, and pulling the paper. If it slips out easily it shows the pad's leaking from that side (see photograph, page 136). If so, it'll need 're-seating'.

Sometimes pads drop out at most inopportune moments. A second oboe player in the Hallé Orchestra was once asked to give the 'A' in a rehearsal as the first oboist had been called outside—(somebody had bumped his car in the car park). A pad fell out unnoticed making his 'A' come out as a B♭…(Well, that's his story!) It was, strangely, the only 'A' he was asked to give during his time in the orchestra!

Repairs, like everything, become easier with practice—but don't try major operations for the first time just before a performance…in case you don't have a 'natural' talent. Contrarily, some DIY enthusiasts go to extremes such as extending or adding keys— using silver teaspoons and the like, or 'thickening' the oboe, by painting it overall around the keys, which then resemble sunken manhole covers in a re-tarred road, with shellac or similar. (This, apparently, affects the instrument's sound.) I've seen oboes which are barely recognisable.

Basic care of instruments seems generally to be inadequately taught, especially at schools, where they're often on loan. I've been horrified by the treatment I've seen school oboes get, followed by a comment like, "My oboe's not working, somebody must have tampered with it."

When I tutored oboists and bassoonists on the Lancashire Schools Symphony Orchestra's Summer and Easter courses, my colleague and I once inspected each student's instrument. We found keys hanging off, pillars out of instruments, even a broken clarinet barrel. I blew half a teaspoon of food out of one girl's bassoon crook—and she'd wondered why her pitch was flat!

My one-time clarinet teacher flatmate used to arrive at her East End schools to find the children fencing with their clarinets—black kids versus whites.

Few players can afford to keep a good quality spare oboe, so it's imperative that yours—especially if it's the tool of your trade—is kept in good working order, mechanical imperfection—and resulting frustration—avoided at all costs (and care doesn't cost much).

There's no point in flying to Timbuctoo to play, after all, if your oboe's not working when you get there.

Chapter 16

Languages and Vocabulary

Different sounds; Different interpretations; Repertoire

Different sounds

Just as everybody's speaking voice is different, so is the sound or 'voice' of every musician. As you can identify a person from hearing them speak you will, as an oboe-player, learn to recognise other oboists by their playing. Besides these individual differences there are also universally recognised 'schools' of playing associated with different countries. One can usually tell the nationality of a composer from his music; it is often easy to recognise the nationality of an oboist by his sound. Styles and tone qualities vary between countries almost as much as the languages themselves. Not only teaching methods, but reeds and reed-making too—which, of course, largely govern the sound produced, differ around the world. For detailed comparisons read Sprenkle's *The Art of Oboe-Playing* (see 'Recommended Publications').

The two most easily distinguishable oboe tones are the very contrasting French and German. A 'typical' French sound (associated in particular with the playing of Pierre Pierlot) has a thin but mellow, fluent and 'reedy' quality—perfect for the music of Poulenc and other compatriots. The richer, thick, warm and dark tone quality of many German players (notably Lothar Koch, principal oboist with the Berlin Philharmonic Orchestra for many years) is ideally suited to the music of Brahms, Bach or Beethoven. The German sound is popular with many British students, some of whom choose to finish their studies in Germany (though it is sometimes considered to be less distinguishable from other woodwind instruments than the French sound, which is more individual).

Reeds, too, vary as much as the sounds they produce. German players, for instance, favour a broader reed, producing their 'rich' tone—French prefer delicacy, and a slimmer reed. Very basically a narrower, thinly scraped reed with a longer scrape will produce a more French sound, and a wider, thicker, more open reed, with a shorter scrape and thicker 'heart' and 'back' a more German sound. (For more details see chapters 9 and 12.)

The diameter of the tube cane also affects the aperture—and sound—of the finished reed (see 'Cane', Chapter 11). German players generally use narrower diameter cane, producing a more open reed, than we do in Britain, but use round, not oval necked staples, to compensate. It's interesting to experiment, or buy reeds made by different reed-makers. Compare the differences for yourself.

It is natural to associate the sound of an oboist with his country's music, and to think of one player above all others as being the typical example of his nation's playing, for instance, the sweet refined sound of the French with

Pierre Pierlot and Poulenc—and the full luxuriant sound of the Germans with Lothar Koch and Brahms.

An English sound is not quite so easily definable, but comes somewhere between these two, neither as rich as the German, nor as reedy as the French. A full clear sound rather than a thin clear sound—'plummy' even—(but these are merely generalisations). Many would think of the sound of the late Terence MacDonagh, principal oboist with the BBC Symphony Orchestra for some years after the war, as being typically English, though there are various accepted styles and sounds in Britain today.

Another, perhaps less markedly different 'voice' is that of many American players—to English ears a less full sound, with a faster vibrato than we are used to perhaps?

Contrast this with the soft, delicate and almost vibrato-less Viennese playing. (Their oboe, which differs from ours, see 'The Oboe's Relatives', Chapter 17, and its sound can be more likened to the baroque instrument—warmer and less cutting than our modern oboe.) Or (more appealing perhaps to British ears) the fuller Dutch sound associated with the Concertgebouw Orchestra, or the Russians' clearer, thinner playing, the brighter, more penetrating Czech tone, etc.

It's impossible to describe different sounds satisfactorily, and you may well disagree with my attempts to do so—but do, at least, be aware that these, often very different, 'languages' and 'dialects' exist, and observe them for yourself. Study and compare as many oboists' playing as you can—on records, broadcasts or live concerts and recitals—and familiarise yourself with their individualities and tone qualities. You'll soon find you can identify many of them easily. See how well you can imitate their different sounds yourself—an excellent 'tone' and 'listening' exercise. It will open your eyes—and ears—to the many different ways you can 'speak' with your instrument.

Sounds and modes of playing are not only matters of taste, and culture, but of fashion, too—and fashions change. Listen to old recordings—of singers as well as players. Even the style of the spoken 'BBC English' has altered enormously over the years. Notice, for instance, how vibrato has changed. On old records singers' vibrato seems deep and fast compared to what we are used to nowadays (though, of course, recording was less reliable a generation ago). At the beginning of this century, however, little or no vibrato was used by oboists, until Léon Goossens gradually made it accepted. I don't think that would be very popular in this country today—vibrato is currently considered an important and accepted part of oboe-playing. We have to change with the times—even in the way we play music. You can tell an old recording from a new one not only by the technical standard of the recording itself.

Whatever one's country of origin, or basic training, it's important to be able to adapt sound and rendition, depending on the music being played. Don't always sound stereotyped English (if there is such a thing) when playing, for instance, French, German or American music, when an English sound may not be suitable.

Try to sound like a flute when playing a flute cue or second flute part—'soften' your tone.

Since we play music by composers from all over the world, as well as from different periods in time, it's my opinion that we should endeavour to vary our playing accordingly, both with reeds and playing techniques (see above, also chapters 9 and 12).

When playing French music, such as Poulenc's oboe sonata or Debussy's orchestral music, I try to produce as French a sound as possible, using a freer, narrower reed, such as the composer would surely have had in mind. I associate the music with this sort of sound. It's almost as important as playing the notes and dynamics accurately, if you think about it. For the beautiful oboe solos in Brahms' symphonies or Bach's works, I aim for a fuller tone, by selecting a wider, thicker reed—for Ronald Binge's 'The Watermill' a full, but free English sound—neither thick nor tinny. You may not share my views, but I find this approach makes playing much more interesting. I certainly make my reeds according to what I have to play, not only for reasons of technical difficulty—quiet low notes, fast staccato, etc. (see chapters 9 and 12), but with sound in mind as well.

You will need to adapt your playing when performing a mixed programme. It's not really practical to be changing reeds all the time. (A test for your ingenuity.) Don't go too far, though! In baroque and pre-baroque days the oboe's sound was far less refined than it is today. Instruments and reeds, as well as playing technique, have advanced enormously since then. I am not suggesting your tone should sound raucous, or that you should play out of tune when performing early music, just because that was how it probably sounded at the time.

Many oboists nowadays learn to play 'baroque' instruments (or modern copies) in order to produce, as nearly as possible, the authentic sound that composers of that period would have been used to. Unfortunately, we have little evidence of what reeds were like then. (It's optimistic to expect any to have lasted long enough for us to have genuine samples today!) Nor have we any recordings or photographs, of course—only a few drawings to go on. So our reproduction baroque reeds—and sound—are partly guesswork (see 'The Oboe's Relatives', Chapter 17).

When playing music from this period on a modern oboe however, try to bear in mind the sort of sound baroque oboes would probably have made, and (although I'm sure Bach and his contemporaries would be delighted to see and hear how the instrument has developed—Mozart too) perhaps not choosing your most refined, modern-sounding reed for this music.

As an actor must adapt his or her voice to suit each part he plays—often using totally different accents or dialects—we must try to adapt our sound (and our playing) according to the music we are performing (see 'You the Musician', Chapter 7). Don't let's forget though, that music is itself a universal language, linking us all whatever our colour or creed.

Different interpretations

Music, like everything else, has altered considerably over the years, with not only different and changing styles of playing, but different interpretations—even notations.

Medieval music was written without bar lines—other 'early' music with uneven bar lengths and no time signatures (we seem to have come full circle there).

In much music of the baroque period, written single dots were interpreted as double dots—or even triplets—(the opposite of one bad habit today—see 'Bad Habits', Chapter 5). We are now taught to play strictly what is printed. (The meaning of appogiaturas has changed, too—see also chapter 5.)

Another baroque fashion was that composers wrote only the bare bones of slow movements. The rest, filling in and ornamenting, was left (and still is, except where editors have added 'their own thing') to the player to improvise, for instance, on repeated sections (something else to be prepared for when playing this music). What a contrast from contemporary music, when every detail of what he wants is indicated by the composer, including exact metronome markings, articulation, sometimes even vibrato! Most composers today wouldn't be very pleased if you started adding to their music!

In many small seventeenth- and eighteenth-century works, parts were just marked 'treble instrument', so could have been played equally on the flute, recorder, violin, *or* oboe.

Ornaments in baroque times were played in specific ways, and trills often measured, with a dictated number of notes, or pattern, or a turn, 'correctly' starting on the upper, or lower note, depending on what preceded it. Certain rhythmic interpretation and improvised ornamentation (see above)—even articulation—was left to the player, but there were understood ways of playing them. As music from this period is such a major part of the oboe's repertoire, it is worth giving its correct (as far as we know) interpretation some study. Certain basic rules in playing this music stylishly and correctly are pretty well accepted, though even here some experts differ. In later music, many of these traditional interpretations changed, along with the meanings of some musical terms. Mozart's or Beethoven's tempo markings, for instance, are not taken to mean the same as Handel's—and trills should not be played the same way for Handel's music as for Haydn's.

Interpretation, and the various accepted authentic ways of playing music from different periods, is far too complicated to go into in detail here, but a useful guide on the subject is Thurston Dart's book, *The Interpretation of Music*; you will also find helpful information in Léon Goossens' and Edwin Roxburgh's book *Oboe* (see 'Recommended Publications').

Repertoire

Despite a relatively limited solo repertoire there is plenty of wonderful music for us to play.

The oboe, described as 'queen of orchestral instruments'—the first oboe as 'prima dona of the orchestra', is also a key member of the opera and ballet orchestras, with a wealth of expressive and glorious solos. Perhaps the most famous orchestral example is the slow movement of Brahms' violin concerto:

The oboe is also a prime member of the chamber orchestra, as well as the wind band and 'light' orchestra. One of the most beautiful solos in this field is surely Ronald Binge's 'The Watermill' for oboe and strings:

Oboists also enjoy a considerable variety of chamber music, from the wind serenades of Mozart, Dvořák, Gounod and Richard Strauss, to wind octets and quintets, quartets and quintets for oboe and strings, and works for two oboes and cor anglais (a popular idiom during the late eighteenth and early nineteenth centuries), as well as numerous baroque trios and quartets. Bach gave us a wealth of obbligati and delicious solos in his cantatas, choral works and Passions, and his contemporaries, a host of sonatas and concertos. Among the best known oboe solos from Bach's choral works is from his 'St Matthew Passion':

see also 'The oboe d'amore', Chapter 17.

The cor anglais has it's own repertoire, too (see 'The Oboe's Relatives', Chapter 17). For other examples, see throughout this book.

Jazz and pop are about the only areas in which the oboe does not play a prominent role.

Following the oboe's importance during the baroque period, the clarinet became fashionable, and composers such as Mozart and Brahms wrote major chamber and solo works for it, forsaking the oboe as a solo instrument. An oboist named Baumgärtel once asked Brahms why, when he'd written such fine chamber music for the clarinet, he didn't write something for the oboe. Brahms replied, "Do you think I want to write for the desk drawer?" implying that it would not be played.

There are very few classical and romantic solo oboe works, apart from Mozart's oboe quartet—a splendid chamber work—his concerto (which flute players try to steal from us) and a few others, although composers such as Schubert, Schumann, Brahms, Beethoven and, later, Dvořák, Mahler, Bruckner, Tchaikowsky, Delius, Shostakovich and many others, gave the oboe major and beautiful solos in their orchestral works.

In the earlier part of the twentieth century the oboe again became prominent, thanks to the supreme artistry and worldwide reputation of Léon Goossens. Leading composers including Richard Strauss, Vaughan Williams, Elgar, Hindemith, Bax, Malcolm Arnold, Gordon Jacob and Britten, were inspired to write concertos or solo works for the instrument. More recently the oboe has been given much notoriety by many first-class players, who in turn have prompted composers to write for it.

This rather imbalanced solo repertoire makes recital programming a problem. Baroque music is more suited to a harpsichord than a piano accompaniment (to be authentic again), though it's not always possible to find a versatile accompanist or have the opportunity of using both instruments in the same programme.

The gap or shortage of romantic works can be 'bridged' by including piano solos by nineteenth-century composers such as Chopin or Mendelssohn. Otherwise, one falls into the temptation of using arrangements, or pinching music written for other instruments, but these usually need doctoring because of the oboe's limited range. Among the few serious nineteenth-century pieces for oboe and piano are Schumann's three 'Romances', often featured for this reason. (Clarinettists and violinists even try to take this 'precious' work from us, saying it was written for their instrument.) Nielsen's early 'Humorésque and Romance' and Grovlez' 'Sarabande and Allegro' also make useful 'bridging' pieces of a more serious nature. In my opinion the two best major romantic oboe works are the sonatas by Poulenc and St. Saëns.

There are also various popular Victorian flavour fun pieces such as variations on 'Carnival of Venice', 'Don Pasquale' and 'la Cenérèntola', and concertos and other works by Hummel, Kalliwoda, Bellini, Pasculli and others (though I never find performing concertos with a piano very satisfactory—certainly not if the accompaniment is orchestral or heavy). More and more soloists are now arranging pieces themselves to widen and fill gaps in the oboe's solo repertoire.

Though so beautiful, the oboe's sound is not easy to listen to for too long—however it's played—so when compiling a programme it's a good idea to have a keyboard (or 'cello if you're using a continuo player) spot to give you, and the audience, a rest from the oboe—or a cor anglais group to give your programme variety and interest—unaccompanied oboe makes a change, too, and gives the accompanist a rest.

It is even harder to plan a cor anglais group since most of its very limited solo repertoire consists of slow romantic or slushy tunes, due to the instrument's character and sound quality. Thought and care then, are needed to plan a varied and interesting recital programme. Meanwhile, let us all revel in our beautiful orchestral solos—for both cor anglais and oboe (particularly in so many nineteenth-century works) and in the wealth of wonderful melodies by Bach.

Chapter 17

The Oboe's Relatives

The cor anglais; The oboe d'amore; The baroque oboe; Others

The cor anglais

The oboe's best known close relation is the cor anglais, English horn (or 'cor blimey'), the alto member of the family. It's name is a misnomer; it's neither a horn, nor English. Theories are a) that as the instrument was originally curved it should have been cor anglé (angled horn), b) that its sound resembled the old hunting horn (hence 'cor'), or c) it translates as 'horn of the angels'. It seems strange to me that in England we use the French name (cor anglais) instead of the English (or American) English horn. I shall refer to it as a 'cor', not to be confused with the French variety. (One player, constantly reprimanded during a rehearsal—directed by a violinist—for not coming in, had to explain politely that 'cor' in a musical score means a French horn, not an English one.)

The fingering is the same as on an oboe (it's really just a larger version) but being longer the pitch is lower—one fifth below the oboe's. Every note fingered sounds a fifth lower.

For example, fingered C″ 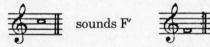 sounds F′

It is, therefore, a 'transposing instrument', its music being written in a different key (a fifth higher), though *you* only need to worry about transposing if you leave yours at home and have to play the part on the oboe! Other transposing instruments include: clarinets 'in A, B♭ or E♭', trumpets 'in B♭' and French horns, like the cor, 'in F'. (The key refers to the note sounding when C is fingered. Non-transposing instruments are 'in C'—C sounding when C is fingered.)

The cor anglais has a beautiful mellow tone, most effective in slow melancholy music, and is consequently renowned for its many great expressive orchestral solos, the most famous being the Largo from Dvořák's 'New World Symphony':

This solo seems to be famous—or infamous—for other reasons than its beauty (see 'Nursing Care', Chapter 15). One player, refused his customary doubling fee (ten shillings in those days) for playing two instruments, was so cross he played it as written but on his oboe—i.e. in the wrong key! Another's reed came off the crook in his mouth, and his lips were trembling so much it dropped down inside the front of his shirt. He missed the whole solo. When I had to play a shortened version (the tune only, not the whole movement)—having played it whole so often I forgot to make the cut, 'sailing up' when I should have been 'sailing down'. I felt awful (until told that the previous player had made the same mistake).

Other popular works featuring prominent cor anglais solos include: Rossini's overture 'William Tell', Berlioz' overture 'Carnival Romain', 'Symphonie Fantastique' and 'Harold in Italy', Rodrigo's guitar concerto, Franck's symphony in D minor, Stravinsky's 'Rite of Spring', Tchaikowsky's overture 'Romeo and Juliet', Wagner's 'Tristan and Isolde', overture 'The Flying Dutchman', Sibelius' 'Swan of Tuonela', Strauss' 'Ein Heldenleben'—and many more. It is sadly neglected as a solo instrument outside the orchestra, though I'm glad to say I am among players who have persuaded composers to write pieces for it. For recitals, solo 'demos', etc. we usually have to arrange or pinch music from another instrument's repertoire.

The cor is not as prone to 'sounding dreadful' as the oboe can be, for instance when one has reed trouble. It is, therefore, good for the morale—encouraging a relaxed embouchure—in turn producing a better sound (as psychological as thinking you'll sound awful on the oboe—causing your embouchure to tense up, making you sound awful). It feels generally 'smoother' to blow than the oboe, especially on the lower register, which is easier to control quietly, but high notes can sometimes be a problem.

Top E‴ [musical notation] sounding A″ [musical notation] is unstable on many instruments, sometimes almost non-existent, or very flat, needing considerable 'lipping up', or 'belting out' (something to watch for when choosing a cor anglais). Luckily this note doesn't crop up too often—except, unfortunately, in the fun (and rather virtuoso) 'Concertino' by Donzinetti (all rather high, being originally written for a higher pitched instrument, now obsolete). Sympathetic composers don't write too many important cor solos on very high notes, but (written) top F‴s do appear, for example in Britten's 'Sinfonia da Requiem'.

Fast fingerwork is harder on the cor than the oboe, it being larger and heavier (more awkward for small hands)—the action on long rods slower, but, because of its tone quality, its repertoire is predominantly slow. Control, intonation and tone are, therefore, of paramount importance—not fast fingers.

There's little need to practise fast difficult studies then, or scales in thirds, fourths, etc. on the cor; slow study should take precedence. *Elementary* exercises are most useful, especially when listening to a new reed (for example, Hinke or Langey first pages, see 'Recommended Publications'). Play them slowly, listening to every detail of your sound, and accustoming yourself to the instrument's feel. Start and end notes pppp—slow scales for instance—in anticipation of those quiet controlled entries (and exits) in the orchestra, and practise not only beautiful melodies—but everything— beautifully, 'con espressione'.

A cor player must be able to come in cleanly and confidently with a quiet solo—and be in tune—after hours of silence, and play expressively. Aim for perfect intonation and an even sound—especially in solos such as Sibelius' 'Swan of Tuonela' or Dvořák's 'New World Largo', which seem to be written on bad or uncomfortable notes. (How I long to re-write these lovely tunes in 'happier' keys!)

Some of the instrument's orchestral solos (for example, 'The Swan of Tuonela') are concerto-like, virtually unaccompanied (like Wagner's 'Tristan and Isolde')—or at least very exposed—so confidence is essential.

There's little scope for faking or cheating. Such antics are for busy oboe music, not slow cor anglais solos. Every detail can usually be heard, including wobbles or cracks. It was once *not* heard, however, when a player in the BBC Symphony Orchestra had an off-stage part to play, and to save taking a music-stand into the wings had cleverly pinned her music onto the curtain. At least it seemed a clever idea…until the curtain rose!

There are two physical differences (apart from size) between the cor and the oboe. a) The cor's bell is pear-shaped—sometimes almost round—contributing to its special sound. (I tested this by playing mine with a (flared) clarinet bell fitted to it, comparing it to its own.) I expect you've seen Gerard Hoffnung's witty portrayal of a cor laying an egg, to the surprise of the player. (A flared bell like the oboe's, of the proportionally larger size of the cor, would be less practical, needing a much larger billet of wood.) b) The cor uses a 'crook', a curved conical tube about four inches long—a continuation of the instrument's bore—made of brass, nickel-silver, or even silver, with cork around it's lower part. It fits into the instrument as the staple (reed)—also a continuation of the bore—fits into the oboe. The cor staple (reed) fits over the outside of the crook. Named after a shepherd's crook (a likeness more apparent with the bassoon) it is used for purely practical purposes; the instrument is too long and heavy to be played at the same angle as the oboe. Cor crooks vary considerably, as do bells and, unlike the bell, affect tuning. Look for the 'right' one for your instrument.

The cor's reed is wider and shorter than the oboe's—the staple like a shorter, wider oboe staple, but without the cork (that's on the crook).

Cor anglais reed   Oboe reed

Staples won't always fit every crook exactly. To help secure the reed, wet the crook's end in your mouth, then twist it on. It's most unnerving when the reed comes off in one's mouth, especially just before a solo (as described earlier). Always check that it is firm before playing. A short piece of rubber bicycle-valve tube around your crook and 'unfolded' over the staple can be a useful stabiliser.

You can alter pitch considerably, without upsetting intonation, by pulling the crook out (mark the place on the cork with a pencil). The reed's pitch is therefore less critical. Tune carefully though, as this permits huge discrepancies, and allow time for this longer instrument to warm up 'right to its toes'.

Professional players and music students will need their own cors. Secondhand ones are uncommon, but worth looking for as they're more expensive than oboes and there are no cheap student models (the oboe being played first). You'll need a double case—for oboe and cor, but a single case is useful, too, as you won't always need both instruments. Together they're heavy, and valuable. Don't carry all your eggs in one basket, or transport instruments—and subject them to vibration—unnecessarily (see 'Nursing Care', Chapter 15).

Although fingered the same, there are blowing and playing differences between an oboe and a cor anglais. The larger cor reed requires a slacker embouchure similar to 'relaxing' for low oboe notes (see 'Embouchure', Chapter 1). This, albeit small, variance makes playing oboe after cor feel easy—but the embouchure seem 'tight', or 'pinched', for the cor, after playing oboe—until you've adjusted. It's important to know the 'feel' of each instrument, and be able to swap, and adapt, quickly—essential when doubling (playing both instruments in one piece), when quick changes often mean launching into a solo on one straight after playing the other. When doubling, usually on second or third oboe, and cor, be sure both reeds are kept moist, and both instruments warm. Blow down whichever's not being played occasionally (without the reed—or with the reed in, but *silently)* to warm it, and suck the reed constantly to stop it drying out, especially in hot conditions—or if your next entry is a solo, which, if you're playing cor, it probably will be.

A student was once sent to 'dep' in the ballet 'Coppelia' in Dublin at short notice, sitting in on one show to learn it. At one point an oboe solo is followed quickly by a cor solo. The oboist, exaggerating to the student all he needed to remember, played the oboe solo bending forward to 'drop' the oboe impressively onto its stand and pick the cor up quickly—but, alas!—his cor wouldn't come off the stand...The conductor was now pointing at him—so he sang the cor solo instead, unfortunately, in his panic, at the wrong pitch and twice as fast.

Many use a sling to support the cor. This is an adjustable strap worn around the player's neck and which hooks into a ring on the (right) thumb rest (they are also used with bassoons, saxes, and other heavier woodwinds). It is especially useful to support and balance the instrument when resting (saving your thumb) or to suspend it temporarily during a quick change to oboe and back, when there isn't time to put it down or unhook the sling in time to pick up the oboe. But a sling *can* make your neck uncomfortably hot and get in the way of necklaces, hair-dos or collars—or worse!..

A tall slim friend of mine was at one time the only female member of a wind quintet. They gave several concerts at prisons, and one afternoon played to an audience of long offenders at Maidstone Jail, where the sight of a woman provoked many bawdy remarks. (It was also in the days of mini-skirts.) They played one piece with cor, for which she used a sling. When they stood up to acknowledge enthusiastic applause its hook caught the hem of her dress, and as she rose to her full height, the prisoners were treated to a view that caused a near riot. (Cor!)

Extra mechanism soon adds weight to a cor…something else to remember when choosing one, or having keys added. Don't get weighed down with 'heavy metal'.

Cor players seem best remembered for disasters (maybe because of the 'solo' nature of the instrument). They've befallen us all. As a student I once played in a concert performance of Delius' 'A Village Romeo and Juliet' in London (a moderately important cor part), and after the rehearsal invited a violinist home for a meal. As always I took my instruments with me, never risking leaving them unattended, but my friend left hers there. On leaving my flat it seemed natural that neither of us was carrying an instrument—I didn't remember until we got to the hall. We drove back at full speed, hooting before driving through red traffic lights, miraculously making it in one piece, and arrived just a quarter of an hour late for the performance. (They'd delayed the start a little.) I felt very  foolish walking through the audience and orchestra to take my place. (My colleague, a string player, so less indispensable…waited till the interval to join in.) Years later, playing cor in another London concert, as I was going on stage the lead 'cellist said loudly, "I once played in a performance where the girl forgot her cor anglais…ha! ha!" not recognising me as the culprit. (I wondered how far he'd already spread the story.)

Cors don't have a low Bb 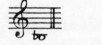 sounding Eb

but it's rarely needed. There is one, however, in a Mahler symphony. To play it, cheat by fitting an 'extension' (made from a cardboard lavatory roll) between the bottom joint and the bell (feasible, as the cor—having no low Bb has no keys on the bell). This flattens the B′ to Bb′. Luckily, B′ isn't needed in this example—which, some suspect, was probably a joke. Cor low Bb's are certainly not worth losing sleep over.

The reeds are less fragile and not such a problem as with the oboe. (Let's be thankful for small mercies!) They certainly last longer, partly because the instrument is played less, consequently fewer players make their own. I never have done, and have usually been able to buy ones I like. Making oboe reeds, I find, takes quite enough time, and adrenalin.

For most cor playing, a responsive, sensitive reed is needed, with a sweet, attractive sound for 100 per cent 'safe' quiet entries. One solo, however, which requires a totally different—very open, hard reed—is the 'Miller's Dance' from

Manuel da Falla's 'Three Cornered Hat'—very much harder than it looks, and totally unaccompanied:

This is a notorious audition piece, to catch you out when you arrive with a 'New World type' reed, expecting typically 'dolce' solos (totally unsuitable for this). It's advisable to be prepared with an appropriate 'Hat' reed for an orchestral audition—just in case—one that can belt out those loud accented Ds without squawking (wiring can help). Some oboists even cheat by changing or adding a note to make this easier! A player I know went to audition for a cor anglais job in one of the regional orchestras. His confidence wasn't improved on his meeting a more experienced player at the station, also doing the audition (this never helps). Then he got this solo to play and made a disastrous job of it. Deciding to cut his losses he dramatically—or so he intended—walked out of the audition. But, in the heat of the moment he took the wrong door, walking into a cupboard instead…He didn't get the job.

Finally, remember that, though a close relation of the oboe, the cor anglais *is* a different instrument, with its own embouchure, feel—and problems. Different notes may need lipping up or down, or require extra diaphram support, etc. than they do on your oboe. It is therefore imperative to feel and play it differently, especially when getting used to it initially. Keep oboe and cor practice—and music—separate. 'Think' the right instrument. 'Think cor'.

The oboe d'amore

Another relative of the oboe, closer in size, but less often heard than the cor anglais, is the oboe d'amore—the mezzo-soprano voice of the family. Bernard Shaw described it as a 'love-oboe', which I consider apt because of its glorious sound. Its bell has been called 'liebesfuss'—'love-foot', but there are no theories as to the real origin of its name.

The oboe d'amore, too, fingers like an oboe, but in size, and therefore pitch, is halfway between the oboe and the cor—another transposing instrument, sounding a minor third below the note written—and below the oboe—and pitched 'in A'.

Fingered C″   sounds A′

Like the cor anglais it has a pear-shaped—or rounded—bell (which has little effect on its tone, except lowest notes)—a crook, about two and a half inches long—and no (fingered) low B♭. The staple (reed) fits over the outside of the crook, and resembles a small cor reed.

Oboe d'amore reed   Cor anglais reed

It's even possible to play the cor using a d'amore reed, or vice versa.

Crooks vary and can radically affect tuning—they're more temperamental than cor crooks. It's essential, therefore, to find one to suit your instrument. Some players will even saw the bottom off a crook if the pitch seems flat (a treatment which *can* also be applied to cor crooks or oboe staples), but not only is this irreversible but if done too drastically the crook (or staple) will no longer be an accurate continuation of the instrument's bore, upsetting intonation and creating endless problems. Trying different crooks (or altering the reed) is more advisable. Relatively few oboe-players have their own oboe d'amore.

Second-hand ones are rare, and there's always a waiting list for new instruments.

Despite its physical resemblance to the cor, the oboe d'amore feels very different—generally quite 'stuffy' and resistant in comparison, with diminuendos and low notes harder to control. Intonation is less reliable too, because of the bore size, which is less satisfactory than that of the oboe or cor, making it the hardest of the three to play. Often considerable lipping (or tuning) of notes is needed. Plenty of practice is, therefore, vital on this instrument, again *not* thinking of it as an oboe, but as a separate entity—what it is, after all. Once more it is essential to familiarise yourself with individual shortcomings—lippings, notes which seem harder to blow or need extra pressure, and, of course, with the feel of the embouchure.

It seems harder to adapt to changing from oboe to d'amore, than oboe to cor (or vice versa), the reed (embouchure) and fingering (comparable distance between the keys) being so near the oboe it can be confusing. The oboe and cor differ enough not to be.

Get to know *each* instrument so you can pick it up and play it with the correct embouchure, a good sound, and in tune, adapting to it straight away. I emphasise this separate practising particularly with the oboe d'amore. Many players advertise that they can play it (which any oboist can, theoretically, as they know how to finger the notes) without owning one. They rush out on Good Friday to borrow or hire one for Bach's 'St Matthew Passion', having possibly not touched one since Christmas (when they borrowed another for 'The Christmas Oratorio') or even since the previous Easter—(possibly never having played that particular instrument before) with no time to get to know it—thus tending to play it like an oboe. It is different, and must be treated differently. 'Think d'amore'.

Most of the instrument's repertoire is the music of Bach. It's worth investing in one if only to play this wonderful music. (For samples see Evelyn Rothwell's *Difficult Passages*, see 'Recommended Publications). Ask any oboist who their favourite composer is and most will reply "Bach". He really did leave us a legacy! Here are tastes of three of his better known d'amore obbligati, from 'The St. Matthew Passion':

'The Christmas Oratorio':

and 'The B Minor Mass':

One or two (occasionally even four) oboes d'amore play big roles in Bach's Passions, oratorios, masses and cantatas (besides the oboe and *oboe da caccia*—a similarly pitched instrument to the cor anglais, now obsolete, whose parts are played on the cor today).

One player, demonstrating instruments on television, was asked the difference between an oboe da caccia and a cor anglais. He replied, unhelpfully, "Five guineas" (probably referring to the hire fee involved). Another, asked by the conductor during a rehearsal of 'Bolero', the exact difference between a d'amore and an oboe, replied, mercenarily, "About one and sixpence" (obviously a while ago).

There are, regrettably, few parts for the instrument in works other than those by Bach (or Telemann). For some time the instrument was neglected (see 'A Brief History') and since its revival only a handful of composers have written for it. Its part in Ravel's 'Bolero' is often cut to save the doubling fee or because nobody has an instrument. Strauss uses an oboe d'amore in his 'Sinfonia Domestica', and Holst in his 'Somerset Rhapsody' (sometimes called 'Somerset Raspberry', depending how it's played. Two more misnomers I can't resist are 'burnt bottom' = czardas, and 'F in Melody' = 'Melody in F'!).

I have enjoyed performing transposed baroque sonatas, however, on oboe d'amore, with harpsichord accompaniment, and our audiences seemed to appreciate the opportunity of hearing this less common 'solo' instrument.

The oboe d'amore's tone is richer than the oboe's—less mellow than the cor anglais—a wonderful carrying timbre. A pair of d'amores playing in harmony in church acoustics is a sound hard to beat.

Note that most of your playing on oboe d'amore is likely to be in churches—which are often cold. DON'T be flat. You can *flatten* your pitch by pulling the crook out, but it's impossible to *sharpen* (without reed alteration, or changing the crook). Consider this when choosing or making reeds, or crooks. One sharper crook might be a useful investment. It's better to err on the side of sharpness, than be flat.

Fingered C″ sounding A′ is often a flat note, hard to control, and unfortunately (being 'concert A') the customary note to tune to. I prefer to tune the d'amore to more reliable notes—but instruments vary.

The reeds seem to last quite well—the best of the three instruments—though obviously influenced by the fact that you'll be playing it least.

If you own an oboe d'amore you'll almost certainly be asked if you hire it out. I'm against this. I feel I didn't buy (and study) it for others to get work on (and possibly 'tamper' with), but you may disagree.

The baroque oboe

There has recently been a trend towards the use of period instruments (or modern copies) for performing music authentically, especially baroque music, the instrument having developed and changed so enormously since that time (see 'A Brief History').

The baroque oboe has a sweet sympathetic quality—less penetrating than today's, so blends well with other instruments, whereas the present day oboe tends to stand out. We're spoiled with our modern mechanism making playing fast, in difficult keys, and especially, *in tune,* easy, compared to the instrument of those times. Nevertheless there is some feeling today that these complicated mechanics have detracted from the oboe's sound quality.

The baroque instrument, having few keys, uses many complicated cross-fingerings, and needs much lipping to play it in tune. Trills and turns, so much a part of music of the period, are often awkward and can sound clumsy. It's a shock to play (or listen to) a baroque oboe when you're used to a modern one! Cross-fingerings, and compromising use of 'extra' fingers, need experimentation. One does not acquire knowledge of them, or achieve 'clean' fast fingers or an ability to play in tune, overnight—only with hours of work. Extensive concentrated practice is, therefore, essential if you're going to play the baroque oboe seriously.

Reeds, too, are quite a problem, even worse than on the modern oboe (their design is partly guess-work, see 'Languages', Chapter 16), and they can vastly affect individual notes. So there are headaches to overcome.

If you take up this instrument it will open up interesting new fields in your playing, whether you're professional or amateur—but do give it serious thought first, and ask yourself whether you really have time or patience to master it to a satisfactory degree. If not, I'd advise concentrating your efforts on improving your standard on the instrument(s) you already play, rather than embarking on another, if it results in a quality of playing unsatisfactory to you and those you make music with, or who listen to you.

Other relatives

Eb oboe. A shrill high-pitched instrument (similar to the Eb clarinet)—or 'descant' oboe. It sounds a minor third higher than the notes written, so is a transposing instrument pitched 'in Eb'.

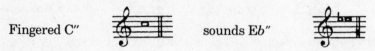

Fingered C″   sounds Eb″

It used to be used in military bands but is rarely heard today.

Baritone or Bass oboe

Another rare relation—not, as one might be misled into believing, two different instruments. It's pitched an octave below the oboe, 'in C' and written for in the treble clef, any note fingered sounding an octave lower. It is of French descent, developed mainly by Triébert and Brod. Earlier models in the eighteenth century had upturned, bulbous bells, but in 1889 Lorée built a straight version as we have today. It has a slim bell, and a crook with an extra bend in it, otherwise is rather like a giant cor anglais, with a similar tone quality. It has a sweet, relatively light sound, with little power or volume, therefore is effective in chamber music but rather lost in the orchestra—definitely an 'indoors' instrument. It uses a reed rather like a cor anglais reed, and descends to B

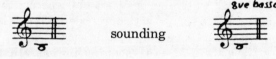

sounding

Heckelphone

Another instrument pitched an octave below the oboe (between the cor anglais and bassoon). Named after its inventor of 1904, a man called Heckel, it was designed to produce an 'oboe-ish' bass sound and is effective in a large orchestra. Richard Strauss 'christened' it in 'Salomé' in 1905, and it was used by Wagner and others. It is of German design, its bore not only twice as long as the oboe's, but twice as wide, producing a sonorous, unrefined tone, described as a 'loud bass voice' (too 'rough' for chamber music). It is a straight instrument, over four foot long including the crook, with a spherical bell, and a short metal 'foot' which rests on the floor. Its reed is larger than the bass oboe's, more like a bassoon reed, and it descends to A

          sounding

Parts scored for either bass oboe or heckelphone, such as Holst's 'Planets' and works by Strauss, Delius and Hindemith, can be played on either instrument. Often when a score says bass oboe the part is played on the heckelphone, despite the different tone quality—sometimes unsatisfactory.

Viennese oboe (Wiener oboe)

This instrument, which looks and sounds—and is structurally different from our own, is virtually unique to the city of Vienna, where the only professional orchestras are which still use it, though they are now made in Japan and other places. It is a German style instrument, which has not developed far from its eighteenth-century classical ancestor; the modern oboe is of French descent. Its bore shape differs, being wider at the top, and conical, becoming straighter and more cylindrical towards the bell—giving it an individual sound. It is shorter, lighter in weight, and there is no low Bb. The reed is different too—freer, with a longer scrape—and some fingerings. Lower notes are smoother and 'effortless', and top notes and large jumps also easier to play, though tuning is not easy, and it is technically harder, so less 'virtuoso'. Its sound is soft and small, better for German and Austrian orchestral music than the modern French oboe, and it blends well with other instruments.

Shawms

Modern copies of these ancestors of the oboe are *occasionally* used in film music today, as well as for music of their period (see 'A Brief History'). The shawm is also a popular folk instrument in Spain, in particular Barcelona.

Chapter 18

Mixed Bag

Reminders and tips: reeds, instrument care, playing, tuning, breathing, teaching, miscellaneous

Reeds

Don't waste your best reed on daily practice—even though it's good for the morale.

Don't use too easy a reed for practice, and be fooled into thinking your technique is A1. On the other hand, don't (if you can avoid it) continually practise on *too* bad a reed—it's so depressing.

Vary your practice reeds. Don't practise for three hours on a very open, hard or half scraped reed, or you'll ruin your lip and risk mouth sores. Use an easier, 'kinder' reed for long practice and playing sessions.

When blowing in a new reed keep to short stints (short *not* sharp!) Don't blow in a new reed so enthusiastically that you blow it out at the same time. Know when to stop.

Practise *before* blowing in new reeds; don't kill your lip first, especially before long note or tone practice. Avoid long blowing in sessions or over-practice on hard reeds before a performance—especially of anything requiring precise embouchure control or delicacy of playing. You'll do better if you and your lip are rested. Always practise before making reeds; *don't* sacrifice practice time for reed-making. Play each reed as if 'twere thy last'.

Note each reed's best side. If a reed feels stiff in the instrument, grip its binding—not the cork which might break—when turning it round or removing it (but apply grease, to ease it). If the cork does break off, don't throw the staple away, it can be re-corked. If a reed is loose in the oboe, wrap paper around the cork, or swell it (see 'Nursing Care', Chapter 15).

Keep a spare reed (or two) in your instrument case for emergencies—such as when you leave yours at home. But…always check that you have your reeds when you leave the house—both (all) sets if playing cor (and oboe d'amore). Make it a subconscious habit—like checking your dress before walking on stage, or seeing that you have your front door keys or have locked the car. After all, what use is an oboe-player without a reed?

A saxophonist, once, forgot his reeds when playing a show on stage, and as there was nobody to borrow from, did the only thing possible—'mimed' the entire show—so convincingly that nobody noticed. His resulting disillusionment, however, prompted him to give up being a musician altogether. Perhaps he was lucky to get away with it—there are occasions where one could not. Try miming a silent recital. Well—you'd have to be a very talented comedian—or ventriloquist. More about 'faking' and 'cheating' later.

Try to be prepared with a reliable spare or number two reed for every occasion. Remember how psychology and fate intervene? You'll be sure to break your best one the day before a recital or audition, but the day *after* you'll probably find a 'winner'!

At a recent reed trio concert I managed to get through the whole of the 'flute' part of Beethoven's variations on Mozart's 'La ci darem la mano' on a reed split from top to toe—I don't know how! The accident must have occurred just as we started the piece, which allows *no* reed changing time...

It is not only wise to be prepared for an accident during a concert, but also, when playing second oboe, for the other player to drop out—or not turn up—when you might have to take their place.

On one grand occasion, the Hallé Orchestra was playing at the Belle Vue in Manchester to a huge audience. The programme included Brahms' violin concerto. The second oboist, having little to play, was getting by on a poor reed, adequate—or so he thought—for the programme. Towards the end of the Brahms first movement, with the big oboe solo approaching, the first oboist turned to the second and said, "I'm going to faint". He knew he couldn't possibly get through it on his reed—and did *not* have a better one with him, so he did the only thing he could think of—shoved her head between her knees and, just in time, she recovered enough to be able to play.

Shortly after leaving college, I was given a trial for the post of second oboe in the Ulster Orchestra, and afterwards stayed on as a deputy second oboe player. Having little of importance to play, I was enjoying the Irish Guinness and change of scenery, and using very second-oboe-type reeds indeed. Arriving at one rehearsal I was alarmed to see no principal oboe, but the manager approaching to tell me he was ill and ask me to play first, for which I was totally unprepared. Ever since, when playing second oboe I subconsciously decide which reed I'll use *if* I suddenly have to play first, and always prepare myself for any difficulties or solos in the first part—just in case. If playing second when I have a good 'first' reed, I find myself almost wishing misadventure on my colleague. But it never happens then!

Do you ever get reeds which seem to 'buzz'?—I call these 'telephone reeds' as, when practising on one I keep stopping, thinking the 'phone's ringing. (It's probably only something in the room vibrating—but is very distracting.)

Carry a little pot of water with you (a pill bottle perhaps)—for wetting reeds in, especially when you're playing in a hot dry atmosphere or under television spotlights—or doubling on more than one instrument. But suck out any water before playing anything, so that your first note is a note, and not a splutter—or silence! Do this GENTLY, NOT with a huge, embarrassing 'kissing' sound, commonly heard. This is also useful for rinsing a good or precious reed after playing. Dip the tip in water, suck up a reedful, then blow it out from the bottom (all over your colleagues if you're not careful—not how to win friends...)

I feel it's unpleasant to put a reed away 'dirty', especially if you've had cups of tea or—worse—food, before playing. "The life of a reed is governed by the state of your stomach", a teacher once told me when I was complaining about the short lives of mine. All the more reason to 'wash them out' after use (especially if you suffer from 'nervous tummy'). With a new reed though, saliva somehow seems to accelerate that smooth, blown in feeling. (Maybe it's really more a question of becoming familiar with it?) Knowing your reed is almost as important as its actual quality!

When a newish reed appears dark-looking and no longer see-through when held up to the light it should be blown in. If it's no good by then don't count on further improvement with playing.

If you have to play on a 'duff' reed, as we all do only too often, don't panic! Put more into your playing to compensate. Give it all you've got. You may even sound good to anyone who is not 'feeling' the agony you are experiencing! I've been favourably surprised, hearing myself on recorded broadcasts. I've also done some of my best and, more important, most musical playing on bad reeds, through sheer effort and will-power—to 'make up for' them. Often it's not as bad as you think (but try convincing a panicking reedless oboist).

When your reed is unsatisfactory, concentrate—use your technique, breathing, embouchure—and wits—to overcome its shortcomings. Treat it as a challenge. Make an extra effort with your appearance and presentation. Ladies, have your hair done. Such things can boost your ego at times like these!

It's easy to let a reed's feel influence your idea of its sound; you sound different to others than to yourself. Often a reed which sounds poor—even harsh or tinny to you 'close'—will come over well to an audience, or on a broadcast. A 'too nice close' type reed which sounds good in a small room, on the other hand, may *not* come over or carry well. Try to 'stand back' and listen to yourself. A reed which is soaking up water, for instance (and sounds 'hissy' to you) probably won't be noticed by your audience, though you will be very conscious of it. A 'weedy' sound (to you) can be surprisingly penetrating to others. Ask them. So cheer up, keep calm—and don't despair unnecessarily.

(Having another anxiety can actually distract you from a reed worry, like having a pain in two places. If you're concentrating on a mechanical problem, or feeling ill, you may forget to worry about your reed!)

When reed-trying at home, give it time. Sometimes new ones sound good for two minutes, then collapse, and turn out to be useless (especially if made from over soft cane). So don't get excited too soon.

A more open reed is safer as it will have more air going through it. (Think about it!)

Avoid disinterested, aimless 'reed-bashing'. It's better to have an occasion in mind, or at least the music you anticipate playing, as far as possible.

If you're a garlic lover like me, spare a thought for your neighbours in the orchestra—in case they're not—and for your garlicky reed and oboe. But a wine or beer flavoured reed—now that's a different story! Don't let a 'tasty' reed make your mouth water—fatal while playing.

Don't be tempted, in anger at a reed's non-performance, to bash it dramatically against the music-stand or floor after a show or concert, 'killing it dead'. Save the staple for re-use. Don't murder that, too!

Test all reeds for leaks (see 'Choosing a Reed', Chapter 8 and 'Mixed Bag', Chapter 18). I do this instinctively every time I put one into my mouth, along with sucking any moisture from it. Carry goldbeater's skin (or its equivalent) in your case for emergency leaks. If necessary, pinch some from another reed.

Keep skin dry—preferably in an airtight tin. Cane sometimes stays damp under Clingfilm, though this is widely used.

Avoid putting damp cane (or reeds) away in an airtight container to 'mouldify'; let it dry completely first. I must admit though that once I did this with some wet, newly gouged and shaped cane (which went black) and years later, trying it in desperation when all else had failed, produced some of my best sounding and longest lasting reeds. One of these survived thirteen weeks of nightly performances happily, with only occasional reviving treatment…a personal record. I've never tried to repeat this phenomenon. Perhaps I should? See-through cylindrical plastic containers in which individual reeds are sometimes sold, are airtight.

If you re-use these to store damp reeds after use, puncture them first if you don't want mouldy black reeds.

Try not to let the dog, baby, or other household 'pet', get at your reeds—or instrument. A pupil of mine always used his baby as an excuse for his chewed reeds. (As with medicines, it's advisable to keep out of the reach of children.)

When a chunk drops out of the reed's tip during a performance (their favourite time for doing this) and you have no time to get your spare out (though it's there 'warmed up' of *course*) it's useful to know that it'll probably speak and play better nicked side upwards.

When your reed-cutting block loses colour with use, making it hard to see the reed's tip clearly against it, licking the surface will make it temporarily black again (but get a new one). If it gets rough it'll make an uneven 'chewed' tip to your reeds. Try sanding it.

Buy a good reedcase with a decent fastener. If you prefer to improvise, use strong tins (nothing airtight) and proceed with care. Enough reed breakages occur as it is—don't encourage more.

Finally, try not to get too depressed (or obsessed) by reeds (famous last words).

(I am resolved never to accept a proposal of marriage from any Mr Reed. Definitely not Wright…)

Instrument care

Carry an emergency repair kit—thin cork, stick of shellac, pads, screwdriver—AND repairer's telephone number.

Get pheasants' tail-feathers for 'drying' the bore after use, from a poulterer if you have no tame game-shooting friends. Cut the tip off a feather to make it stronger, less flimsy and easier to use in the top joint without it bending.

If you carry your oboe on a bicycle or motorbike, strap it to your body (or 'wear' it in a rucksack) rather than to the bike itself. Protect instruments from vibration as much as possible. I remember arriving at a performance at Sadler's Wells Theatre on my moped, getting my oboe out and two keys dropped off. That was after only a short journey and perhaps underlines the point. Examine your oboe regularly for screws working loose. Don't let this happen. (A repairer, recently handed an oboe thumb rest was told, "This fell off the back of a Lorée.")

A proper fitted oboe case, though expensive, is a worthwhile investment in my opinion. There are some excellent lightweight ones on the market, or you can make your own if you prefer by fitting-out a hard brief-case. (N.B. Foam rubber is inadvisable to use for this. It absorbs damp from the instrument after playing, so that it never dries out. This is okay for the wood, but not the other bits.) A waterproof cover is advisable, too. You can make one from Rexine, or any tough waterproof material, with strong zips or Velcro fasteners, adding pockets for your personal requirements (music, reedcase, stand, spare bow tie, etc.) but don't carry anything too heavy for the handle. A range of covers, some with pockets and useful shoulder-straps, is available to buy.

Check frequently that keys prone to sticking (especially octaves) are working, and have no water or dampness in them. Keep cigarette-papers in your case and mop up whenever you suspect water, and always before putting your instrument away after playing. Store cigarette-papers dry (i.e. not in your coat pocket on a rainy day). Otherwise when you need one urgently you'll find they're just a stuck-together mass. (There are usually plenty on the floor around the woodwind chairs.) When you buy them ask for ones with corners.

To see whether a joint of an oboe is airtight, close all the keys, block the bottom end with your hand, and blow down it, or suck to create a vacuum (as in testing a reed for leaks). You will hear a hiss or notice lack of pressure if it does. A good way of finding *where* an instrument is leaking is to inhale a mouthful of smoke—if you are a non-smoker and can bear to. Then blow it down the joint, with keys closed and the end blocked. Look in a mirror, or have somebody there to see where the tell-tale smoke is eddying out (far quicker than testing each pad with cigarette-paper). Avoid doing this too often though, or sticky nicotine may get onto the pads. Smoke will eventually make the oboe smell, too.

Leaks, or unco-ordinated keys, may be due to worn or missing cork adjusters, tired springs, loosened screws or rods, etc. This occurs with general use, wear and tear, and transportation, or to shrinkage of corks due to age, hot dry conditions or a dry climate.

If, despite regular oiling and maintenance, the instrument generally becomes harder to play than usual, it is probably time to have it serviced, usually necessary every few years, depending on treatment and use.

Keep your instrument case right way up when storing or transporting it. A good fitted case can stand quite a lot of jolting, but upside down knocks and vibration can be fatal (remember this if you make your own case). Don't leave instruments assembled on chairs or the floor where they might be overlooked. *Don't* sit on a valuable oboe (or stand on one). This has actually been done—more than once.

If the corks on the joints of your oboe feel loose, even after 'swelling' treatment (see 'Nursing Care', Chapter 15) they can be replaced (as can cork on staples and crooks).

It's useful to keep a shammy leather on your knee when playing, to wipe perspiration off hands and keys. The acid damages silver-plating quickly—(the oboe can also otherwise make water or oil marks on your 'concert' clothing). It also provides added soft protection for the instrument(s) in the case, if not too bulky.

Make sure anything hard or bulky in your instrument case (tuning-fork, knife, cor sling, etc.) cannot damage the instrument when the case is shut. Even the hard 'stems' of feathers can be fatal. A fitted case doesn't allow much leeway for 'junk', except the usually catered for essentials such as reedcase (crook), grease pot and small screwdriver.

One manufacturer will no longer replace cracked oboe joints on guarantee in Iceland. The country is renowned for instruments cracking (stringed as well as wind) in the extremely dry atmosphere, so be warned if you're thinking of going there.

I once spent a winter season in the Icelandic Symphony Orchestra, and I thought I had taken every precaution. I made a thermal instrument case cover, oiled the bores of my instruments regularly, kept them away from radiators and windows, allowed warming up time in room temperature before playing, and even kept small damp sponges inside pricked polythene bags in the instruments' bells to counteract the dryness. Nevertheless, the three instruments I took with me all cracked in several places, though one was over fifty years old. Although they were all 'pinnable' (so suffered no permanent damage), it was an upsetting experience. It seems there is no sure prevention. Orange peel in the case can also help, or the small humidifiers found in cigar boxes. To combat damp conditions, try a small sachet of Silicagel in your instrument case (the crystals used in packing of electrical goods and cameras).

Insure your instruments adequately. Consider not only their monetary value but the inconvenience of finding a replacement quickly, and the daunting prospect of having to adapt to a different instrument—especially if it is your livelihood. Even if one could afford a good spare, no two oboes are identical and both would have to be kept 'in practice'. Read the small print on your policy and make sure it covers your instruments if you take them abroad. Check this in good time—*not* after you've arrived there. *Always* label your case.

Never leave instruments unattended, especially in a car overnight. Thefts are increasingly common, and an unnecessary risk as the oboe is so easy to carry and fits conveniently into a bag or brief-case. Don't drive off with them on the car roof. (I even know a double bass player who did this!)

A strange case of theft happened to Léon Goossens. His oboe was in a dispatch case in the back of the car when he stopped on the way home after a concert to cross the road to a garage to see if it was open. When he returned, the case (plus instrument) was gone. The case was later found washed up by the sea, but the oboe was not recovered despite advertising and wide enquiries. Two years later he received an anonymous telephone call telling him his oboe was for sale in an East End junk shop as a clarinet. He rang the shop to ask if he could see the instrument on approval and sent someone to collect it. It *was* his long lost oboe, easily recognisable as when he'd purchased it as a boy he had carved his initials on each joint. Who the caller was remains a mystery, but Goossens was so overjoyed to get his oboe back he was happy to ask no questions. This happened in the 1920s, and he subsequently played the instrument for the rest of his life.

Playing

Listen to other players in an orchestra or ensemble for balance and intonation, but listen to your own tuning, too. Learn to play 'out of tune' so you are always in tune with the person next to you.

Aim for the first beat of each bar in very 'notey' passages, such as the last movement of St. Saëns' oboe sonata, rather than trying to count all the intermediary notes. The general flow of the music is more important:

ending:

This is especially important on runs which don't start on the first beat, e.g. the end of Rossini's overture 'Semiramide':

tutti

Use your tongue more firmly ('more tongue') and stomach muscle pressure ('more tum') to ensure quiet low entries are clean, especially if your reed is uncertain on attack. Keep your tongue ready to make a positive entry 'on time' and your fingers 'agog' for quick neat action. (A car will get away more quickly 'on the lights' if the driver has anticipated by having his hands and feet poised, ready, over the controls—if he is in gear he will get away on the 'downbeat'.)

Use more fingers, i.e. move less—to facilitate a downward slur, especially with a diminuendo—for instance G′ to low Db′. . . (you can play G′ with your Db key on).Or, play middle C″ descending to low Db′, D′ or C′ with the right-hand fingers down for the C″. Less movement of fingers means less risk of clumsiness, and enables you to concentrate on embouchure and breath control, especially on a descending interval, lessening the likelihood of splitting the low note.

Using the right-hand G#/Ab key for G#′/Ab′ descending to low B′. . .

 avoids a slide (or use left-hand G#/Ab and low B keys together), leaving your left-hand G#/Ab key on facilitates playing G#/Ab descending to C″. . .

and so on.

It's helpful to anticipate a nasty slide. Try, mentally, to move the slide finger (or a lazy or weak finger) ahead. Anticipate too, with finger action, for smoother downwards intervals, allowing for the low note not to speak, and avoiding clumsy breaks in sound—not forgetting the embouchure change (see 'Embouchure', Chapter 1)—for instance, slurring from middle D″ to low E′

or C″ to C′, as in the first movement of Poulenc'sSonata:

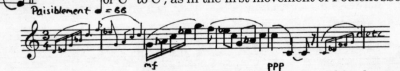

A relaxed embouchure and thinner reed also help to save cracking low notes in such instances.

You can keep the left-hand G#/A♭ key down for other right-hand notes (for instance the arpeggio of C#/D♭ major). For top C‴-C#‴ you can keep the right-hand fingers on for C‴—and, on some oboes, leave your D♭ finger on for low B♭′ when D♭′ follows (or vice versa), or the left-hand E♭ finger on for playing E♭′ to low C′ to E♭′—useful too for C# to D# trills. Keep your right-hand fingers on for C″, for middle C″ to D″ to C″, or C″ to C#″/D♭″ to C″, or your C# finger on for low B′ to C#′ to B (if you have a B′-C#′ coupling) especially to trill. This sort of thing is particularly useful for awkward trills such as C″ to D#″ when you can leave your right-hand fingers down...

'Open C#‴' can be a useful fake fingering when you are 'in a hurry'—if it's in tune—(no fingers), e.g. in Ferling's exercise number 34 (see Recommended Publications). These and other examples, of course, depend on your oboe.

Use of extra fingers can 'improve' the sound of a note, or help to tune or stabilise it, besides making certain passages or entries easier or safer—worth investigating and experimentation. For instance, in the opening of Tchaikowsky's ballet 'Swan Lake' (see page 37) which starts on F#″, adding your E♭ key will stabilise the note if it's an unreliable one on your oboe. (The same note begins the famous solo in the ballet.) If you use your right-hand fingers, as for E♭, on the first note (written C″) of the cor anglais solo in Dvořák's 'New World Symphony' (see page 163) it will be more stable, less 'bright', and better matched to the E♭″ following it, besides making the move easier (as you will be moving fewer fingers). Adding your D finger for G#/A♭ will flatten it slightly, your right-hand fingers as for F (on a conservatoire oboe) will flatten the note B♭″...

Using different fingerings to 'lighten' or 'darken' the sound, is a matter of taste (or what sounds best on your instrument). Some players 'add' as many fingers as possible to avoid a bright sound, others use fewer to avoid a dull sound.

For a fast accented trill such as that from top A″ to B♭‴ near the end of the Scherzo in Poulenc's oboe sonata, use the right-hand trill key, and for extra speed—and effect—keep your wrist stiff and use wrist action rather than finger action.

'Nose grease' is a useful 'aid' to make awkward slides smooth, e.g. slurring from bottom B♭′ to D#/E♭′

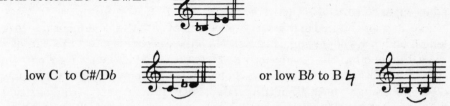

low C to C#/D♭   or low B♭ to B ♮

Rub the slide finger down the side and lower corner of your nose, where we all have skin greasy enough to lubricate the finger nicely—an old trick. (Have you ever wondered why oboists have blackheads on the sides of their noses?) More observant members of audiences must wonder why we all seem to have this habit of rubbing our noses...

A tape recorder can be useful and, like a camera, cannot lie (in things such as tempo and intonation). But don't let hearing yourself on an inferior model put you off the oboe for good if the sound reproduction is too depressing.

When preparing at home try to allow for concert conditions, i.e. stress. Things are naturally easier when you're relaxed in your own surroundings, so—for anything to be safe in a concert it must be 100 per cent dead certain at home every time.

Consider the acoustics you'll be playing in—an echoey church? or a 'dead' theatre pit? Anticipate this in your choice of reed for the occasion (see 'You the Musician', Chapter 7). When listening to new reeds at home, try different acoustic tests. Play 'into' something soft (especially if the room is resonant) as well as 'into' hard surfaces (which will 'reflect' your sound). Listen to yourself in different parts of the house, such as the bathroom or hall. High or low ceilings, furnishings, etc. all alter the effect. (As a performer you will have to get used to adapting to *all* sorts of acoustics.)

You are more limited in this sort of experiment with the cor anglais due to its length and angle of playing. If you practise the cor sitting down in a carpeted room, the sound will be mostly absorbed into the carpet. When you get onto the concert platform you'll get a shock when your sound comes back at you 'loudly' off the bare stage—most off-putting. I find it essential to practise the cor standing up, and to hold it as high as possible, to listen to myself. Hold it over a low coffee table if the room is carpeted, to make your sound easier to hear.

To hear yourself better in a concert or rehearsal, play 'into your music' for a sample test. (When I first saw somebody do this I thought they were having a fit.) During a rehearsal ask somebody to listen from a distance and comment.

186

Don't be put off if, like the oboist rehearsing the Cimarosa concerto who asked the conductor to listen from the back of the hall, the comment is "b..... awful"!

Violinists certainly have the advantage over us in that they can listen to themselves right 'in their ear'.

A top violinist, comparing the violin with the double bass on television, which the bass player claimed is the hardest stringed instrument (its sound being 'furthest away') admitted, "the older we (violinists) get the more out of tune we play, through deafness." So there are disadvantages, too.

As an oboe is played actually 'in one's head' its vibrations travel through our body as well as our hearing them through our ears. If excess wax in your ears becomes dislodged, as I've experienced, causing temporary deafness, it is most disconcerting 'feeling' your playing through this vibration, without actually hearing yourself. (I believe deaf people are now learning, successfully, to play woodwind, brass and other instruments, proving there is something in this.) I once gave a recital at Scunthorpe Music Club while suffering from deafness caused by catarrh, not knowing that sulphur fumes—which we could smell in the hall—given off by steel works, are a good cure. During the concert my ears suddenly 'popped' and the volume (to me) doubled, giving me quite a shock!

If you find yourself 'pinching' the reed, especially when you need to relax your embouchure even more for low notes, e.g. when you are tense or your lip tired, a *slight* pressure with the *upper* lip helps your *lower* lip (or jaw) relax. Using more vibrato temporarily can help to disguise bad tone if you're struggling on a terrible reed (a last resort). Thank God, too, for vibrato to cover up faulty intonation!

If your fingers feel stiff, especially in cold weather, soak your hands in hot water before playing, to 'ease' and relax them.

Check key and time signatures, repeats, dynamics, etc. *before* starting to play. Look ahead for key and time changes, and other traps. To remind yourself of the key, look back to the beginning of a line, BUT also beware key changes that lurk in the middle of one (common in light music selections, Strauss waltzes, etc., as well as in more contemporary music, which often has frequent switches).

It's embarrassing to miss or make an 'extra' repeat, or be in a different key—even worse to play the wrong piece. (On one occasion the wind section of an orchestra thought it was playing 'Flight of the Bumble Bee' and the strings 'Eine Kleine Nachtmusik'. It wasn't as bad for the oboist, only having one note to play, as for the flautist 'going berserk' with the hectic 'Bumble Bee' to an accompaniment of 'Eine Kleine'.) Be very sure that you know the order of the programme, and beware joining in loudly in 'tacet' or 'strings only' numbers.

A conductor who hated extra rehearsals was begged one day to rehearse, since there were several 'deps' in. He did so half-heartedly. In the performance half the orchestra made a repeat—the rest did not. Afterwards he stormed into the bandroom and bawled, "Now you see what happens when you rehearse."

If you play out of doors and use wind irons to anchor the music, don't obliterate the key signatures down the left-hand side of the page with them (unless you know the music very well).

To make a V.S. ('quick') page turn easier, position the music overlapping the right-hand edge of your music-stand, so that you can flick it over quickly. If the last few notes on the page require the left-hand fingers only, you can (for once) briefly rest your oboe on your knee to play, while turning the page with your right hand. Or, if more appropriate, memorise the last—or first—notes of the page and turn a couple of bars early—or late.

Use a pencil to ring key or time changes, dynamics, or an unexpected 'SOLO' so you're not caught unawares. (Use the traditional pair of specs $\bigcirc\hspace{-0.6em}\mathcal{U}$.) Mark your own personal death-traps or danger spots to remind you to watch or watch out:

For instance 'use trill key' (TK), 'left-hand fingering' (LH), 'forked F' (F, 2 or°), breathing places ($\checkmark$ or ?), repeats ('Yes', 'No', 'straight on' or 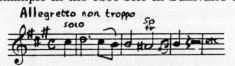), a quick page turn (VS), or 'use spatula key' (Sp). (Slide your left index finger across the C″ key onto the spatula to trill from B ♮ to B♭/A#—for example in the oboe solo in Sullivan's overture to 'Yeomen of the Guard':

Allegretto non troppo

Indicate $\longleftarrow$ to remind you to hold back where you may rush, $\sim\sim$ for a rit., $\rightarrow$ for accel. or 'move', the beats over a rhythmically complicated bar (see page 80) and any accidentals you might miss, especially at the start of a line, or over the page. It's useful, too, to note numbers of bars' rest to count from a previous page at the top of the next, e.g. 26/10 etc., or 1, 2, 3, etc. above a line of repeated bars:

And 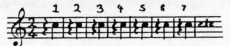 = 'do *not* look at the conductor' can sometimes be useful!

Note anything which has caught you out already—there's no excuse to make the same mistake twice. Always take a pencil to rehearsals. I've seen often-performed music which is more pencil than print.

If a reed is sharp, mark the place on the cork where it should be pushed in to. This applies more to crooks, which are often not pushed right in.

Fake fingerings, extreme lippings and other feats can produce chords and various weird effects on the oboe. Such things are sometimes demanded by contemporary composers (Berio, for example, in his 'Sequenza' for solo oboe). They're also fun to use for sound effects of a less serious nature, such as an ambulance, bells, animal noises, etc., which I have enjoyed including in musical stories for children, which I and my bassoon-playing piano accompanist wrote, and have performed in lecture recitals at infant and junior schools all over the country. (At one school we visited, a teacher told us her class had begged to be excused from their lesson to see the 'magicians'. I hope they weren't too disappointed to discover we were mere 'musicians'.)

Harmonics are a fake fingering which can be useful for certain effects, such as soft high entries. There are eight on the oboe (see page 54)—but none if you have automatic octave keys.

Make a cardboard lavatory roll extension to fit between the bell and bottom joint of the cor anglais, to play a written low Bb'

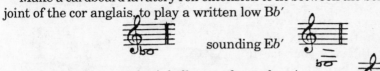

sounding Eb'

or push one into your oboe's bell to produce a low A (by fingering bottom Bb)—as scored—(probably as a joke) in one of Mahler's symphonies. In another piece with a low A in an oboe solo, the composer was at the rehearsal. The oboist told him, "This note will take me off the oboe." Whereupon a loud voice was heard to say, "You should have been taken off the oboe years ago," followed by unkind laughter.

It's especially hard on some old oboes to play a soft low B'. One player used to cheat by pulling the bell and bottom joint out a little to flatten the pitch, and finger C' instead. One day, finding himself a bit sharp he went just too far, and the bell dropped to the floor with a loud clatter!

For a very difficult fast passage in B major, I've known players pull their reeds (and oboe bells) out and play the entire piece in C, impressing the conductor who personally congratulated them on their technique. It was very out of tune, of course, but in a loud 'busy' piece they got away with it—the effect was there.

An effective 'cheat' in Berlioz' 'Symphonie Fantastique' in the rather awkward trill passage in the 'Witches' Sabbath' movement (where both oboes play in unison) is for one player to play the note while the other trills—with exactly the same effect, but twice as easy:

Miming can be used, not only as a last resort when you've forgotten your reeds or a note doesn't speak, but after a note ceases—creating an impressive diminuendo to nothing. (It's sometimes easy to fool audiences—even conductors—sh sh!) Occasionally, actually changing a note here and there in a very fast or awkward passage (e.g. 'The Three Cornered Hat', see page 169) will make it easier but still give the same overall effect without being noticed. (I mention these incidents as hearsay, of course—*not* personal experience.)

Tuning

When giving an 'A' in the orchestra use a tuning-fork. It's easy to hold it to your right ear—though most of us have one 'flat' and one 'sharp' ear— while playing the note using your left hand. Do this for effect—even if you don't actually listen to it, or have perfect pitch, to look convincing to those who, whatever your 'A', will complain that it is 'up' or 'down'—or both!If it's your job to give the 'A' make sure you arrive in time to get warmed up enough to give it accurately—especially in cold weather. There's no creeping in late and unobserved for first oboe players.

Second oboe—don't be smug! Be ready, too, in case your colleague is late and *you* are suddenly called upon to give the 'A'. Don't get caught out.

Compare 'A's with more stable and reliable notes, such as Ds and listen to the intervals. During practice check your pitch with the tuning-fork *after* playing something ending on an A or other easily related note, especially when making or testing reeds. If you listen to the fork first, you'll probably adjust automatically to it with your lips.

After banging the fork, hold it against your teeth, or the bone in your lower ear to hear it more easily. N.B. Don't bang it on hard surfaces such as your chair; use your knee or the rubber sole of a shoe. And don't habitually drop it. Such treatment will eventually make it go *out* of tune!

Sir Malcolm Sargent once stopped the orchestra and said, "Oboe, you're flat," to which the oboist—that well remembered character, Alec Whittaker (who had a pronounced north-country accent)—responded by holding up his oboe and saying to it sternly, "Dyer 'ear that yer booger?…Yer're flat!". The obvious answer, of course, is always to be in tune.

I was once in digs where the cat mewed constantly on top C#‴—which I found most annoying when practising. A possibly more reliable way of 'picking up pitch', if you have no fork handy—but are near a 'phone, is to dial its number to get a G. I believe that one of BT's more dependable—and free—qualities is that the engaged tone is always a G.

Finally, 'play in tune and spend less time tuning'...Playing in tune is the most important thing of all. Often playing 'A's is a waste of time.

Breathing

All active sport (in moderation of course) is beneficial to oboe-playing, as well as to health. But I consider swimming to be the best of all. It certainly improves breathing. Try playing after swimming... you'll feel the difference. I once knew a trombone player who claimed that if he played immediately after exercising with a chest expander, he produced a much better sound.

Breathing for oboists is in many ways similar for singing.—So if you do both, one should help the other. But don't *ever* forget that when playing the oboe you must breathe OUT first.

Before a long solo, or an exposed passage needing particular control (such as 'Swan Lake', 'Barber of Seville' overture (see page 35) the slow movement of Beethoven's 'Emperor Concerto' (see page 83) or Bizet's 'L'Arlesienne', or the solo in the second movement of Schubert's 'Unfinished Symphony', breathe out, then in, before you start (allow time for this). For extra control, let a little air out so you're not playing with very full lungs. The passage in 'L'Arlesienne', for instance, should then be easily played in one breath, even at a slow tempo. As this is with the flute, you may prefer to breathe together to match the phrasing—it's too long for a flautist to play in one breath. This can also help you control those exposed dying away notes at the end of quiet pieces, and stop them 'dying away' too soon (for example, Mahler's fourth symphony, see page 83). (I have even learned—with practice—to sustain a note while burping, something I often find useful.)

Teaching

It's a good idea if you are a professional or advanced player to teach a few pupils—and it's good for us *all* to have lessons occasionally, too. Teaching others often brings home to you that a) you don't stick to all those excellent methods you are preaching, and b) you actually can't do half the things you're telling your pupils off for not being able to do. You may suddenly discover this, to your embarrassment, when you offer to demonstrate in a lesson. A little teaching certainly keeps you on your toes, and keeps you practising, too. It can also serve as a morale booster—if you compare your own playing with that of your elementary pupils! As a teacher try to ensure that you play to, and with, your pupils as much as possible. This is important, and should encourage beginners especially, to imitate your sound—but make sure it's worth imitating.

I advise students to listen to good players and model their sound on that of the experts. If you teach beginners all day you may need to do the same for yourself (if only to remind yourself what an oboe really sounds like), otherwise you might find yourself sounding like a beginner next time you play.

After leaving school I had lessons with a local professional before starting at the Guildhall School of Music. At my first lesson, to dispel my nervousness, he

warned me light-heartedly that the cat hated the oboe, and I mustn't be put off if it fled when I played. As soon as I began, to his embarrassment, it rushed up to me and behaved in a very friendly fashion.

A fellow Guildhall student caused some surprise when he arrived for his second lesson with our teacher, at his house in north London.

At the first lesson, the professor told him if no one was about when he arrived the following week, to come in and get ready. The next week, the student went into the room as instructed and started to practise. Presently a lady came in looking startled...It was the wrong house!

Miscellaneous

If you play a loud wrong note, or make an embarrassing squawk during a concert DON'T blush or giggle. Carry on as if nothing had happened. Or, better, glare at your neighbour.—If you do it confidently enough, everyone should be convinced it was them, or, if they were absorbed in the music, even wonder afterwards if it happened at all. Making a bad mistake and being able to carry it off is a difficult art—as important to master as playing your instrument.

When newsreaders or broadcasters make a slip, if they carry on nonchalantly you wonder if they really said that, or was it your imagination? It's only obvious if they are thrown, and stammer, hesitate, or worse, apologise. Even the worst performance is greeted with tumultuous applause if artists beam at their admiring public with an air of achievement, stretch out their arms with seeming pride and turn on 'that smile' and that 'I'm the greatest' look. This 'act' doubles the applause immediately—I've witnessed it many times. (Try it and see—I dare you!)

If you're being televised, don't assume that because you're not playing a solo you won't be in the picture, like the oboist who was picking his nose when the cameraman took a close-up of him.

If you type, learn to use *all* your fingers, as right now, my C and F# fingers are worn out! Typing using only my two third (G and D) fingers might have been an excellent excercise and probably helped my playing, but it would have been very 'largamente'.

If you combine oboe-playing with home decorating, carpentry, gardening, etc., leave time for your hands to unstiffen and loosen before trying to play straight afterwards. (Playing the oboe, especially low notes, is an excellent remedy for constipation.)

Make a loop for the hook on your cor anglais sling in the lid of your cor case, and slip the leather ('collar') part in the feather slot—a useful carrier.

If, in your instrument case, you keep a mop, cleaner, or an instrument stand, up the bell of your oboe DO remember to take it out before playing. It's a common tale. No note…panic…then… finding the mop in the instrument. It's not an unheard of trick to play on poor, unsuspecting woodwind players either—putting something up the instrument's bell when they're not looking (e.g. a tangerine in a cor anglais' bell), or threading some cotton through a key, which causes untold panic and fear of some major mechanical disaster. (An equally effective way of 'shutting up' string players is to grease their bows.) It's another argument for putting instruments away during intervals.

If you are of a nervous disposition don't practise next to the telephone and jump so much when it rings that you answer it with a bleeding mouth and broken reed. 'Mute' it by putting it on a carpet or cushion, or find a less dangerous spot to practise.

If anyone is rude enough to complain about your practising, the answer, of course, is, "You're lucky, others *pay* to hear me..." Proper practice, though, to be fair, *should* consist of things one *can't* play, and other boring-to-listen-to items such as scales and long notes. Or, worse for listeners, testing new or half scraped reeds, constantly repeating the same loud notes or phrases—very rarely one's 'party piece'. Time your practice for when the neighbours are out when possible. Try to do it in generally sociable hours to keep good relations with all within earshot. If you follow the sound advice of taking deep breaths by an open window before practising, close it afterwards, before you play. And if others share your house, be considerate and polite and give them warning if you're planning wind octets or 'band practice' at home. I'm fortunate—my neighbours seem to enjoy my music making (or pretend to anyway). At least, unlike pianists, we can, if necessary, practise in a different room, or point the instrument away from neighbours' walls, which helps a little if they are disturbed.

It's easy when rushing out of the house to catch a train, loaded with overnight bag, evening clothes, etc. to take the wrong instrument (or reeds), especially if you're constantly changing from a double to a single case, for example, to take your double case with no oboe in it, or a heavy brief-case containing everything *but* your oboe...or even to leave both behind.

One player arrived at Eastbourne to open his bag and find neither oboe nor cor anglais.He was able to 'phone his wife, who rushed them to East Croydon station and gave them to a guard on the train. They arrived in time for the evening's performance, but another player lost her instruments in Spain, and they had to play Handel's two oboe 'Entry of the Queen of Sheba' using two violins, until she was able to borrow an oboe. Her own turned up, two weeks later, in the freight department at Barcelona Airport. An oboist arrived at Sadler's Wells to find he'd taken an empty case and (again at Sadler's Wells) another found he had left the bell of his oboe at home, eventually finding it down his bed...

Leaving part of an instrument behind is perhaps a greater risk for clarinettists. One, who'd been working on his instruments at home during the day, got to the Royal Festival Hall with half a Bb and half a bass clarinet, and, another time, after working on mouthpieces, left the mouthpiece at home and had to improvise by sticking the reed onto the instrument with Sellotape.

An oboist travelling south for a concert, stopped in Manchester to dash into a chemist for some toothpaste and—like most of us, never letting his oboe out of his sight—took it with him. After driving about fifty miles down the M6 he noticed it was not on the seat beside him. He knew he would never find the chemist again in all the one-way systems in Manchester, so had to enlist the help of the police. His oboe was exactly where he'd left it, in his brief-case in the middle of the shop. But the building had been evacuated!

Forgetting reeds, instruments—or even parts of them—is, as you see, a common occurrence. Don't let it happen to you.

Be careful with kissing before a concert—don't ruin your embouchure! A better aid, perhaps, for musicians who suffer badly from nerves than taking alcohol before playing is 'Betablockers' ('Propanalol' or other pills) which lower the adrenalin and blood rate slightly. They are used by many musicians, but it must be stressed that in rare circumstances (such as with some asthma sufferers) they *can* be dangerous. Try them first under medical supervision, starting with small doses (10mg) and sampling different sorts, at an unimportant time. Get them from a doctor, not your colleagues. Swallowing 20mg quickly about an hour before playing stops those knee-knocking shakes which can really spoil a performance. Don't 'chew' them or they'll 'numb' your tongue. And be cautious…An 'overdose' will make your fingers go to sleep, if not you as well. If used sensibly these *can* make all the difference on special or 'solo' occasions.

On a less serious note, it sometimes takes a disaster to break the atmosphere, making everyone relax. So, for your 'party trick' drop the music, knock over the music- stand, or trip up the steps and 'fall' onto the stage—it's a knockout!

Chapter 19

Finale

THE 'PRO' BIT

Concert dress; Professional etiquette; Coda

Choosing concert clothes

What you wear to play is all-important. It's essential to feel comfortable and be able to perform 'safely'. Choose garments with plenty of breathing space—your chest needs expansion room—playing is impossible while restricted. Take deep breaths when trying on concert clothes, not only to test comfort, but whether zips stay up, etc. I've had to leave the stage crab-wise with a gaping zip at the back (though my long hair was useful camouflage) and have watched singers' dress zips travel downwards with uncanny regularity on every breath. I have even gone home stuck in my concert dress and had to choose between going to bed in it, going into the street and asking a stranger to undress me, or breaking the zip.

Ladies—avoid lacy sleeves which may catch in your oboe keys. If you indulge in curtseys, check that you won't split—or reveal—anything you shouldn't, that ribbons, bows, etc. won't catch in your shoes—or your hair (if long) in hooks, bows or buttons.

Choose dresses that are easy to walk and climb stairs in carrying your oboe, music, etc., elegantly, without risk of tripping. Shoes or sandals that catch in a long dress hem when you walk will kill that air of confidence stone dead.

Non-crease clothes are advisable for any musician, but pack a travel iron.

Avoid outfits which may be too hot or cold (easier for women, though men can vary the material of a tail suit or dinner-jacket, i.e. have summer and winter versions, if funds allow—or wear a vest or waistcoat underneath).

Shawls, stoles or wraps, though attractive, and theoretically a good idea when you can't foresee the temperature of a venue, can turn playing the oboe into a feat. They may catch in keys, or slip down, and you'll be too busy worrying about them to concentrate on your playing.

Avoid wearing a cor anglais sling together with elaborate collars, necklaces or hairdos, and beware the empty hook catching your clothing, especially mini-skirts.

Gentlemen—avoid tight neckties or collars, or cummerbunds or trousers which a large breath might burst. At least you have the advantage of being able to wear braces, eliminating the worry of coming undressed during a performance (a strong belt might be the best answer). Bow ties and black socks often get forgotten—keep spares in your case or pocket, along with that emergency spare reed.

In pits, often only one's top is visible to the public, so dinner-jackets, white shirts and bow ties are sometimes worn over cords or jeans (why wear out dress trousers unnecessarily?), and ladies can wear what they like on their lower half as long as their top half is 'black'.

At hot summer concerts when 'shirtsleeves' may suddenly be dictated for men, be prepared with a 'white all over' (not just white-fronted) shirt—without torn sleeves or bad sweat stains. (It's easy, and embarrassing—to get caught out here.)

One oboist who left his white shirt at home played in a performance *on stage,* with evening suit, tie, etc. and a bare (white but hairy) chest.

When a member of a string quartet forgot his evening trousers, once, there was no alternative but to explain to the audience why he was wearing his tail-coat over jeans. This broke the ice beautifully, creating a relaxed atmosphere and a consequently splendid and *much* enjoyed performance! Perhaps we *shouldn't* worry quite so much about 'safe' clothing...

Professional etiquette (or 'How to get asked again')

Here are some suggestions which you may consider obvious, but which are perhaps best observed—until you're well-established, confident of always being 'booked' again:

Never argue with conductors—even when you *know* they're wrong. Malcolm Sargent, once, rehearsing Beethoven's fifth symphony, kept telling the oboist—Alec Whittaker—(renowned for his 'cheek in tongue') how he wanted the little oboe cadenza played, but Whittaker kept repeating it the same. Finally, Sargent told him, "If you won't pay any attention to me I might as well not be here"…to which Whittaker replied, "Now yer're 'ere yer might as well stay." (Only a top player could get away with this sort of behaviour—Don't try it too soon.) Don't ridicule a

foreign conductor's pronunciation either, as one player did when the maestro said, "Oboe, could we pleeze have sex before three" by replying "We'll have to hurry—it's a quarter to, now." Rather, flatter the conductor by pretending to watch him *intently*, even when you have *absolutely no idea* what he's doing…

Sometimes you have to take the initiative yourself, as in a chamber concert I played in at the Queen Elizabeth Hall, London. The composer 'conducted' the (quite playable) music, but instead of beating each bar, he just followed odd leads, jumping bars and beats all over the place. We 'came in' when we felt we hadn't played for some time! It was hard not to giggle in those formal surroundings! (I never saw the crit of this concert!)

As a student, I played in a performance of Handel's 'Messiah' when the conductor beat everything 'down, up…down up', whether it was in two, three or four, (i.e. $\frac{3}{4}$ numbers were beat 'down, up, down',—'up, down, up', etc.!—an unnerving experience).

Don't argue with the first oboe, if you're playing second. Remember, he or she could have a say in whether you're asked back, or your name's passed on for other work. It's imperative to fit in and get on with the other musicians and help create a friendly, pleasant atmosphere to work in. You may pass an audition with ease if you're a capable oboist and musician, but fail a trial through incompatibility with the other players. *Never* allow personal enmity to affect your job, or your performance.

Nowadays it's work that's scarce, not musicians. It was a different story in 1829 in this country, when an actor in Hamlet in a prominent theatre 'descended from the stage and played the fiddle between acts' ('doubling' with a difference). These days it's so competitive we cannot afford not to be on our best behaviour, always.

When playing second oboe, DON'T continually look over the first's shoulder at his music, or, worse still, finger his solos (an obnoxious habit of some know-all students). Respect his experience; don't try to undermine his confidence.

DON'T stand on your chair and rattle off the opening bars of the Strauss concerto (oboists' favourite show-piece!). Especially not just when the conductor's asking for 'hush'. Certainly not if it's your first date or it'll almost certainly be your last.

'A great [oboist]—like a great beauty, sometimes imagines others will be pleased with him as long as he is pleased with himself'…(but perhaps *not* if he's *too* pleased with himself…). Rather, exercise modesty. When 'double encores' first appeared in 1808, a singer asked the conductor to cut an oboe cadenza in 'The Duenna', as 'the great applause given to [it] stopped the encore of his song which followed'. The oboist agreed, and 'never interfered again with his enemy'…

In the last century improper use of power was common (there was no Union until 1921). A wealthy singer asked for her brother to play first oboe at the Opera House, removing the then principal player, who had for several years 'filled the post with great ability'. He, fortunately, agreed to play second, and furthermore, when there were passages the new first oboe couldn't play (as happened frequently) 'kindly agreed to play them for him'!

There's a tendency, especially among advanced students who've achieved a good finger technique, to think that fast fingers (though impressive to non-musicians) mean you're a real expert. Yet all students leaving college after three or four years' concentrated study should be able to get their fingers round any music, however technically demanding. Playing second oboe in something simple, say, Haydn or Mozart, perhaps after a lengthy, trying, journey, in adverse or uncomfortable conditions, when over-tired, hungry or not feeling well, and being expected to blend beautifully with a first oboe you've never met—or even heard—before (i.e. not untypical freelance conditions!...) is far harder than being able to finger fast, or technically difficult music—which, after all, is simply a matter of practice. A shock after perhaps enjoying the exalted position of principal player at college.

Before the war, John Butterworth (a wealthy oboe-player) was a senior student and sub-professor at the Royal College of Music, and very full of himself. He arrived for his first lesson with a new professor with a pile of concertos, asking, "Which would you like me to play?"..."A scale of C major," was the stern reply. He was so taken aback he squawked on bottom C. "Try again"... After three attempts the professor said, pointing at the music, "Two years on long notes, then, perhaps, I'll hear one of those..."

Arriving on time and at the right place certainly helps your name not to get struck off lists. Musicians have been known to go to the wrong town, like the player who arrived at the Winter Gardens at Bournemouth, instead of Eastbourne. Or the oboist who went to the Pavilion at Bournemouth (B'm'th) instead of Bath. One, I believe, even turned up in the wrong country! Listen carefully to telephone instructions and confirm details. I've experienced standing in station ticket queues not exactly sure what destination to ask for, having taken down details hastily...

Try to arrive on the right day, too. Not like the sixteen piece band which travelled from Scarborough to Skegness to play at a police ball, to find they were a day early... Unfortunately most weren't free the following day, leaving a headache for the fixer.

A trio of well-known musicians, arriving to rehearse for a concert at the Free Trade Hall in Manchester one wet November afternoon, were surprised to see no posters advertising their programme. They'd got the date right, but were a year early!

One hot summer afternoon an oboist was dozing in the sunshine in his garden after a morning rehearsal, when the 'phone rang. "You're supposed to be at a session"… Throwing on his clothes he 'slammed' down to the studio as fast as he could, apologised all round, got out his oboe, and opened the folder. The first number…'cor anglais', second number…'cor anglais'…and the poor man hadn't taken his cor with him! He 'phoned home and had it put in a taxi. The taxi got stuck in rush-hour traffic—and finally arrived after the session was over. They had to over-dub the part.

Check what the dress is if you've been booked for a concert over the 'phone. Or take 'the wardrobe' and be prepared for anything. Not all orchestras require ladies to wear 'long black' nowadays, preferring long coloured dresses. And if you're the only man wearing tails when the rest are in dinner-jackets, you'll feel very conspicuous.

DON'T haggle over money—except when you're offered less than Union rates (and you are a member of the Union—aren't you?). If this applies to everybody don't be the one with the loudest voice if you're the least experienced musician present.

Sir Thomas Beecham once engaged an elderly oboist who stuttered, saying, "I can offer you this engagement for five pounds per week." The oboist started to reply… "Going up to nine pounds", Beecham added hastily, presuming he was going to argue about the fee. In fact, he'd only been trying to say 'thank you'.

Money should *never* be seen as compensation for a bad performance. An Italian opera singer, receiving a poor reception for his singing, told his colleague, who was trying to console him, "Oh sare, dey may hissa me as much as dey please, if I getti di money".

Professional musicians do, regrettably, sometimes get used as a source of free music. A nineteenth-century 'noble lord' was so impressed with the playing of Fischer, a virtuoso oboist of the day, that he invited him to dinner, saying, as an afterthought, "You'll bring your oboe of course". To which Fischer replied, "My lord, my oboe doesn't sup". A distinguished player, finding himself frequently invited for weekends with a 'P.S. Do bring your oboe', became so fed up that he once sent a crummy oboe with a note. It said, 'Sorry I can't make it this weekend—but here's my oboe'. Another, offered little money to play at a music club, agreed, but said he 'couldn't guarantee a personal appearance'.

Don't take newspaper 'crits' too seriously…I once gave a recital with an accompanist who played nineteenth-century piano solos, to contrast with my repertoire. Although I was certain no critic had attended, our concert had a wonderful review in the local newspaper, praising *my* performances of works by Chopin, Mendelssohn, Schubert, etc… One oboe-player was described in a newspaper as 'well-known 'cellist'. When asked what he was going to play he had replied, "Marcello"…

Even competition judges make mistakes. An oboe competitor, playing

Mozart and Handel, reached a semi-final. He received congratulations from the oboist judge, whose only criticism was that he'd 'taken the Britten too fast'.

Few members of the public realise how small a part of being a musician performing is. Some even believe it's a glamorous life! Hopefully, performances are stimulating and fulfilling enough to make up for the rest...It wasn't me who christened the LSO the 'Life Sentence Orchestra'. When I asked colleagues for amusing experiences or anecdotes to recount here, one long-time orchestral oboist looked at me aghast, and said, "What can possibly be funny about playing the oboe?" Oh dear! That's what it can do to you.

Being a musician is a job, like any other. But it's one few of us would swap. It can take you anywhere in the world, offering unique experiences. On a ballet company's foreign tour, for instance, one of the dancers defected and the whole Company found itself locked into the theatre after the performance. Music is certainly a truly international language and musicians come from every sort of background.

I've been asked, 'Isn't it easy for you after all these years?' Little do folks realise how much harder it is to play something freshly or thrillingly for the ninety-ninth time, than when it's new and exciting, and no hang ups have had time to creep in.

If I hear a bad performance—broadcast or live—especially by an artist whose playing I normally admire—I feel sympathy rather than snobbery. Maybe they're under stress, are suffering from toothache, have forgotten their reeds—or just broken their only good one—and had to borrow or use a dud, couldn't find the venue or a parking meter, or missed the train, or their husband or wife walked out on them the night before. Make allowances. Don't always be over-critical. We all have 'off' days...possibly even you?

After many years in the profession when, between playing, travelling, teaching and reed-making (possibly raising a family, too) there's rarely time for the exhaustive practice you had opportunity for as a student, your fingers probably won't be as agile as when you left college. Experience gained since, however, should more than compensate. So, respect your superiors and you'll find they respect you in return. DON'T, then, react with obvious scorn if a more experienced player messes up something *you* think is easy—there's probably a jolly good reason. Wait until it's *your* turn. The best teachers are experience and playing with better musicians than oneself. I felt I'd learned more—in some ways—after a few months playing second oboe and cor anglais with the Royal Ballet (which I joined when I left college) than in four years' hard study.

Don't always assume others are ignorant. On one early Sadler's Wells tour two oboists went to the pub after a performance. They noticed a little chap staring in wonderment at their dinner-jackets. Eventually he came over and asked if they were in the orchestra..."Yes," they said. His eyes widened. "What do you play?" "Oboe." They widened further. One of the oboists started to explain. "It's like a clarinet but with a double reed..." There was an interruption, then the other player offered the man a drink saying, "You're obviously interested. Do you play anything?" "Yes...Oboe...In the Hallé" He was a top player of the day!

If you want to work as a freelance player you must not only be available, but easily reached. Answerphones and 'diary services' are helpful (see 'Useful Addresses'), unless you have a husband, wife, flatmate or children to accept dates for you. Don't say 'No' too often. Make sure your 'phone number (and address) is correct in any directory or list, especially if you move house. Don't hide away. Sell yourself. Let other players—and fixers—know you're looking for work. It's 'who you know' as well as 'what you know' that counts. Luck, and opportunity play a part, too.

Ensure that your oboe (and you) is in working order. And that you have a reed (or preferably two) worth playing on. Finally, keep in practice... especially when playing is scarce. Always remain a 'practising oboist'.

CODA

In conclusion, I wish you joy, happiness and success in your music making. Enjoy our beautiful instrument, and pass on some of that pleasure to others through your playing.

'FINE'

D.C. ad lib...

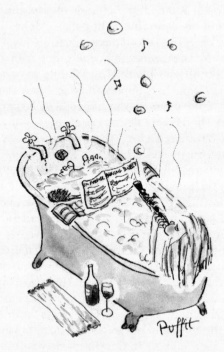

A Brief History

There is evidence of double reed instruments all over the world as far back as prehistoric times.

The ancestors of the oboe, 'the most ancient of reed instruments', date back to primitive civilisations in the Middle East and Europe. They varied considerably but all used a double reed. Though of Hindu origin there are also traces of them in ancient Egyptian and Greek sculpture and painting.

The early oboe, or *shawm,* was played in Europe as long ago as the thirteenth century. It first appears in English history in the early 1300s. By the sixteenth century there were basically two families of double reed instruments—*crumhorns (krummhorns)*—with cylindrical tubes, and shawms and *pommers*—with conical tubes. In Elizabeth I's reign the word *howeboie* was used for the shawm. ('Shawm' comes from the Latin 'calamus': reed). During the seventeenth century shawms and higher pommers became known as 'haut bois' ('high wood')—they were loud and raucous, and usually used in military bands—and large pommers, 'gros bois' ('big' or 'low wood').

These terms referred more to volume than pitch—high meaning loud; low, soft. The oboe developed from the treble shawm during the second half of the seventeenth century. It was redesigned by Jean Hotteterre and Philidor in about 1657 to meet the demand for an instrument for indoor use, and used at the court of Louis XIV and to portray scenes of 'ill omen' in Shakespeare's plays.

Oboe-making reached a new peak at this time, arousing German and French courts' interests, and the instrument was first used in the orchestra around 1671. It became a regular member by the end of the century when it was also introduced, and became popular, in England (inspiring obbligati by Purcell). The first tutors then appeared, with varied fingerings, showing that players were becoming particular about intonation. Between 1600 and 1750 oboes had three keys. They also became split into three sections. By then many inbetween instruments had disappeared and the ranges of the oboe and bassoon were extended to compensate.

During the eighteenth century indoor chamber orchestras became common. Oboes were used extensively by Bach, Handel, Telemann and their contemporaries (Handel himself played the oboe when young), and there were many virtuoso players. Music from this 'baroque' period shows that an advanced technique had already been developed. It is still an important part of the oboe's repertoire (see 'Vocabulary', Chapter 16).

The construction and design of the instruments were substantially improved by Delusse at the end of the nineteenth century. Oboes became more individual, making it less easy, as had been customary, to double on bassoon, clarinet etc., and specialisation resulted.

By about 1820 some oboes had six keys, and by 1860 up to thirteen. It was only during the last hundred years or so that the present system, with its complicated mechanism, was developed—mainly in Paris by Triébert, and more recently, by Lorée. Brod further improved its design, giving it a reputation as the 'first of the woodwind instruments'. Later Gillet brought reed-making and playing technique to a 'high degree of perfection'. Manufacturers today are still constantly modifying and 'improving' the instrument's design (though many recent alterations have been made for ease of manufacture, rather than efficiency of playing). Centuries of loving care and skill have brought the oboe to its present high standard with over one hundred fingerings (some feel, however, that the earlier 'simpler' instruments were, after all, superior, and that today's weighty mechanics actually produce an 'inferior' sound, as well as many headaches!).

The systems, including bore lengths, vary, even today. Reeds have changed considerably, too. Originally larger and wider, more like the bassoon reed, today's are small and slender in comparison.

The cor anglais appeared in Vienna in 1760 and was developed from the alto pommer. Opinions differ as to the origin or the name (see 'The Oboe's Relatives', Chapter 17). Its immediate predecessor, the *oboe da coccia* ('chase' or 'hunting' oboe) was used extensively by Bach. Today these parts are played on the—similarly pitched—cor anglais. This instrument had a flared bell, later changed to pear-shaped, and was curved...

Brod developed the present straight cor anglais during the last century. At the end of the 1800s the instrument began to be much used in orchestras by Wagner and his contemporary 'romantic' composers because of its warm and generous tone (it's described as 'resembling the human voice')—a continuing tradition.

The oboe d'amore, originating from about 1720 in Germany and given major roles by Bach in many of his works, especially to describe 'pastoral' scenes, was forgotten during the romantic period and revived in the 1870s. Ten years later the instrument as we know it was being made in England and France by Lorée. It is used in only a few modern works, Bach's music still being its main repertoire, and it has a soulful, 'lovelorn' quality. The origin of its name is unknown.

For a detailed history I recommend *Woodwind Instruments and Their History* by Anthony Baines (see 'Recommended Publications').

Recommended Publications
and Bibliography

Studies and exercises; Further reading (referred to in text, and others)

(Bracketed publishers = British Agents.)

Studies and exercises

Hinke: *Elementarschule.* (Elementary exercises, simple studies in all keys.) Published by Peters Edition Ltd., 10-12 Baches Street, London N1 6DN. Tel 071-253 1638.

Otto Langey: *Practical Tutor for Oboe and Cor Anglais.* (Rudiments, simple fingering chart, useful finger exercises.) Published by Boosey and Hawkes Ltd.

Louis Bleuzet: *La Technique du Hautbois.* (Volume 1, scales, fingerwork, long notes/tonework, articulations, trills; Volume 2, scales in thirds, fourths etc., chromatic; Volume 3, arpeggios, staccato.) Published by Alphonse Leduc, Éditions Musicales, 175 rue Saint-Honoré, Paris. (U.M.P.)

Luft: *Studies.* (24 studies, in all keys, moderately hard, based on scales and arpeggios. Good fingerwork practice.) Published by Peters Edition Ltd.

W. Ferling. *48 Études pour Hautbois ou Saxophone.* (Useful slow and fast studies, in every key, moderately hard.) Published by Éditions Billoudot, 14 rue de L'Echiquier, Paris. (Kalmus).

W. Ferling: *144 Preludes and Studies.*

Fifty Classical Studies for the Oboe: (A cross-section of studies, in different styles, by Blatt, Ferling, Parma and Schmitt. A mixed bag, several study books in one. Mixed grades. Many 'fun'.) Published by Universal Edition Ltd.

Vade-Mecum of the Oboist, by Albert J. Andraud. (Over 200 technical and orchestral studies for oboe and cor anglais.) Published by Southern Music Co., San Antonio, Texas 78292, U.S.A.

25 Studien und Capricien für oboe, by Karl Mille. (A combination of slow and expressive, and lively music, in all keys. Moderately hard. Great fun!) Published by Veb Friedrich Hofmeister Musikverlag, Leipzig. Germany.

Fernand Gillet: *Studies for the Advanced Teaching of the Oboe.* (25 studies, technically advanced, includes comprehensive 'Practice Method'—how to work at each study, and detailed fingering chart.) Published by Alphonse Leduc, Éditions Musicales, 175 rue Saint-Honoré, Paris. (U.M.P.)

Trente-Deux Études pour le Hautbois: 32 hard studies on awkward notes! covering all tricky fingerings. (For advanced students wishing to 'perfect' their finger technique.) Published by Alphonse Leduc, Éditions Musicales, 175 rue Saint-Honoré, Paris. (U.M.P.)

Orchestral Studies. *Difficult Passages for Oboe and Cor Anglais,* by Evelyn Rothwell. (Solo passages from standard orchestral works. First volume, 'Classical', Beethoven to Brahms; Second volume, 'Classical', Franck to Weber;

Third Volume, 'Modern', Bartok—Stravinsky.) Published by Boosey and Hawkes Ltd.

J.S. Bach. *Difficult Studies for Oboe, Oboe D'Amore and Oboe da Caccia (Cor Anglais).* Same series as above. (Excerpts from obbligati and other solos from Bach's cantatas, masses, Passions and other works. Good 'tone practice', useful reference and gorgeous music to 'revel' in!)

Orchesterstudien für Oboe, in two volumes. Published by Breitkopf, (Kalmus Ltd.)

Strauss Orchesterstudien aus den symphonischen werken (including two oboes and cor anglais.) Published by Peters Edition Ltd.

Oboe Excerpts, in several volumes. Published by Belwin-Mills Music Ltd.

Soli' é passi tecnici (orchestral excerpts) by Crozzoli. From opera; from J.S. Bach. Published by Casa Musicale Sonzogno, Milano. (Available from T.W. Howarth and Co., Ltd.) Good clear print.

The Essential Oboist, by John Williams. (A concise approach to daily practice. Detailed look at certain aspects of playing and reed-making. A 'different' book.) Published by Cinque Port Music Publishers, Bank House, Queen Street, Deal, Kent CT14 6ET.

Tone Development Through Interpretation, by Marcel Moyse. (Famous slow melodies, transposed through different keys (for flute). Excellent tone development, and intonation practice.) Published by Hinrichsen Editions (Peters Edition Ltd.)

Any of these publications should be available from major music shops, or can be ordered by them.

Further reading

Oboe Technique, by Evelyn Rothwell. (An excellent guide, aimed at students, but including basic instruction for beginners, in a concise, easily readable style. Full of good, sound advice, including simple reed-making guidance, and a list of oboe and cor anglais music, with publishers.) Published by Oxford University Press, 1953 (first edition).

Guide to Oboe Reed-Making, by Evelyn Rothwell. (An invaluable comprehensive guide with many photographs.) Published by Nova Music.

Oboe Reed-Making and Problems of the Oboe Player, by Alio. Published by Jack Spratt Music Co., Connecticut, U.S.A.

Oboe Reed Styles, Theory and Practice, by David Ledet. (A unique study, analysing reeds by 81 artists from 14 countries, with photographs and drawings.) Published by Indiana University Press, 1981.

The Art of Oboe-Playing, by Robert Sprenkle and David Ledet. (An American publication, full of technical facts and advice for serious students, with interesting statistics and comparisons between reeds used by players throughout the world. Excellent larger than life photographs of every stage of preparing cane and reed-making, and fingering chart, including trills, for oboe and cor anglais.) Published by Summy-Birchard Co., Illinois, U.S.A., 1961.

Oboe Player, by James L. Weil. Published by Golden Quill, U.S.A., 1961.

The Oboe Reed Book, by Jay Light (A clear guide by a Canadian oboist.)

Available from Forrest's Music Shop, 1849, University Ave., Berkeley, C.A., U.S.A.

Oboe Reeds: How to make and adjust them, by Robert Mayer. Published by Instrumental Co., U.S.A.

The Art of Oboe Reed-Making, by Berman. (A simple step by step guide by a Canadian oboist.) Available from Forrest's Music Shop, 1849, University Ave., Berkeley, C.A., U.S.A.

Oboe, by Léon Goossens and Edwin Roxburgh. (Technical advice on playing, interpretation and reed-making from the world's finest oboe player. History and interpretation of eighteenth-century, among other, music, and explanations of modern techniques by a specialist. Includes a fingering chart.) Published by MacDonald and James, 1977, as part of Yehudi Menuhin's Music Guide Series. Now published by Kahn and Averill, 7 Harrington Gardens, SW7.

The Oboe and the Bassoon, by Gunther Joppig. (Interesting, thorough, easy to read. Detailed account of the instruments' development. Reference to soloists over the years. 'Tips' for beginners. Photographs. Translated from German.) Published by B.T. Batsford Ltd., 1988.

The Oboe, by Philip Bate. (Detailed history, construction and development, including reed-making, with fascinating photographs of instruments from different periods.) Published by Ernest Benn Ltd., 1956 (first edition).

Woodwind Instruments and Their History, by Anthony Baines. (Comprehensive general background, history and development of all woodwind families, including mechanism and reeds.) Published by Faber and Faber Ltd., 1957 (first edition).

Musical Instruments through the Ages, by various contributors. (Edited by Anthony Baines.) Published by Penguin Books Ltd., 1961 (first edition).

The Adventure of the Cor Anglé, by Bo Eriksson, principal cor anglais in Swedish Radio Symphony Orchestra. (An extensive list of all major music published for the instrument—solo, chamber and orchestral, plus list of accessory suppliers. Invaluable reference for any cor player.) Published by Älta Music Co., Sweden. Available from T.W. Howarth and Co. Ltd.,

How to Make Double Reeds for oboe, cor anglais and bassoon, by J. Artley. Published by Selmer, Paris.

The Singing Reed, by Alain Girard. (Introduction to reed-making in three languages; English, French, German.) Published by Musik-Academie de stadt, Basel, 1983.

Music in the Wind, by Barry Wynne. (The story of Léon Goossens, with interesting family background; how he fought to overcome a serious car accident which badly damaged his mouth and jaw, and how he returned to playing. A captivating book.) Published by Souvenir Press Ltd., 1967 simultaneously by The Ryerson Press, Canada.

Musical Memoirs, by W.T. Parke. (An intriguing, sometimes amusing, day to day diary of musical events in the nineteenth century, historically interesting, too. Parke was principal oboist at the Theatre Royal, Covent Garden, for forty years. In two volumes. A good read if you can get hold of a copy. (Volume 2 is available from Central Music Library in London). Volume 1 covers 1784-

1805, volume 2 1806-1830. Published by Henry Colburn and Richard Bentley, 1830 (Vol 2).

The Interpretation of Music, by Thurston Dart. (Invaluable guidance on how to play music from different periods 'authentically'. Written in a style easy to understand.) Published by Hutchinson, 1954.

Dental Problems in Wind Instrument Playing, by Maurice M. Porter. Published as a monograph (containing all the papers he ever published). Published by and available from the British Dental Association.

Tensions in the Performance of Music. (A symposium by nine or ten contributing authors. Edited by Carola Grindea.) Published by Kahn And Averill, 1978.

A Method for Adjusting the Oboe and English Horn, by Carl J. Sawicki (comprehensive instruction for basic adjustments). Published by Carl J. Sawicki, Box 248, Delhi, NY 13753, 1986.

We Make Music , a video. (The Oboe: History and Development, and Reed-Making. Available from Anvil Films, Beaconsfield, Bucks.)

Music for Oboe (1650-1800) by Bruce Haynes. A bibliography of solo and chamber music. Published by Fallen Leaf Press, Berkeley CA. U.S.A.

Useful Addresses

INSTRUMENT DEALERS (new & second-hand) (UK)

OBOE MANUFACTURERS

SPECIALIST OBOE REPAIRERS (UK)

REED-MAKERS (UK)

TUBE CANE GROWERS

MAJOR STOCKISTS & SUPPLIERS OF WOODWIND MUSIC (UK)

WOODWIND PUBLISHERS (UK)

SPECIALIST SUPPLIERS OF ACCESSORIES & TOOLS

COLLEGES & SCHOOLS OF MUSIC/COLLEGES OFFERING
SPECIALIST COURSES (UK)

SOME SPECIALIST MUSIC SCHOOLS (UK)

YOUTH ORCHESTRAS & CHILDREN'S ORCHESTRAS (UK)

SUBSIDISED CHILDREN'S CONCERTS
& YOUTH ORGANISATIONS (UK)

SOURCES OF GRANTS SCHOLARSHIPS & SUBSIDIES (UK)

SUMMER SCHOOLS & COURSES

SOCIETIES & ASSOCIATIONS

MAGAZINES & PUBLICATIONS (sources of information)

MISCELLANEOUS (dentistry; medical; main music libraries;
instrument collections/museums; some financial advisors &
insurance; auctioneers/old instruments; publicity photographers;
answering and diary services/radio paging/data base/answer phones/
artists' management)

ALPHABETICAL LIST OF ADDRESSES

*Not all services individually tested or guaranteed by the author.
Addresses correct at time of printing.*

USEFUL ADDRESSES

INSTRUMENT DEALERS

New and Second-hand) (U.K.)*

Boosey & Hawkes Ltd. (Buffet oboes) (Middlesex)

Crowthers (new & second-hand) (Kent)

Peter Davies (second-hand & Rigoutat) (West Yorkshire)

J & L Dawkes (new) (Berkshire)

Chas E Foote Ltd (mainly beginners') (London)

T.W. Howarth & Co Ltd (new & second-hand & hire scheme) (London & Sussex)

Paul Lowdell (new & second-hand) (London)

Musicians' Instrument Agency (second-hand) (Cardiff)

John Myatt (new & large selection second-hand) (Herts)

Michael White (new & hire scheme) (London)

Woodwind & Co (Manchester)

* Most woodwind retailers stock beginners' instruments. (See your local Yellow Pages under 'Music Shops')

* See also 'Oboe Manufacturers'

OBOE MANUFACTURERS*

Bulgheroni Instruments (Italy)

Buffet Crampon (France)

Cabart (see Lorée) (Paris)

Paul Covey Inc. (USA)

Fossati (France)

Fox Oboes (see Sanderson & Taylor)

T.W. Howarth & Co., Ltd. (London & Sussex)

Hans Kreul & Moosmann (West Germany)

F. Lorée, Cabart (Paris)

J. Marigaux (Strasser-Marigaux) (Paris)

Moëck (baroque reproduction instruments) (West Yorkshire)

Fratelli Patricola (student and professional oboes) (Italy)

Josef Püchner (Germany)

Rigoutat (Paris)

Sanderson & Taylor Ltd. (Fox oboes) (Edinburgh)

Strasser (see Marigaux)

W. Schreiber & Söhne (West Germany)

Ward & Winterbourn (London)

Guntram Wolf (Germany)

Yamaha Corporation (Japan)

Yamaha UK distributer (Buckinghamshire)

* Available in U.K. See 'Instrument Dealers'

* See under 'Retailers' in British Music Yearbook (see 'Publications' or your local library ref. section)

* See also 'Music Shops' in your local Yellow Pages

SPECIALIST OBOE REPAIRERS (UK)*

John Coppen (London)

Peter Davies (West Yorkshire)

Tim Davies (Surrey)

J & L Dawkes (Berkshire)

David Fingerhut (Middlesex)

T.W. Howarth & Co. Ltd. (London)

Graham Johnson (London)

Andy Lee (Newcastle-upon-Tyne)

Paul Lowdell (incl. 'emergency night service') (London)

John Myatt (Hertfordshire)

Fiona Stevenson (Hampshire)

Ken Thomson (Edinburgh)

Chris White (Herefordshire)

Michael White Musical Instruments (London)

* Some larger woodwind retailers now provide a repair service (see your local Yellow Pages under 'Music Shops'). See under 'Retailers' in British Music Yearbook (see 'Publications' or your local library ref. section)

* See also 'Instrument Dealers' (see 'Publications'). Instruments can be sent to repairers outside your area by Carrier or Post Office guaranteed next day service safely, if well wrapped with 'bubble wrap' or similar, both inside and outside the case.

REED-MAKERS (UK)

Anthony Aspden (Dorset)

David Blyth ('Regency Reeds') (Hertfordshire)

Janet Brook (Essex)

Jenny Caws (Sussex)

Cooper Canes (West Yorkshire)

Chris Crosby (London)

Crowthers (Kent)

Lynda Harrison (Buckinghamshire)

R. Janney (Inverness-shire, Scotland)

Paul Lowdell (London)

Rosalyn Mace ('Tipple Oboe Reeds') (Suffolk)

Paul Mosby (London)

Adrian Rowlands (London) (Cane and reed blanks only)

Fiona Stevenson (Hampshire)

Peter Wiggins (London)

Michael Winfield (Surrey)

Nicholas Winfield (South Glamorgan, Wales)

TUBE CANE GROWERS*

François Alliaud (France)

Maison Dante Biasotto (France)

Maison Bonazza (Italy)

Mme Marcel Ghys (France)

Francisco Médir (Spain)

* Tube cane from these growers is available from many other sources including some larger woodwind retailers (see your local Yellow Pages under 'Music Shops'). See under 'Retailers' in British Music Yearbook (see 'Publications', or your local library ref. section)

* See also 'Suppliers of Accessories & Tools)

MAJOR STOCKISTS & SUPPLIERS OF WOODWIND MUSIC (UK)*

Blackwell's Music Shop (Oxford)

Linda Cummins Music (Surrey)

June Emerson Wind Music (Yorkshire)

Forsyth Bros. Ltd. (Manchester)

T.W. Howarth & Co. Ltd. (London and Sussex)

John Myatt (Hertfordshire)

* See also 'Woodwind Publishers'

* See Music Publishers' Assn. for comprehensive list (see 'Assns.')

WOODWIND PUBLISHERS (UK)

Associated Board of the Royal Schools of Music (London)

Bärenreiter Ltd. (Essex)

Belwin-Mills Music Ltd. (Essex)

Boosey & Hawkes Ltd. (London)

Camden Music (London)

Chester Music Ltd.(London)

Alfred Kalmus Ltd. (Kent)

Alfred Lengnick & Co. Ltd. (Buckinghamshire)

International Music Publications (IMP) (Essex)

New Wind Music Co. (Middlesex)

Nova Music Ltd. (Sussex)

Novello & Co Ltd. (London)

Oxford University Press (OUP) (Oxford)

Peters Edition Ltd. (London)

Phylloscopus Publications (Lancashire)

G. Ricordi & Co. Ltd. (Buckinghamshire)

Schirmer Ltd. (London)

Schott & Co. Ltd. (London)

Spartan Press Ltd. (Oxford)

Stainer & Bell Ltd. (London)

United Music Publishers Ltd. (UMP) (London)

Universal Edition Ltd. (London)

Josef Weinberger Ltd. (London)

Woodwind Plus (Yorkshire)

* See Music Publishers' Assn. for fully comprehensive list (see 'Assns.')

SPECIALIST SUPPLIERS OF ACCESSORIES & TOOLS*

Tony Allcock (gouging machines, guillotines, profilers, shapers, pre-gougers, reed-making accessories) (Nottinghamshire)

David Blyth (most accessories) (Hertfordshire)

Barry Chiltern (knives, gouging machines, shapers) (Derbyshire)

Crowthers (general accessories) (Kent)

Barrie Gregson (knife maker, sharpener and refurbisher) (Hampshire)

T.W. Howarth & Co. Ltd. (tools, accessories, gouging machines. (Mail order service) (London and Sussex)

Stephen Lickman (cor anglais bocals) (USA)

F. Lorée (reedcases, knives, mandrels) (Paris)

Paul Lowdell (reedcases & other accessories) (London)

K. Michel (reed-making machines, gouging machines, shapers, profilers) (West Germany)

Paul Mosby (knives, staples & most accessories incl. 'ticketers' used in knife sharpening) (London)

John Myatt (general accessories) (Hertfordshire)

Pisoni (staples, tools) (Italy)

George Reiger (gouging machines) (Germany)

Michael White Musical Instruments (general accessories) (London)

Windcraft (cane, general tools & accessories) (Berkshire)

Nicholas Winfield (cane, knives) (South Glamorgan, Wales)

* Many retail woodwind shops now stock a good range of tools & accessories (see your local Yellow Pages under 'Music Shops').
See under 'Retailers' in British Music Yearbook (see 'Publications' or your local library ref. section)

COLLEGES & SCHOOLS OF MUSIC/ COLLEGES OFFERING SPECIALIST COURSES (UK)*

Birmingham Conservatoire (Birmingham)

Chichester College of Technology (Sussex)

City of Leeds College of Music (Yorkshire)

City of London Polytechnic (instrument making & repair courses)

Dartington College of Arts (Devon)

Goldsmith's College (University of London)

Guildhall School of Music and Drama (London)

Huddersfield Polytechnic (Yorkshire)

Kent Music School (Kent)

London College of Music (London)

Merton Technical College (instrument repair courses) (Surrey)

Morley College (courses at all levels, orchestral, chamber music etc.) (London)

Newark & Sherwood College (woodwind making & repair courses) (Nottinghamshire)

Royal Air Force School of Music (Middlesex)

Royal College of Music (London)

Royal Marines School of Music (Kent)

Royal Academy of Music (London)

Royal Military School of Music (Middlesex)

Royal Northern College of Music (Manchester)

Royal Scottish Academy of Music and Drama (Glasgow)

Trinity College of Music (London)

Welsh College of Music (Cardiff)

* For further courses see British Music Yearbook & British Music Education Yearbook (see 'Publications' or your local library ref. section)

SOME SPECIALIST MUSIC SCHOOLS (UK)

Ardingly College (Sussex)

Bedford School (Bedfordshire)

Bradfield College (Berkshire)

Broughton High School (Edinburgh)

Chetham's School (Manchester)

Cricklade College (Hampshire)

Music School of Douglas Academy (Glasgow)

Pimlico School (London)

Purcell School (Middlesex)

St. Mary's Music School (Edinburgh)

Wells Cathedral School (Somerset)

Yehudi Menuhin School (Surrey)

* For further schools see British Music Education Yearbook (see 'Publications' or your local library ref. section)

YOUTH ORCHESTRAS & CHILDREN'S ORCHESTRAS (UK)*

British Youth Symphony Orchestra

European Community Youth Orchestra

National Children's Orchestra

National Children's Wind Orchestra of Great Britain

National Wind Band of Scotland

National Youth Orchestra of Great Britain

National Youth Orchestra of Scotland

National Youth Orchestra of Wales

National Youth Wind Ensemble of Scotland

National Youth Wind Orchestra of Great Britain

Young Musicians' Symphony Orchestra

* Further addresses available from the National Assn. of Youth Orchestras (see 'Assns.')

* For local instrumental teachers see your nearest M.U. branch (via your telephone directory or Central branch, or the Assn. of Woodwind Teachers (see 'Societies & Assns.')

SUBSIDISED CHILDREN'S CONCERTS & YOUTH ORGANISATIONS (UK)*

The Children's Music Club

Ernest Read Music Assn. (ERMA)

Hallé Concerts Society

Music for Youth

Young Person's Concert Foundation (free concerts at schools)

Youth & Music (London)

Youth Music Centre (children's Saturday morning music school) (Middlesex)

Youth & Music (North East)

Youth & Music (Yorkshire)

* Many orchestras offer 'junior' & student ticket discounts. Enquire to orchestras.

* For children's youth summer courses see 'Summer Schools'

SOURCES OF GRANTS, SCHOLARSHIPS & SUBSIDIES (UK)*

Arts Council of Great Britain (publishes lists of competitions, scholarships & awards for music students)

Arts Council of Northern Ireland

British Council (scholarships to study abroad)

Countess of Munster Musical Trust (grants max. age 27)

Craxton Memorial Trust

Dept. of Education & Science (publishes leaflets on State School Scholarships)

Directory of Grant-Making Trusts

The Grants Register

Loan Fund for Musical Instruments

Martin Musical Scholarship Fund

Scottish Arts Council

Welsh Arts Council

* For Handbook of Music Awards & Scholarships see Musicians' Benevolent Fund (see 'Assns.')

* For further details of grants & scholarships see British Music Yearbook & British Music Education Yearbook (see 'Publications', or your local library ref. section)

SUMMER SCHOOLS & COURSES*

Aberystwyth International Summer School (mainly chamber music) (Wales)

Alston Hall (year round courses incl. chamber music) (Lancashire)

Baroque Chamber Music Week (Oxford)

Beauchamp House Music & Drama Holiday courses (Gloucestershire)

Benslow Music Trust (many courses per year, mainly chamber music, all standards) (Hertfordshire)

Canford Summer School of Music (Dorset)

Chamber Music Holidays & Festivals (Bournemouth)

Charterhouse School of Music (symphony & chamber orchestras, chamber music) (Surrey)

Children's Wind Orchestra of Great Britain (summer courses)

The City Lit. (Music dept.) (London)

Coleg Harlech Summer School (August) (Wales)

Countrywide Holidays Assn.

Dartington International Summer School (chamber, orchestral & other music) (Devon)

Emscote Lawn Music School (for children)

Ernest Read Music Assn. (ERMA)

Gloucestershire Education Offices (young orchestras, July/Aug) (Gloucestershire)

Gloucestershire Summer Music School (July) (Cheltenham)

Guildhall Summer School (wind band course)

Hawkwood Adult College (various year round & summer courses) (Gloucestershire)

Keele Summer Schools (Staffordshire)

London Wind Consort (end July) (Wilts)

Malden School of Musical Instrument Repair (Easter & Summer 2 day & 1 week courses, no experience necessary) (Surrey)

Musicale Holidays & National Children's Wind Orchestra course & summer school (various centres)

Musicamp (Aug) (Berkshire)

National Centre for orchestral studies, Goldsmith's College (London)

National Children's Orchestra courses

National Youth Wind Orchestra of Great Britain orchestral courses

New London Music Society Sumphony Orchestra (Aug) (Buckinghamshire)

New Wind Summer School (adults) (Kent)

North East of Scotland Music School (courses throughout the year) (Scotland)

Rehearsal Orchestra (spring & summer orchestral courses during Edinburgh & Brighton Festivals, 1 & 2 day courses throughout the year at various venues)

Scarborough Summer School (Aug) (wind quintet & piano accomp) (N. Yorks)

Shell Expro Music School (for young students, Aug) (Aberdeen, Scotland)

Summer Music Summer School

University of London summer school & courses

White Hart Summer School (Yorkshire)

Winchester Summer Music (chamber & orchestra, Aug) (Hampshire)

* A list of Summer Schools may be obtained from the Workers' Educational Assn. (see 'Assns.')

* A comprehensive list can be found in British Music Yearbook & British Music Education Yearbook (see 'Publications' or your local library ref. section) with addresses for applications, venue, nature of course & approximate dates)

* For summer courses abroad see British Music Yearbook

* Major annual courses are announced in Musical Times from Jan each year (see 'Magazines')

* Weekend & similar courses are advertised in the New Statesman magazine (see 'Magazines')

* For holiday, weekend & evening courses see University Music Depts., or extramural depts., or University of London Institute of Education (University Centre for Teachers)

* Music Courses for teachers are organised by Dept. of Education & Science (see 'Grants')

* The UK Council for Adult Education & Training publishes information about residential short courses

SOCIETIES & ASSOCIATIONS*

Amateur Music Assn.

Assn. of British Orchestras (ABO)

Assn. of Medical Advisors to British Orchestras (AMABO)

Assn. of Woodwind Teachers

British Assn. of Concert Agents

British Assn. of Performing Arts Medicine (BAPAM)

British Assn. of Symphonic Bands & Wind Ensembles (BASBWE)

British Double Reed Society (BDRS) (for all double reed players, teachers, pupils & students)

British Federation of Music Festivals

British Performing Arts Medicine Trust (BPAMT) (see BAPAM)

British Society for the study of Orthodontics Dept.

The Children's Music Club Ltd.

The Concert Artists' Assn.

Educational Development Assn.

Ernest Read Music Assn. (ERMA)

Feldenkrais Guild (UK)

Incorporated Society of Musicians (ISM)

International Assn. of Music Libraries, Archives & Documentation Centre

International Double Reed Society (IDRS)

International Society for Music Education

International Society for the Study of Tension in Performance (ISSTIP)

Musicians' Benevolent Fund

Musicians' Social & Benevolent Council

Musicians' Union (MU)

Music Publishers' Assn. Ltd.

National Assn. of Youth Orchestras

National Federation of Music Societies

Performing Right Society (PRS)

Royal Society of Musicians of Great Britain (financial help for musicians' families)

Schools Music Assn.

The Society of Teachers of Alexander Technique

Workers' Educational Assn.

Workers' Music Assn. (WMA)

* For further Assns. see the National Music Council

MAGAZINES & PUBLICATIONS
Sources of information + *

British Music Yearbook +

British Music Education Yearbook +

Classical Music

The Double Reed (journal of IDRS) (USA)

Double Reed News (journal of BDRS)

Exchange & Mart

The Gramophone

The Instrumentalist (USA)

ISSTIP journal

Musical Opinion

The Musical Times

Musician (journal of MU)

The Musician's Handbook + (compendium of advice for pro musicians)

Music Teacher

The New Statesman

Oboe-Faggott (Germany)

Winds (journal of BASBWE)

+ = non magazines

* (see 'Societies & Assns.')

* For further information & addresses see your local library ref. section.

MISCELLANEOUS

Dentistry; Medical; Main Music Libraries; Instrument Collections/ Museums; Some Financial Advisors & Insurance; Auctioneers/Old Instruments; Publicity Photographers; Answering & Diary Services/Radio Paging/Data Base/ Answerphones/Artists Management

Dentistry

G.W.T. Bryant, MSc., B.D.S. (dental surgeon with special interest in wind players)

Brian Karet, B.D.S. (dental surgeon able to advise on prevention of possible damages & problems affecting wind players)

Mouth guards

Medical

Assn. of Medical Advisors to British Orchestras (AMABO) (available to musicians outside these orchestras)

British Assn. for Performing Arts Medicine (BAPAM) (clinics in different areas offering specialist help for all fields of medical problems of performing artists)

BAPAM Edinburgh Clinic (for clinics in other areas contact BAPAM London Office)

British Society for Study of Orthodontics (consult your dentist)

Feldenkrais Guild (UK) (a method to restore ease of movement by unlocking habits)

International Society for the Study of Tension in Performance (ISSTIP) (to bring dialogue between scientists, medical pros, therapists and performers)

Musicians' Clinic (consultant physicians working with registered complementary therapists, specialising in problems of orchestral musicians)

Performing Arts Clinic (ISSTIP in collaboration with London College of Music)

The Society of Teachers of Alexander Technique

The Voice Clinic (problems of the larynx)

Main Music Libraries/Information Centres

B.B.C. Music Library

British Music Information Centre (scores, recordings, ref. material, concerts/talks) (London)

Central Library (Birmingham)

Central Library (Music) (Liverpool)

Central Music Library (London)

Scottish Music Information Centre (Glasgow)

Wakefield Library (Yorkshire)

Henry Watson Music Library (Manchester)

Welsh Music Information Centre (Cardiff)

Important Instrument Collections/ Museums*

The Bate Collection of Historic Instruments (Oxford)

Bruxelles Conservatory Collection (world's largest) (Belgium)

Horniman Museum & Library (London)

Kunsthistorisches Museum (Vienna)

Metropolitan Museum (New York)

Municipal Museum, Den Haag (Holland)

Pitt Rivers Museum (Oxford)

Victoria & Albert Museum (London)

* see local Museum Directories

Some Financial Advisors/Insurance

Accounting & tax (Lloyd Pigott Accts) (Manchester)

Accounting for musicians (Sheila Bettaney) (Middlesex)

Finance & Insurance (Trevor Ford & Co.) (London)

Financial advice & management for musicians (Roger Taylor) (Hertfordshire)

Fine Instruments Finance Ltd. (Kent)

Insurance Brokers (Harrison-Beaumont) (specialist insurance against injury to performers) (Oxon)

Insurance & mortgages for musicians (Russell Meers & Co.) (Worcestershire)

Instrument insurance (Charlton Associates) (Wales)

Musical Instruments Insurance (British Reserve Ins. Co. Ltd.) (Kent)

Musicians' Insurance Service (P.J. Jenkins & Co.) (Middlesex)

Musicians' Union Insurance Advisory Service (Victor Knight Ltd.) (London)

Musicians' Union members' insurance, pensions, mortgages etc. (Andrew Harwood & Co.) (Middlesex)

Musicians' Union Pensions Scheme (administration) (Surrey)

Ridgers, Neave & Co. (Accountants)

Solicitors specialising in musicians' legal problems (Seifert Sedley Williams) (London)

Auctioneers/Old Instruments

Tony Bingham (old instruments, books on woodwind instruments) (London)

Christie's (auctioneers of instruments) (London)

Phillips (fine arts auctioneers) (London)

Sotheby's (auctioneers of instruments) (London)

Publicity Photographers

Robert Carpenter Turner (London)

Answering/Diary Services/Radio Paging/Data Base/Answer Phones/ Artists' Management*

Allegro Diary Service (Sussex)

Baker's Diary Service (Surrey)

Callsaver answerphones (London)

The Diary Service & Radio Paging (Julian Morgenstern) (London)

Hazard Chase Ltd. (artists' management & diary service) (Cambridge)

Jackie's Musicians' Answering Service (Herts)

Kantor Concert Management Ltd. (London)

Meridan Artists (diary service) (London)

Music & Musicians' Artists' Management (London)

The Musicians' Answering Service & Radio Paging (Surrey)

Presto Management (Sussex)

* Most artists' agents are licensed by the Dept. of Employment

* Most licensed agents are members of British Assn. of Concert Agents

* for orchestral 'fixers' see British Music Yearbook (see 'Publications') under 'Orchestral Managers/contractors'.

ALPHABETICAL LIST OF ADDRESSES

A

Aberystwyth International
Summer School
Aberystwyth Arts Centre
Penglais, Aberystwyth
Dyfed SY23 3DE
Tel 0970-622882

Tony Allcock
217 Curzon Street
Long Eaton
Nottingham NG10 4FJ
Tel 0602-726377

Allegro Diary Service
3 Hackenden Cottages
Hackenden Lane
E. Grinstead
W. Sussex RH19 3DP
Tel 0342-313436

François Alliaud
Bôite Postale 7
F-84-310
Morières-les-Avignon
224 Rue de la République
France Sud-ouest

Alston Hall, Longridge
Preston, Lancs PR3 3BP
Tel 0772-784661

Amateur Music Assn.
Medlock School
Wadeson Road
Manchester M13 9UR
Tel 061-273 3094

Ardingly College
Haywards Heath
Sussex RH17 6SQ
Tel 0444-892577

Arts Council of Great Britain,
14 Great Peter Street
London SW1P 3NQ
Tel 071-333 0100

Arts Council of Northern
Ireland
181A Stranmillis Road
Belfast BT9 5DU
Tel 0232-381591

Anthony Aspden
29 Benleaze Way
Swanage
Dorset BH19 2SH
Tel 0929-422177

Associated Board of the
Royal Schools of Music Ltd
14 Bedford Square
London WC1B 3JG
Tel 071-636-5400

A.B.O.
Francis House
Francis Street
London SW1P 1DE
Tel 071-828 6913

A.M.A.B.O.
c/o Academic Unit
Royal Free Hospital
Pond Street
London NW3 2QG
(see also B.A.P.A.M.)

Assn. of Woodwind Teachers
100 Common Road
Blue Bell Hill
Chatham
Kent ME5 9RG
Tel 0634-861486

B

Baker's Diary Service
21 Tormead Road
Guildford
Surrey GU1 2JA
Tel 081-549 1706

Bärenreiter Ltd
Burnt Hill
Elizabeth Way, Harlow
Essex CM20 2HX
Tel 0279-417134

Baroque Chamber Music
Week
4 Glebe Gardens, Grove
Wantage OX12 7LX
Tel 02357-3496

The Bate Collection
University of Oxford
Faculty of Music
St. Aldates
Oxford OX1 1DB
Tel 0865-276139

Beauchamp House
Little Acorns
Beavan's Hill, Kilcot
Newent, Glos GL18 1PG
Tel 098982-244

Bedford School
Burnaby Road
Bedford MK40 2TY

Belwin-Mills Music Ltd
Woodford Trading Estate
Southend Road
Woodford Green
Essex IG8 8HN
Tel 081-551 6131

Benslow Music Trust
(formerly Rural Music
Schools Assn.)
Little Benslow Hills
Ibberson Way
Benslow Lane, Hitchin
Herts SG4 9RB
Tel 0462-459446

Sheila Bettaney
78 Harrowes Meade
Edgware
Middlesex HA8 8RP
Tel 081-958 9806

Tony Bingham
11 Pond Street
London NW3 2PN
Tel 071-794 1596

Birmingham Conservatoire
City of Birmingham
Polytechnic
Paradise Place
Birmingham B3 3HG
Tel 021-331 5901-2

Blackwell's Music Shop
38 Holywell Street
Oxford OX1 3SW
Tel 0865-792972

David Blyth
20 Cavendish Road
St. Albans
Herts AL1 5EE
Tel 0727-46055

Maison Bonazza
Via Martovana
32/0 1-38 060 Mattarello
Italy

Boosey & Hawkes Musical
Instruments Ltd
Deansbrook Road
Edgware
Middlesex HA8 9BB
Tel 081-952 7711

Boosey & Hawkes Music
Publishers Ltd
The Hyde
Edgware Road
London NW9 6JN
081-205 3861

Bradfield College
Bradfield, Reading
Berks RG7 1AU
Tel 0734-744407

British Assn. of Concert
Agents
26 Wadham Road
London SW15 2LR
Tel 081-874 5742

B.A.P.A.M.
John Hollingworth
5 South Green, Widdington
Saffron Walden CB11 3SE
Tel 0279-501689

B.A.P.A.M. Edinburgh Clinic
Professor Arnold Maran
Otolaryngology Unit
Royal Infirmary
Edinburgh EH3 9EN

B.A.S.B.W.E. Sec.
3 Northbrook Road
Solihull, West Midlands
BD0 3NT
Tel 021-743 2483

B.B.C. Music Library
Tel for enquiries 071-927 4284

British Council
10 Springfield Gdns
London SW1A 2BN
Tel 071-930 8466

B.D.R.S.
21 Brighton Road, Earley
Reading
Berks RG6 1PS

221

British Fed. of Music
Festivals
Festivals House
198 Park Lane, Macclesfield
Cheshire SK11 6UD
Tel 0625-428297

British Music Education
Yearbook
published by Rhinegold
Publishing Ltd
239/241 Shaftesbury Avenue
London WC2H 8EH
Tel 071-240 5749

British Music Information
Centre
10 Stratford Place
London W1N 9AE
Tel 071-499 8567

British Music Yearbook
(see British Music Education
Yearbook)

B.P.A.M.T.
(see B.A.P.A.M.)

British Reserve Insurance
Co. Ltd, Brooke House
7-9 Mt. Ephraim Road
Tunbridge Wells
Kent TN1 1ET
Tel 0892-515244

British Society for the Study
of Orthodontics
Eastman Dental Hospital
Gray's Inn Road
London WC1X 8LD
Tel 071-837 2193

British Youth Symphony
Orchestra
24 Loxley Green
Wyton Village, Huntingdon
Cambs PE17 2JN
Tel 0480-69832 (eves)

Janet Brook
152 Butt Road, Colchester
Essex CO3 3DR
Tel 0206-562740

Broughton High School
Lothian Specialist Music
Scheme
Carrington Road
Edinburgh EH4 1EG
Tel 031-556 7028

Bruxelles Conservatoire
Royal de Musique de
Bruxelles
30 rue de la Régence
Brussels, Belgium

G.W.T. Bryant BDS MSc
79 Harley Street
London W1N 1DE
Tel 071-935 7498 or
0372-721593 (eves)

Buffet Crampon
3A 5 rue Maurice Berteaux
78200 Nantes-la-Ville
France
Tel 34.77.57187

Bulgheroni Instruments
F. lli Bulgheroni snc
Via 1° Maggio
1-22020 PARÉ (Como), Italy
Tel 031/44.00.53

C

Cabart (see Lorée)

Callsaver Ltd
3 Caledonian Road
London N1 9DX
Tel 071-278 5187

Camden Music
19A North Villas
Camden Square
London NW1 9BJ
Tel 071-267 8778

Canford Summer School of
Music
5 Bushey Close
Old Barn Lane, Kenley
Surrey CR2 5AU
Tel 081-660 4766

Robert Carpenter Turner
63 Hemstal Road
London NW6 2AD
Tel 071-624 2225

Jenny Caws
32 Bigwood Avenue
Hove, Sussex BN3 6FQ
Tel 0273-734756

Central Library
Chamberlain Square
Birmingham B3 3HQ
Tel 021-235 2482

Central Library (Music)
William Brown Street
Liverpool L3 8EW
Tel 051-225 5463

Central Music Library
160 Buckingham Palace Road
London SW1W 9UD
Tel 071-798 2192

Chamber Music Holidays
and Festivals
57 Chatsworth Road
Bournemouth BH8 8SL

Charlton Associates
18 High Street
Johnstown, Wrexham
Clwyd, Wales
Tel 0978-840689

Charterhouse Summer
School of Music
Charterhouse, Godalming
Surrey GU7 2DX
Tel 0483-426791

Chester Music Ltd
8/9 Frith Street
London W1V 5TZ
Tel 071-434 0066

Chetham's School of Music
Long Millgate
Manchester M3 1SB
Tel 061-834 9644

Chichester College of
Technology
Ave. de Chatres
Chichester
Sussex PO19 1SB
Tel 0243-786321

The Children's Music Club
Ltd
98 Mortlake Road
Kew, Richmond, Surrey
Tel 081-876 6728

Children's Wind Orchestra
of Great Britain
(see Musicale Holidays)

Barry Chiltern
175 Warwick Avenue
Littleover
Derby DE3 6HJ

Christie's
8 King Street
St. James's
London SW1Y 6QT
Tel 071-839 9060

City of Leeds College of
Music
Cookridge Street
Leeds LS2 8BH
Tel 0532-452069

The City Lit. Music Dept.
Keeley House
Keeley Street
London WC2B 4BA
Tel 071-430 0548

City of London Polytechnic
Dept. of Music Technology
41 Commercial Road
London E1 1LA
Tel 071-320 1841

Classical Music Magazine
(see British Music Education
Yearbook)
Tel 071-836 2383

Coleg Harlech, Harlech
Gwynedd LL46 2PU
Wales Tel 0766-780363

Concert Artistes' Assn.
20 Bedford Street
London WC2E 9HP
Tel 071-836 3172

Cooper Canes
4 North Terrace, Birstall
Batley
W. Yorks WF 9EU
Tel 0924-444843

John Coppen
50 Kipling Street
London SE1 3RU
Tel 071-378 1952

Countess of Munster Musical
Trust
Wormley Hill
Godalming
Surrey GU8 5SG
Tel 0428-685427

Countrywide Holidays Assn.
Birch Heyes
Cromwell Range
Manchester M14 6HU
Tel 061-225 1000

Paul Covey Inc.
424 East 30th Street
Baltimore
Maryland 21218, USA
Tel (301) 467 5587

Craxton Memorial Trust
50 Hatherleigh Road
Ruislip
Middlesex HA4 6AU

Cricklade College
Charlton Road
Andover
Hants SP10 1EJ
Tel 0264-363311

Chris Crosby
38 Hatchard Road
London N19 4NH
Tel 071-272 4943

Crowthers
10 Longport, Canterbury
Kent CT1 1PE
Tel 0227-763965

Linda Cummins Music
23 Woodcote Road
Wallington
Surrey SM6 0LH
Tel 081-647 2919

D

Maison Dante Biasotto
'La Fréjussienne de Roseaux'
Route de Bozon
F-83 600 Fréjus, France

Dartington College of Arts
Dartington Hall
Totnes, Devon TQ9 6EJ
Tel 0803-862224

Dartington International
Summer School
(see Dartington College of
Arts)
Tel 0803-867068

Peter Davies
Springfield Mill
Norman Road
Denby Dale, Huddersfield
W Yorks HD8 8TH
Tel 0484-866191

Tim Davies
23 Sends Barn Lane
Send, Woking
Surrey GU21 7BS
Tel 0483-211385

J & L Dawkes
652 Bath Road
Taplow, Nr. Maidenhead
Berkshire SL6 0NZ
Tel 0628-604404/7

Dept. of Education
Sanctury Building
Great Smith Street
London SW1P 3BT
Tel 071-925 5000

Dept. of Education &
Science (Music)
Government Buildings
Forest Road
Tunbridge Wells
Kent T2N 5AQ
Tel 0892-515644

The Diary Service
Julian Morgenstern
149 Englefield Road
London N1 3LH
Tel 071-354 2711

Directory of Grant-Making
Trusts
48 Pembury Road
Tonbridge
Kent TN9 2JD

The Double Reed, Ed
Daniel Stolper
610 W. Ottawa Street
Appartment 306
Lansing MI 48933-1049
Tel (517) 355-7727

Double Reed News, Ed
Flat 1
21 Fitzjohn's Avenue
London NW3 5JY
Tel 071-435 8857

E

Educational Development
Assn.
The Castle, Wisbech
Cambs PE13 1ES
Tel 0945-5096

June Emerson Wind Music
(Emerson Edition)
Windmill Farm, Ampleforth
N. Yorkshire YO6 4HF
Tel 04393-324

Emscote Lawn Music School
Emscote Lawn
Warwick CV34 5QD
Tel 0926-478135

E.R.M.A.
9 Cotsford Avenue
New Malden
Surrey KT3 5EU
Tel 081-942 0318

European Community Youth
Orchestra
53 Sloane Street
London SW1X 9SW
Tel 071-235 6641/7671

Exchange & Mart
Link House
25 West Street
Poole, Dorset BH15 1LL
Tel 2020-671171

F

Feldenkrais Guild (UK)
P.O. Box 370
London N10 3XA

Fine Instruments Finance Ltd
32 London Road
Southborough
Tunbridge Wells
Kent TN4 0QA
Tel 0892 511711

David Fingerhut
197 Edgwarebury Lane
Edgware
Middlesex HA8 8QJ
Tel 081-958 5025

Chas E. Foote Ltd
10 Golden Square
London W1R 3AF
Tel 071-437 1811

Trevor Ford & Co
151 Mount View Road
London N4 4JT
Tel 081-341 6408

Forsyth Bros Ltd
126 Deansgate
Manchester M3 2GR
Tel 061-834 3281

Fossati
L'Atelier du Hautbois
136 Rue Paul Doumer
F-45200 Montargis, France
Tel 38.98.45.45

Fox Oboes
(see Sanderson & Taylor)

G

Mme Marcel Ghys
Avenue Michard
Pellissier 2239
06600 Antibes, France

Gloucestershire Education
Office
Colwell Centre for Arts
in Education
Derby Road
Glos GL1 4AD
Tel 0452-330300

Gloucestershire Summer
Music School
(see Gloucestershire
Education Office)

Goldsmith's College
(University of London)
Lewisham Way
London SE14 6NW
Tel 081-692 7171

The Gramophone
General Gramophone
Publications Ltd
177-179 Kenton Road
Harrow
Middlesex HA3 0HA
Tel 081-907 4476

The Grants Register (pub
Macmillan)
Globe Book Services
Houndmills, Basingstoke
Hants RG21 2XS
Tel 0256-29242

Barrie Gregson
42 Linden Avenue
Old Basing, Basingstoke
Hants RG24 0HS
Tel 0256-24065

Guildhall School of Music &
Drama
Barbican, Silk Street
London EC2Y 8DT
Tel 071-628 2571

Guildhall Summer School
(see Guildhall School of
Music & Drama)

H

Hallé Concerts Society
30 Cross Street
Manchester M2 7BA
Tel 061-834 8363

Lynda Harrison
14 Avon Crescent
Stratford-upon-Avon
Warwicks CV37 7EU
Tel 0789-268775

Harrison-Beaumont Ltd
4 Meadow Court
High Street
Witney, Oxon OX8 6LP
Tel 0993-703251

Andrew Harwood & Co
290A Hale Lane
Edgware
Middlesex HA8 8NP
Tel 081-958 5579

Hawkwood Adult College
Stroud, Glos GL6 7QW
Tel 0453-764607

Hazard Chase Ltd
25 City Road
Cambridge CB1 1DP
Tel 0223-312400

Horniman Museum & Library
London Road
London SE23 3PQ
Tel 081-699 1872

TW Howarth & Co Ltd
31/33 Chiltern Street
London W1M 1HG
Tel 071-935 2407

TW Howarth & Co Ltd
53 Surrey Street, Brighton
E. Sussex BN1 3PB
Tel 0273-821760

Huddersfield Polytechnic
(Dept. of Music), Queensgate
Huddersfield
Yorks HD1 3DH
Tel 0484-422288

I

I.S.M.
(see British Music Info
Centre)
Tel 071-629 4413

The Instrumentalist
200 Northfield Road
Northfield, Illinois, USA
Tel (312) 446 5000

International Assn. of Music
Libraries Archives &
Documentation Centres
University Library
Stocker Road
Exeter EX4 4PT

I.D.R.S.
Idaho Falls, Idaho
USA

I.D.R.S. Sec
626 Lakeshire Drive
Monroe, LA. 71203-4032 USA
Tel (318) 345-1159

International Music
Publications
(see Belwin-Mills)

International Society for
Music Education
Music Education Centre
University of Reading
Bulmershe Court
Reading RG6 1HY
Tel 0734-318821

I.S.S.T.I.P.
Kingston Hill Centre
Kingston Polytechnic
Kingston upon Thames
Surrey KT2 7LB
Tel 081-547 2000

J

Jackie's Musicians'
Answering Service
42A Shenley Road
Borehamwood
Herts WD6 1DR
Tel 081-207 0007

R. Janney
Bearnock Lodge
Glenurquart
Inverness-shire
Scotland
Tel 045-64-244

P.J. Jenkins & Co
20 Charles Street
Hillingdon, Middlesex
Tel 081-561 8148

Graham Johnson
1C Hartland Road
London NW6 6BG
Tel 071-372 7311

K

Alfred Kalmus Ltd
38 Eldon Way
Paddock Wood, Tonbridge
Kent TN12 6BE
Tel 0892-833422

Kantor Concert Management
Ltd
30 Weymouth Street
London W1N 3FA
Tel 071-580 0309

Brian Karet B.D.S.
22 Wimpole Street
London W1M 7AD
Tel 071-580 3572

Keele Summer Schools
Dept of Adult Education
The University, Keele
Staffs ST5 5BG
Tel 0782-625116

Kent Music School
Westgate Towers
Pound Lane, Canterbury
Kent CT1 2BZ
Tel 0227-464320

Hans Kreul & Moosman
Schwärzlocher Strasse 80
D-7400 Tübingen,
West Germany
Tel 07071/45014

Kunsthistorisches Museum
A-1010 Vienna, Burgring 5
and Neue Burg
Tel (0222)93-06-20

L

Andy Lee
195 Osborne Road
Newcastle-upon-Tyne
Tel 091-281 3585

Alfred Lengnick & Co Ltd
Pigeon House Meadow
2 Grove Road
Beaconsfield
Bucks HP9 1VR

Stephen Lickman
Dallas Symphony Orch
2832 Lawtherwood Place
Dallas
Texas 75214 USA
Tel 214-321 0185

Lloyd-Pigott Accountants
Blackfriars House
Parsonage
Manchester M3 2JA
Tel 061-833 0346

Loan Fund for Musical
Instruments
(see Musicians' Benevolent
Fund)
Tel 071-436 4816

London College of Music
Thames Valley University
St. Mary's Road, Ealing
London W5 5RF
081-579 5000

London Wind Consort
Cantax House, Lacock
Wilts SN15 2JZ
Tel 0249-730468

F. Lorée & Cabart
4 rue du Vert-Bois
75003, Paris, France
Tel (1) 48-87-24-38

Paul Lowdell
42 Woodbastwick Road
Sydenham
London SE26 5LH
Tel 081-778 4941

M

Rosalyn Mace
96 Kimberley Road
Lowestoft
Suffolk NR33 0UA
Tel 0502-500829

Malden School of Musical
Instrument Repair
4 Orchard Avenue
New Malden
Surrey KT3 4JT
Tel 081-942 1543

J. Marigaux
(Strasser-Marigaux)
Boul. de la Villette 144-146
F-75019
Paris, France
Tel 4 20 84 43 45/40 79

Martin Musical Scholarship
Fund
76 Gt. Portland Street
London W1N 5AL
Tel 071-580 9961

Francisco Médir
c/o San Antonio 34
Apartado 108, Palamōs
Gerona, España
Tel 972-314339

Russell Meers & Co
1 Foregate Street
Worcester W1R 1DR
Tel 0905-723753

Meridan Artists
32 St Peter's Close
London SW17 7UH
Tel 081-672 1233

Merton Technical College
London Road, Morden
Surrey SM4 5QX
Tel 081-640 3001/081-542 3931

Metropolitan Museum of Arts
Fifth Avenue & 82nd Street
New York 1008
Tel (212) 879-5500

K. Michel
Sutelstrasse 25, Bothfeld
3000 Hanover 51
W. Germany
Tel (010-49) 0511-6497030

Moëck UK
38 Manningham Lane
Bradford
W. Yorks BD1 3EA
Tel 0274-721646

Morley College
61 Westminster Bridge Road,
London SE1 7HT
Tel 071-928 8501

Paul Mosby
4 Creighton Avenue
London N10 1NU
Tel 081-444 9830

Mouth Guards
E.M. Natt Ltd
45 Friern Barnet Road
London N11 3EG
Tel 081-361 4549

Municipal Museum
(Haags Gemeenremuseum)
Stadhouder Slaan 41
2517 HV, The Hague
Holland
Tel (070) 514181

Music & Musicians Artists'
Management
6 Princess Road
London NW1 8JJ
Tel 071-586 8424

Music Publishers' Assn. Ltd
103 Kingsway
London WC2B 6QX
Tel 071-831 7591

Music School of Douglas
Academy
Mains Estate, Milngavie
Glasgow G62 7HL
Tel 041-956 2281

Music Teacher Magazine
(see British Music Education
Yearbook)
Tel 071-836 2384

Music for Youth
4 Blade Mews
Deodar Road
London SW15 2NN
Tel 081-870 9624

Musical Opinion Magazine
2 Prince's Road
St. Leonard's-on-Sea
E. Sussex TN37 6EL
Tel 0424-715167

The Musical Times
c/o Orpheus Publishing
4th Floor, Centro House
Mandela Street
London NW1 0DU
Tel 071-387 3848

Musicale Holidays,
National Children's Wind
Orchestra and Children's
Wind Orchestra of Great
Britain
'The Bourne'
20 Salisbury Avenue
Harpenden
Herts HL5 2QG
Tel 0582-760014

Musicamp
121 Vale Road
Windsor, Berks SL4 55R
Tel 0753-859845

The Musicians' Answering
Service
173 High Street
Dorking
Surrey RH4 1AD
Tel 0306-880669
Radio Paging Tel 0306-740077

Musicians' Benevolent Fund
16 Ogle Street
London W1P 7LG
Tel 071-636 4481

Musicians' Clinic
7 Park Crescent
London W1N 3HE
Tel 071-436 5961

The Musician's Handbook
(pub. Rhinegold)
(see British Music Education
Yearbook)

Musicians' Instrument
Agency
24 Cathedral Road
Cardiff CF1 9LJ
Tel 0222-786435

Musicians' Social &
Benevolent Council
194 Muswell Hill Road
London N10 3NG
Tel 081-444 0246

Musicians' Union, National
Office
60/62 Clapham Road
London SW9 0JJ
Tel 071-582 5566

Musicians' Union Insurance
Advisory Service
Victor Knight Ltd
9 Wades Hill, Winchmore Hill
London N21 1BD
Tel 081-886 4202

Musicians' Union
Pensions Scheme
Abbey Life, Poplar Road
Shalford, Guildford
Surrey GU4 8DJ
Tel 0483-38883

John Myatt
57 Nightingale Road
Hitchin, Herts SG5 1RQ
Tel 0462-420057

N

National Assn of Youth
Orchestras
Ainslie House
11 St. Colme Street
Edinburgh EH3 6AG
Tel 031-225 4606

National Children's Orchestra
157 Craddocks Avenue
Ashtead
Surrey KT21 1NU
Tel 0372-276857

National Children's Wind
Orchestra
(see Musicale Holidays)

National Federation of Music
Societies (see A.B.O.)
Tel 071-828 7320

National Music Council
(see British Music Info
Centre)
Tel 071-436 0007

National Wind Band of
Scotland
Scottish Amateur Music Assn.
7 Randolph Crescent
Edinburgh EH3 7TH
Tel 031-225 7592

National Youth Orchestra
of Great Britain
Causeway House
Lodge Causeway
Fishponds
Bristol BS16 3HD
Tel 0272-650036

National Youth Orchestra of
Scotland
3 La Belle Place
Glasgow G3 7LH
Tel 041-332 8311

National Youth Orchestra
of Wales
Welsh Joint Ed Committee
245 Western Avenue
Cardiff CF5 2YX
Tel 0222-561231

National Youth Wind
Ensemble of Scotland
(see National Wind Band of
Scotland)

National Youth Wind
Orchestra of Great Britain
32 Park Lawn
Church Road
Farnham Royal
Bucks SL2 3AP
Tel 02814-2223

New London Music Society
3 Lynwood Road
Thames Ditton
Surrey KT7 0DN
Tel 081-398 3227

New Statesman
Perseverance Works
38 Kingsland Road
London E2 8DA
Tel 071-739 3211

New Wind Music Co.
11 Park Chase,
Wembley Park
Middlesex HA9 8EQ
Tel 081-902 2073

New Wind Summer School,
Kent
119 Woolstone Road
Forest Hill
London SE23 2TO
Tel 081-699 1101

Newark & Sherwood College
'Chauntry Park
Newark on Trent
Notts NG24 1PB
Tel 0636-705921 Ext
242/243 (day) 0636-78650
(eves)

North East of Scotland Music
School
1 Kenfield Place
Aberdeen AB1 7UW
Tel 0224-316004

Nova Music Ltd
Unit 3A
Stevenson Road
Freshfield Industrial Estate
Kempton, Brighton
E. Sussex BN2 2DF
Tel 0273-621272

Novello & Co Ltd
8-10 Lower James Street
London W1R 3PL
Tel 071-287 5060

O

Oboe-Faggott Magazine
pub by Hans Kreul
(see Hans Kreul)

O.U.P.
Walton Street
Oxford OX2 6DP
Tel 0865-56767/0536-741519

P

Fratelli Patricola
Costruzioni Strumenti
Musicali
1-15053 Castelnuovo
Scrivia (AL)
Via Magenta 10
Italia
Tel 0131/856616

Performing Arts Clinic
(see London College of
Music, also your nearest
professional orchestra)

Performing Right Society Ltd
29-33 Berners Street
London W1P 4AA
Tel 071-580 5544

Peters Edition Ltd
10-12 Baches Street
London N1 6DN
Tel 071-253 1638

Phillips Fine Arts Auctioneers
101 New Bond Street
London W1Y 0AS
Tel 071-629 6602

Phylloscopus Publications
92 Aldcliffe Road
Lancaster LA1 5BE
Tel 0524-67498

Pimlico School
Lupus Street
London SW1V 2AT
Tel 071-828 0881/071-821 1717

Pisoni
Via 4 Novembre 24
38014 Gardolo, Trento
Italia

Pitt Rivers Museum
South Parks Road
Oxford OX1 3PP
Tel 0865-270927

Presto Management
64 Lime Tree Avenue
Findon Valley, Worthing
W. Sussex BN14 0DP
Tel 081-549 9583/0903-873025

Josef Püchner
6085 Nauheim
bel Gross-Gerau
Beethovenstrasse 18
Bahnstation, Nauheim
Germany
Tel 06152-2725

Purcell School
Mount Park Road
Harrow-on-the-Hill
Middlesex HA1 3JS
Tel 081-422 1284

R

Rehearsal Orchestra
22 Micawber Street
London N1 7TB
Tel 071-251 6472

Georg Reiger
756 Gaggenau
Alois-Deglerstrasse 429
Germany

G. Ricordi & Co Ltd
The Bury, Church Street
Chesham
Bucks HP5 1JG
Tel 0494-783311

Ridgers, Neave & Co
117 Vanmar Road
Witney, Oxon OX8 6LL
Tel 0993-774694

Rigoutat
66 rue de Paris
F-94340
Joinville-le-Pont
Paris, France
Tel (33-1)48.85.70.39

Adrian Rowlands
124 Roundwood Road
London NW10 9UN
Tel 081-451 0184

Royal Academy of Music
Marylebone Road
London NW1 5HT
Tel 071-935 5461

Royal Air Force School of
Music
RAF Uxbridge
Middlesex UB10 0RZ
Tel 0895-37144 Ext 6345

Royal College of Music
Prince Consort Road
London SW7 2BS
Tel 071-589 3643

Royal Marines School of
Music
Deal, Kent CT14 7EH
Tel 0304-362121

Royal Military School of
Music
Kneller Hall
Twickenham
Middlesex TW2 7DU
Tel 081-898 5533

Royal Northern College of
Music
124 Oxford Road
Manchester M13 9RD
Tel 061-273 6283

Royal Scottish Academy of
Music and Drama
100 Renfrew Street
Glasgow G2 3DB
Tel 041-332 4101

Royal Society of Musicians of
Great Britain
(see British Music Info.
Centre)
Tel 071-629 6137

S

St. Mary's Music School
Old Coates House
Manor Place
Edinburgh EH3 7EB
Tel 031-220 1664

Sanderson & Taylor Ltd
6 Barclay Terrace
Edinburgh EH10 4HP
Tel 031-229 2051

Scarborough Summer School
The Spinney, Scampston
Malton
N. Yorks YO17 8NG
Tel 09442-479

Schirmer Ltd
(see Chester Music Ltd)

Schools' Music Assn.
Education Office
Town Hall
Friern Barnet
London N11 3DL
Tel 081-368 1255
Ext 3116

Schott & Co Ltd
48 Gt. Marlborough Street
London W1V 1DB
Tel 071-437 1246

W. Schreiber & Söhne
(see Josef Püchner)

Scottish Arts Council
12 Manor Place
Edinburgh EH3 7DD
Tel 031-226 6051

Seifert, Sedley, Williams
2 & 3 Dyers Buildings
London EC1N 2JL
Tel 071-831 3030

Shell Expro Music School
3 Nutborn House
Clifton Road
London SW19 4QT
Tel 081-946 2995

The Society of Teachers of
Alexander Technique
London House
266 Fulham Road
London SW10 9EL
Tel 071-351 0828

Sotheby's
34-35 New Bond Street
London W1A 2AA
Tel 071-408 5344

Spartan Press Ltd
5 Fairfax Avenue
Oxford OX3 0RP
Tel 0865-251825

Stainer & Bell Ltd
Victoria House
Gruneisen Road
London N3 1DZ
Tel 081-343 3303

Fiona Stevenson
26 Hollow Lane
Hayling Island
Hants PO11 9EX
Tel 0705-463438

Strasser
(see Marigaux)

Summer Music Summer
School
22 Gresley Road
London N19 3JZ
Tel 071-272 5664

T

Roger Taylor
Altofer Ltd
5 Regent Gate
83 High Street
Waltham Cross
Herts EN8 7AF
Tel 0992-654654

Ken Thomson
5 Blackford Glen Road
Edinburgh EH16 6AD
Tel 031-666 0329

Trinity College of Music
11-13 Mandeville Place
London W1M 6AQ
Tel 071-935 5773

U

UK Council for Adult
Education & Training
13 Back Lane
S. Luffenham, Oakham
Leics LE15 8NQ
Tel 0780-721115

U.M.P. Ltd
42 Rivington Street
London EC2A 3BN
Tel 071-729 4700

Universal Edition Ltd
Warwick House
9 Warwick Street
London W1R 5RA
Tel 071-437 5203/6880

University of London
Institute of Education
20 Bedford Way
London WC1H 0AL
Tel 071-580 1122

University of London
Summer School & courses
(see Goldsmith's College)

V

Victoria & Albert Museum
Cromwell Road
London SW7 2RL
Tel 071-938 8500

The Voice Clinic
David Garfield Davies
Outpatients' Department
Middlesex Hospital
London W1
Tel 071-636 8333
Ext 4677

W

Wakefield Library HQ
Balne Lane, Wakefield
W. Yorks WF2 0DQ
Tel 0924-371231
Ext 217/218

Ward & Winterbourn
75 Alexandra Road
London NW4 2RX
Tel 081-203 2678

Henry Watson Music Library
Central Library
St. Peter's Square
Manchester M2 5PD
Tel 061-234 1976

Josef Weinberger Ltd
12-14 Mortimer Street
London W1N 7RD
Tel 071-580 2827

Wells Cathedral School
Wells
Somerset BA5 2ST
Tel 0749-72117

Welsh Arts Council
9 Museum Place
Cardiff CF1 3NX
Tel 0222-394711

Welsh College of Music
Castle Grounds
Cardiff CF1 3ER
Tel 0222-342854

Welsh Music Information
Centre
PO Box 78
University College
Corbett Road
Cardiff CF1 1XL
Tel 0222-874000
Ext 5126

Chris White
4 Stage Coach Mews
West Street, Hereford
Tel 0432-352144

Michael White Musical
Instruments
11 Queens Parade
Queens Drive
London W5 3HU
Tel 081-997 4088

White Hart Summer School
White Hart
Cold Bath Road
Harrogate
Yorks HG2 0NF
Tel 0423-505681

Peter Wiggins
20 Barrington Road
London N8 8QS
Tel 081-348 0740

Winchester Summer Music
37 St. David's Road
Clifton Campville
Nr. Tamworth
Staffs B79 0BA
Tel 0827-86586

Windcraft Ltd
(see J & L Dawkes)

Winds
Ed. Wally Horwood
2 Jubilee Lane, Boundstone,
Farnham
Surrey GU10 4SZ
Tel 025-125 3010

Michael Winfield
Century Cottage
Byers Lane
S. Godstone
Surrey RH9 8JH
Tel 0342-893388

Nicholas Winfield
Foxwell Cottage
21 Forrest Road
Penarth, S. Glam.
S. Wales CF6 2DP
Tel 0222-709 335

Guntram Wolf
Im ziegelwinkel 13
8640 Kronach, Germany
Tel 09261/4207

Woodwind & Co
208 Liverpool Road
Cadishead
Manchester M30 5DB
Tel 061-775 1842

Woodwind Plus
19 Denton Avenue
Leeds 8, Yorks
Tel 0532-665388

Workers' Educational Assn.
44 Crowndale Road
London NW1 1TR
Tel 071-387 8966

Workers' Music Assn.
240 Perry Rise
Forest Hill
London SE23 2QT
Tel 081-699 2250

Y

Yamaha Corporation
10-1 Nakazawa-cho
Hamamatsu 430, Japan
Tel (053)460-2081/460-2581
UK distribution by
Yamaha-Kemble Music
(UK) Ltd
Sherbourne Drive
Tilbrook
Milton Keynes MK18 1XF
Tel 0908-366700

Yehudi Menuhin Music
School
Cobham Road
Stoke d'Abernon
Cobham
Surrey KT11 3QQ
Tel 0932-864739

Young Musicians' Symphony
Orchestra
Flat 4
11 Gunnersbury Avenue
London W5 3NJ
Tel 081-993 3135

Young Persons' Concert
Foundation
95 Wellington Road
Enfield
Middlesex EN1 2PW
Tel 081-360 7390

Youth & Music
28 Charing Cross Road
London WC2H 0DB
Tel 071-379 6722

Youth & Music North East
9 Black Swan Court
67 Westgate Road
Newcastle-upon-Tyne
NE1 1SG
Tel 091-230 1130

Youth & Music Yorkshire
Dean Clough Industrial Park
Halifax HX3 5AX
Tel 0422-345631

Youth Music Centre
132 Wemborough Road
Stanmore
Middlesex HA7 2EG
Tel 081-907 8018

Index